DATE DUE

JE 1 0 '94			

DEMCO 38-296

HOSTAGE TO REVOLUTION

HOSTAGE TO REVOLUTION

*Gorbachev and
Soviet Security Policy,
1985–1991*

Coit D. Blacker

COUNCIL ON FOREIGN RELATIONS PRESS

NEW YORK

COUNCIL ON FOREIGN RELATIONS BOOKS

The Council on Foreign Relations, Inc., is a nonprofit and nonpartisan organization devoted to promoting improved understanding of international affairs through the free exchange of ideas. The Council does not take any position on questions of foreign policy and has no affiliation with, and receives no funding from, the United States government.

From time to time, books and monographs written by members of the Councils research staff or visiting fellows, or commissioned by the Council, or written by an independent author with critical review contributed by a Council study or working group are published with the designation "Council on Foreign Relations Book." Any book or monograph bearing that designation is, in the judgment of the Committee on Studies of the Councils Board of Directors, a responsible treatment of a significant international topic worthy of presentation to the public. All statements of fact and expressions of opinion contained in Council books are, however, the sole responsibility of the author.

If you would like more information on Council publications, please write the Council on Foreign Relations, 58 East 68th Street, New York, NY 10021, or call the Publications Office at (212)734-0400.

Library of Congress Cataloging-in-Publication Data

Blacker, Coit D.
    Hostage to revolution : Gorbachev and Soviet security policy, 1985–1991 / by Coit D. Blacker.
        p.   cm.
    Includes bibliographical references and index.
    ISBN 0-87609-143-5 : $16.95
    1.   Soviet Union—Politics and government—1985–1991.   2. Soviet Union—Foreign relations—1985–1991.   3. Soviet Union—National security.   4. Soviet Union—Military policy.   I. Title.
DK288.B58   1993
947.085—dc20
                                                                    93-9800
                                                                       CIP

93   94   95   96   97   EB   5   4   3   2   1

Cover Design: Michael Storrings

Contents

Acknowledgments   vii

Chronology   ix

Introduction   1

1   The Brezhnev Legacy   10

2   Military Doctrine and the Restructuring   55
of the Armed Forces

3   Arms Control and Regional Security   88

4   Perestroika and the Soviet Military   144

5   Gorbachev, Security Policy, and the   183
Soviet Collapse

Notes   207

Suggestions for Further Reading   227

Index   229

Acknowledgments

It is a pleasure to acknowledge the assistance of so many colleagues and friends in the preparation of the manuscript. I owe a special debt of gratitude to Michael Mandelbaum, of the Council on Foreign Relations and the School of Advanced International Studies of the Johns Hopkins University, who first proposed that I write a book on the revolutionary developments in Soviet security policy during the Gorbachev era. Neither of us knew, of course, how complex and prolonged a task this would turn out to be or that I would end up writing a book on contemporary history and not, as we had first agreed, an analysis of developments in progress. For his steadfast support and extremely valuable comments throughout the preparation of the manuscript, I am deeply grateful. Edward L. Warner III chaired the Council's Henry A. Kissinger Study Group that supported my efforts, and to him as well, I express my sincere appreciation.

Andrew Bennett, Andrew Goldberg, and Deborah Yarsike prepared background papers for the study group that I found extremely helpful in the development of my own thinking on the subjects they addressed. Also providing critical commentary at various stages in the writing process were Leon Aron, Keith Bickel, Kurt Campbell, Tyrus Cobb, Sidney Drell, Joshua Epstein, Stephen Flanagan, Francis Fukuyama, Raymond Garthoff, Rose Gottemoeller, Dale Herspring, Robin Laird, Jan Lodal, Michael MccGwire, Col. Thomas Neary, Nicolai Petro, Cynthia Roberts, Dmitri Simes, Major Alan Stolberg, Strobe Talbott, and Marc Zlotnick. The book is immeasurably better for their having taken the time to read some or all of the chapters and I am pleased to acknowledge their critical contributions.

To my colleagues at the Center for International Security and Arms Control at Stanford University, including Lynn Eden, David Holloway, and, in particular, Condoleezza Rice, I am also indebted. Their comments were immensely helpful, especially in the development and refinement of the book's central themes and arguments. I am indeed fortunate to have such colleagues, with whom I have been able to discuss issues and share ideas for the better part of a decade, located literally "down the hall." Martha Little, in the early going, and Brian Davenport, during the final two years, provided critical research assistance. I thank Davenport, especially, for his tireless support and cheerful labors on my behalf. That he could juggle both the tasks that I assigned and his own dissertation work with such ease is noteworthy; that he managed to complete his own manuscript while helping me with mine is little short of remarkable. Theresa Weber, program associate of the Council's Project on East-West Relations, managed with apparent ease the often complicated logistics that the writing of the book seemed to entail. To her, as well, I offer my special thanks.

This book is part of the Council on Foreign Relations Project on East-West Relations, which is supported by the Carnegie Corporation.

Chronology

1985

March
Politburo member Mikhail S. Gorbachev is elected CPSU general secretary, succeeding Konstantin Chernenko.

U.S. and Soviet arms negotiators begin Nuclear and Space Talks (NST) in Geneva

April
Gorbachev announces a unilateral moratorium on the further deployment of intermediate-range nuclear missiles, proposes a moratorium on all nuclear weapons tests, and expresses interest in a summit meeting with U.S. president Ronald Reagan

July
Eduard A. Shevardnadze succeeds Andrei A. Gromyko as Soviet foreign minister; Gromyko is named USSR president

Soviet Union announces imposition of five-month moratorium on nuclear weapons tests and states that an extension is contingent upon a similar U.S. response

Source: *The Foreign Affairs Chronology of World Events: Second Edition, 1978–1991* (New York: Council on Foreign Relations Press, 1992)

September   Moscow proposes at Geneva disarmament talks that the United States and USSR reduce long and medium-range nuclear weapons by 50 percent; United States must agree to a conditional ban on spaced-based weapons research and a permanent ban on testing and deployment of such systems

November   U.S. president Ronald Reagan and Soviet general secretary Gorbachev meet in Geneva for five hours of private talks

1986

January   Gorbachev proposes a ban on all nuclear weapons by the year 2000

February   At Twenty-seventh Congress of the Communist Party of the Soviet Union, Gorbachev announces his sweeping plans for economic reform, "perestroika," changes in Moscow's conception of foreign policy, "new thinking," and introduces the military concept of "reasonable sufficiency"

April   Reactor Number Four at the Chernobyl nuclear power plant explodes

June   Warsaw Pact Political Consultative Committee meets in Budapest, proposes mutual Warsaw Pact–NATO troop reductions of 100,000 to 150,000 men and advocates the reduction of military capabilities to those "necessary for defense"

July   Gorbachev delivers a speech in Vladivostok, announcing a five-point plan for cooperation in the Asia-Pacific region and advocating closer ties with China

October   Reagan and Gorbachev meet in Reykjavik, Iceland, but arms control talks end without agreement due to differences over restrictions on SDI research

November   Supreme Soviet passes legislation allowing for some private enterprise in manufacturing and basic services

1987

January   Gorbachev charges the Communist party with stagnation and systemic failures at a plenum of the Central Committee

May   Soviet Defense Minister Sergei Sokolov is dismissed after a West German teenager, Mathias Rust, lands a small aircraft in Red Square; Gorbachev ally and relative unknown army general Dmitri Yazov is named defense minister

Warsaw Pact Political Consultative Committee ends its meeting in East Berlin with a call for talks with NATO on the reduction of conventional forces and tactical nuclear weapons

July   NATO calls for the replacement of the MBFR (mutual and balanced force reduction talks) with a new round of negotiations within the confines of the CSCE (Conference on Security and Cooperation in Europe)

August   The USSR confirms deployment of rail-mobile SS-24 ICBM

November   At the seventieth anniversary celebration of the Bolshevik Revolution, Gorbachev defends the progress of perestroika and announces his intention to complete a strategic arms control treaty with the United States

December   Gorbachev travels to Washington to sign the INF treaty with Reagan eliminating all 2,611 Soviet and U.S. intermediate-range nuclear forces

1988

January   After meeting with Czech Communist party chairman Milos Jakes, Gorbachev announces the need for "innovative policies" in Eastern Europe

February   A two-day Central Committee meeting concludes with the removal of Boris Yeltsin as a candidate member of the Soviet Politburo

March   U.S. defense secretary Frank Carlucci and Soviet defense minister Yazov meet in Bern, Switzerland, to discuss both countries' military doctrines

May   Reagan arrives in Moscow for a summit meeting with Gorbachev; they sign nine separate agreements on arms control and exchange the formal documents of ratification of the INF treaty

June   Nineteenth All-Union Party Conference convenes in Moscow at which Gorbachev advocates a strong presidency and a more representative national legislature, along with multicandidate elections

September   Gorbachev gives a speech at Krasnoyarsk, discusses problem of security in the Asia-Pacific region and offers to place the controversial radar station located there under international supervision

November   The Supreme Soviet approves constitutional changes proposed by Gorbachev transforming the body into a bicameral legislature and giving the chairman of the Presidium (president) more power over economic, social, and foreign policy

December   Gorbachev announces in a speech before the United Nations General Assembly in New York a unilateral reduction of Soviet forces by some 500,000 men, 10,000 tanks, 8,500 artillery pieces, and 800 combat aircraft

            Chief of the General Staff Marshal Sergei Akhromeyev retires, assumes new position as Gorbachev's personal military adviser

1989

March   Elections are held nationwide for the 2,250-seat Congress of People's Deputies, leading to the defeat of many party members by populist, liberal, and nationalist candidates

               MBFR talks end in Vienna and are replaced by Conventional Forces in Europe (CFE) negotiations

April   Soviet soldiers crack down on Georgian nationalists in Tbilisi, killing 20 demonstrators and wounding 200

               Solidarity is legalized in Poland

               Unilateral withdrawal of Soviet forces begins from Hungary

May   The new Congress of People's Deputies convenes in Moscow; Gorbachev is reelected to the strengthened chairman of the Presidium (president)

               Hungary dismantles barbed-wire fence separating itself from Austria

               Gorbachev addresses Council of Europe in Strasbourg, indicating that the Soviet Union will not intervene militarily in political events in Eastern Europe

July   Gorbachev announces in a nationally televised speech that ethnic violence and nationalism pose an "enormous danger" to the USSR

               Conservative Politburo member Yegor Ligachev denounces multiparty democracy in the Soviet Union

August   Solidarity activist Tadeuz Mazowiecki confirmed head of a predominately noncommunist coalition government in Poland

               East Germans begin to flee into Austria through Hungary

Lithuania declares Soviet annexation of the country in 1939 "illegal"

September In Washington, Shevardnadze announces that U.S.–Soviet disagreements over "Star Wars" should not prevent the conclusion of a strategic arms agreement

October Shevardnadze proclaims before the Supreme Soviet that the Soviet invasion of Afghanistan in 1979 "violated the norms of proper behavior" and that Krasnoyarsk radar installation is illegal under the 1972 ABM treaty

November U.S. president George Bush and Gorbachev meet in Malta to discuss a timetable for the conclusion of nuclear and conventional arms control agreements

The Berlin Wall falls; travel restrictions on East German citizens end

"Velvet Revolution" in Czechoslovakia; communist government falls

December First meeting of "Big Four" (the United States, France, Great Britain, and the Soviet Union) in eighteen years to discuss the status of Berlin

Romanian revolution; Premier Nicolai Ceauşescu and wife are executed

Playwright Václav Havel elected president of Czechoslovakia

1990

January Soviet troops are deployed and a state of emergency is declared in Azerbaijan in the wake of massive anti- Armenia demonstrations

February "Two Plus Four" talks on German reunification announced

March Radical former Moscow party chief Boris Yeltsin is elected to the Russian Supreme Soviet

Lithuania declares its independence from the Soviet Union; Gorbachev declares the move "illegitimate"; Soviet paratroopers seize headquarters of the Lithuanian Communist party and round up army deserters

The Third Congress of People's Deputies in Moscow repeals the constitutional guarantee of a Communist party monopoly of power in the Soviet Union; Gorbachev is elected by the body to the new, more powerful executive presidency

April   Estonian parliament votes to end the conscription of its citizens into Soviet army

May   Boris Yeltsin is elected president of the Russian Federation by the Russian Parliament

Gorbachev arrives in Washington for a four-day summit, signing accords on trade and chemical weapons as well as discussing strategic arm reductions with President Bush

June   USSR Supreme Soviet establishes freedom of the press

July   The Twenty-eighth Congress of the Communist Party of the Soviet Union opens in Moscow; Gorbachev is reelected general secretary; Yeltsin announces his resignation from the party

Gorbachev and West German chancellor Helmut Kohl announce agreement to allow reunified Germany to belong to NATO; Soviet troops to remain in eastern Germany for three to four years

Gorbachev decrees that ethnic militias disarm immediately

August   The "Shatalin Plan" for 500-day move to a market economy in the Soviet Union announced

October   East and West Germany unite as the Federal Republic of Germany

November   Second CSCE Summit convenes in Paris; NATO
             and Warsaw Pact states in attendance sign the CFE
             Treaty; heads of all the CSCE member states sign
             the Charter of Paris, ending the division of Europe
             and endorsing democratic freedoms and human
             rights

             Gorbachev proposes a new Union Treaty to re-
             define the relationship between the USSR
             government and the fifteen republics

             Defense Minister Yazov states that Gorbachev has
             approved the use of deadly force by the armed
             forces to defend military installations and service-
             men in the fractious republics

December   Shevardnadze resigns as Soviet foreign minister and
             warns in a speech before Supreme Soviet of an im-
             pending dictatorship; Politburo member Gennadi
             I. Yanayev is named USSR vice president

1991

January   Soviet Defense Ministry announces that army para-
             troopers will be used to round up draft dodgers in
             at least seven republics

             Soviet army troops kill fifteen protesters in Vilnius,
             Lithuania, in a crackdown on pro-independence
             forces; at least four are killed in Latvia by "black
             beret" Interior Ministry troops in similar actions

February   Foreign ministers of Warsaw Pact states meet in
             Budapest to sign an agreement dismantling the
             alliance by March 31, 1992

March   In the USSR's first national referendum, voters
             choose to preserve the union; three Baltic states,
             Armenia, Georgia, and Moldova boycott the vote

June   CSCE foreign ministers meet in Berlin, formally
             announcing an end to the Cold War

Differences in CFE treaty discussions, specifically over the reclassification of certain Soviet army units, are resolved

Boris Yeltsin becomes the first popularly elected president in Russian history, garnering 60 percent of the popular vote

Gorbachev and seven republic leaders sign a draft that decentralizes many USSR government functions

July   Warsaw Pact is formally disbanded in Prague

At Group of Seven economic summit in London, Bush and Gorbachev reach an agreement on the Strategic Arms Reduction Treaty (START); the two leaders meet again in Moscow at the end of the month to sign the START Treaty

Gorbachev announces that he and the leaders of ten Soviet republics have reached agreement on power-sharing provisions in a new Union Treaty; a signing ceremony is set for August 20

August   On the 19th, a State Committee for the State of Emergency declares Gorbachev incapacitated and seizes power; while Gorbachev is held in the Crimea, Yeltsin resists and military forces begin to switch loyalties to the Russian president; the coup collapses on the 21st, but at least three are left dead in its aftermath

Gorbachev resigns his post as general secretary, but does not quit the party; Russian Supreme Soviet bans the CPSU for an indefinite period

September   President Bush announces unilateral elimination of approximately 24,000 primarily tactical U.S. nuclear warheads, as well as a halt to the rail-based MX missile program and an end to 24-hour alert status for strategic bombers

October   Gorbachev responds to the Bush initiative in kind

November   The Russian Federation gains political and financial control of most Soviet ministries

December   Ukrainian voters approve a referendum on independence; Leonid M. Kravchuk is sworn in as president of an independent Ukraine

The leaders of Russia, Belarus, and Ukraine meet in Minsk on the 8th to proclaim the formation of the Commonwealth of Independent States (CIS), decreeing that the Soviet Union no longer exists; Yeltsin meets with military leaders four days later to gain their support for the new entity

On the 21st, eleven of the former Soviet republics, except the Baltic states and Georgia, formally constitute themselves as the Commonwealth of Independent States

On the 25th, Gorbachev resigns as president of the USSR; the red hammer-and-sickle flag is lowered from the Kremlin and is replaced by the Russian tricolor

Introduction

WHEN WORK ON THIS BOOK BEGAN IN SPRING 1990 MIKHAIL Sergeyevich Gorbachev had just completed his fifth year as general secretary of the Communist Party of the Soviet Union (CPSU). He was also head of state, having replaced the venerable Andrei Gromyko as chairman of the USSR Supreme Soviet in October 1988. Of the world's leading political figures, Gorbachev was enormously popular, especially outside his own country, and highly visible. As this book nears completion, Gorbachev is a private citizen and the Soviet Union is no more, thanks largely to political and social forces that Gorbachev himself unleashed and to the determined efforts of Boris Nikolayevich Yeltsin, president of the Russian Federation and the Soviet leader's one-time ally and comrade-in-arms.

The collapse of the Soviet Union, and the revolution in world politics that this remarkable development denotes, transformed the character of this study—from an analysis of events in progress to a study in contemporary history. The purpose of the book changed as well. What began as an effort to provide an informed analysis of developments in Soviet security policy, then ongoing, has become an attempt to construct a concise explanation for the causes and consequences of the Gorbachev revolution, particularly as it affected the related issues of military reform, arms control, regional and international security, and civil-military relations. Given that barely a year

1

separates us from the dismantling of the Soviet empire and the establishment in its place of a loose collection of sovereign states—some more collected and more sovereign than others—the analysis should also be considered exploratory rather than definitive in nature.

A considerable number of issues are examined in the pages that follow. Precisely because the temptation has been to include in the discussion virtually everything that may be of interest and value to the reader—thereby obscuring the larger purposes that motivated the book's writing in the first place—a conscious decision has been made to keep the scope of the study limited. Three major propositions inform the discussion and constitute the book's analytical core.

First, it was the urgent need to revitalize the Soviet economy—and by so doing restore the people's faith in the renewability of the socialist system as a whole—that led Gorbachev to undertake a fundamental reappraisal of the country's security requirements and to press for far-reaching reforms in the armed forces and in military doctrine.

The rapid deterioration of the Soviet economy in the early to mid-1980s left Gorbachev with no option but to press for significant reductions in military expenditures early on, both to free up badly needed resources for new investments in the country's aging scientific, technological, and industrial infrastructure and to make available to the USSR's long-suffering consumers more goods and better services. Without a significant shift in resources, Gorbachev and his advisers understood, a broadly based renewal and regeneration of Soviet society would be impossible to accomplish.

In the ongoing Western debate over how to account for the abrupt departure of Gorbachev's foreign and military policies from those that had come before, the book comes out squarely, then, on the side of those who point to the causal nature of so-called "domestic-level"—as opposed to "international-level"—variables, that is, to the determinative impact on Soviet decision-makers during this period of the multiple and reinforcing crises that they confronted at home.[1]

Various external factors, such as the Reagan defense buildup during the first half of 1980s, certainly influenced the kinds of security-policy initiatives, in arms control for example, that Gorbachev undertook after 1985. The growing economic might of the developed, noncommunist world played a part as well. As Raymond Garthoff has observed, it was a welcome paradox from Moscow's perspective that as the West had grown more powerful over the preceding decades, it also had become less dangerous, opening up new opportunities for accommodation and cooperation and for the resolution of important regional conflicts.[2] The most decisive factor, however, in Moscow's turn toward radical reform in foreign and military policy was the urgent need to restore the vitality of the USSR's economic and social systems, which the leadership believed it could only do by easing the burden of defense spending and rapidly improving the lot of the ordinary citizen.

Second, domestic change of the magnitude proposed by Gorbachev could only be undertaken without endangering the security of the state by containing the political and military rivalry with the West. Bringing that competition to an end required, among other actions, the full normalization of relations with Moscow's principal adversary, the United States.

This vital objective Gorbachev sought to accomplish in three steps. The first step was to communicate to Washington Moscow's unambiguous acceptance of the political ramifications of the nuclear revolution, namely, the understanding that in the nuclear age security between the superpowers could only be mutual and that under contemporary conditions neither side could hope to attain a position of meaningful military superiority. From this emerged the Soviet leader's commitment to what was later termed "the new political thinking." The second step was to affirm this understanding with the United States through the conclusion of substantial arms control agreements—such as an accord on intermediate-range nuclear forces (INF), a new treaty on the reduction of long-range, strategic nuclear systems (START), and a NATO–Warsaw Pact agreement on conventional forces in Europe (CFE)—that would bring the combined armed forces (both nuclear and conventional) of

East and West into rough numerical equilibrium for the first time in twenty years.

The third step was to seize upon the progress in arms control to accelerate the establishment of "normal" political relations between the Soviet Union and its erstwhile Western adversaries—relationships in which the USSR, having discarded at last its revolutionary heritage, would begin to function as a reliable, predictable, peaceable, and thoroughly integrated member of the international community of states. With this tectonic shift underway, Gorbachev could then legitimize to his own military reductions in defense spending, facilitate the downsizing of Soviet armed forces, and strengthen the case for the reform of military doctrine. This also helps to explain the Soviet leader's strong support for the concepts of "reasonable sufficiency" (as a guide to the procurement and deployment of military equipment) and "defensive defense" (as a way to limit the demand for personnel).

The improvement in Sino-Soviet relations, which Gorbachev and his Chinese hosts celebrated at the May 1989 summit in Beijing, served similar purposes in the Soviet leader's estimation. It brought to an end three decades of bitter political conflict and military tension with Moscow's powerful communist neighbor—thus, along with the upturn in East-West relations, freeing Gorbachev to turn his attentions inward and to concentrate on the formidable task of rebuilding Soviet society.

Third, Gorbachev's ambitious designs in security and military policy fell victim to the failure of perestroika to spark an economic recovery and to the resulting radicalization of the Soviet domestic political scene. The effect of these latter developments was to divide the Gorbachev era into two, unequal parts: the years of reform, from March 1985 to late 1989; and the years of revolution, from early 1990 to December 1991.

During the first period, Gorbachev's domestic policies should be understood as an attempt to transform the Soviet Union by reference to the logic of what Timothy Colton, writing in 1986, termed "radical reform," or "all-encompassing change containing as an essential component the restructuring of the country's political institutions and central, legitimizing beliefs and myths."[3] While the Soviet leader may not have started out as a radical reformer, by the time of the nineteenth CPSU conference in June 1988 his belief in and commitment to thoroughgoing change were unmistakable. In foreign policy, Gorbachev's goals during this first period were also ambitious, although not so radical as to call into question Moscow's status as the "other" superpower. On the contrary, the essential purpose of Gorbachev's diplomacy, as he himself said, was to assure the Soviet Union's entry into the twenty-first century "in a manner befitting a great power."

During the second period, however, the dynamics of the situation inside the Soviet Union had so changed that Gorbachev became, in effect, not the architect of reform, but a hostage to revolution, struggling against ever-mounting odds to retain control over a system that had begun to spin out of control. Moreover, as the domestic crises deepened, he lost leverage internationally, undermining his ability to manipulate concessions and rewards in order to induce cooperative behavior on the part of his Western negotiating partners. Toward the end—as symbolized by his repeated appeals to the Group of Seven countries in 1990 and 1991 for economic assistance—Gorbachev was forced to abandon the fiction of the Soviet Union as Washington's equal and to accept the reality of Moscow's status as an exhausted supplicant, urging Western assistance to the USSR to help avert the country's outright collapse and disintegration.

Separately and together, these three themes—the centrality of the domestic systemic crisis, the urgent need to delimit the military and political competition with the West, and the sharp discontinuity in the fundamental purposes of Soviet security policy between the first and second phases of Gorbachev's leadership—frame the analysis that follows, providing a context within which the reader may interpret the historical record.

There are, of course, other ways to understand and make sense of these enormously complex events that students of Soviet affairs, comparative politics, and international relations may find more compelling. The purpose in elaborating the book's major themes at the outset is not to restrict the search for answers, but to structure the analysis and to facilitate presentation of the material. It also serves to make explicit what the author regards as the study's principal findings.

The book begins with an analysis of the conditions, both at home and abroad, that confronted Gorbachev at the time of his accession to power in March 1985. Chapter 1 concentrates, in particular, on the mixed legacy in foreign and military policy that Gorbachev inherited from his predecessors and on the dismal state of the Soviet economy. Knowing the scope of the problems that Gorbachev faced when his Politburo colleagues elected him CPSU general secretary is an essential step in understanding not only the choices Gorbachev made, but why he made them. What was it, in other words, that this strong-willed if entirely loyal product of the "Great October Revolution" saw as he assumed office that led him ultimately to run such risks in the pursuit of economic reform and systemic renewal?

The middle three chapters focus on discrete, though related, components of Gorbachev's security policy. Chapter 2 examines the link between the new foreign policy agenda developed by Gorbachev and his closest advisers between 1985 and 1989, in particular, and the effort to reformulate Soviet military doctrine and to reorganize the armed forces in such a way as to reduce their size and to limit their offensive capabilities. Chapter 3 reviews Soviet arms control policies between 1985 and 1991, with special reference to superpower negotiations on nuclear forces; it also assesses Gorbachev's attempts to restructure Moscow's regional security relations in Europe and East Asia.

Chapter 4 is devoted to a discussion of civil-military relations under Gorbachev, particularly the response of the military high command to the reforms in organization and doctrine mandated by the political leadership, the military's reaction to the visible disintegration of Soviet civil society (including their obvious reluctance to be drawn into the country's deepening ethnic and religious conflicts), and the conduct of the armed forces during the failed coup attempt of August 1991.

Chapter 5 offers an assessment of Gorbachev's record in security policy and explores in some depth the connection between the failure to reform the larger system, both economically and politically, and the defeat of the Soviet leader's designs in foreign and military policy. The last section of the chapter speculates on the possible significance of the Soviet Union's collapse, both for world politics and for the study of international relations.

Chapter 5 is meant to serve as a conclusion to the study as a whole; it could just as easily, however, function as the book's introduction. In essay form, it elaborates in considerable detail the arguments and themes that have been previewed here, in the book's first few pages. Some readers, therefore, may wish to begin their consideration of the manuscript by proceeding directly to the conclusion.

For students of Soviet affairs, the passing of the Land of Lenin is bittersweet. It is rather like losing a close, if detested, relative: you may not have liked him, but at least you believed that you understood both his motives and his conduct. What lies ahead for the people of this last, great multinational empire is anyone's guess. Writing this book enabled me to figure out what I thought about this remarkable final chapter in Soviet history and thus to accept the fact that the end had really arrived. This is, for me, sufficient reward.

A NOTE ON SOURCES

The kinds of sources used in the writing of this book reflect the very real changes in Sovietology that took place during the almost seven years of Gorbachev's leadership. Prior to 1985 most treatments of Soviet security policy relied heavily on interpretation of the leadership's key speeches and pronouncements and on a close reading of a relatively small number of authoritative newspapers and journals, such as *Pravda, Izvestiya, Krasnaya zvezda, Kommunist*, and *Kommunist vooruzhennikh sil*. Typically, the analyst took note of a particular development in policy and then sought to "reverse engineer" it, explaining why and how the decision in question might have come about, given the available evidence and some informed speculation. Such exercises took place within a relatively static analytical framework—most Soviet policies changed slowly, after all—that enabled Kremlin watchers to hold most variables constant, or nearly so.

With the opening up of Soviet society in the late 1980s, the old system for keeping track of and making sense of events began to lose its utility. If once we knew too little, suddenly we knew too much. Moreover, it seemed that no one, with the exception of Gorbachev and members of his immediate entourage, spoke authoritatively on behalf of the government. Even this was not always the case. Lower-level officials often contradicted these statements and sometimes ignored them altogether. The once-reliable Soviet press only added to the confusion by simultaneously asserting its independence, while continuing to mouth the views of its powerful sponsors. If, before 1985, the voices of Soviet officialdom all sounded more or less the same, by the midpoint in Gorbachev's tenure as CPSU general secretary the leadership could barely make itself heard over the din of other voices now fully resolved to make their views known.

The book's use of sources reflects this transition in Soviet society. Where appropriate, I have employed the standard tools of Kremlinology—speeches of the leadership, especially those central to the policymaking process, editorials of the major press organs, and published analyses of individuals who, while speaking or writing in an "unofficial capacity," are understood to have reflected the views of those in power. At the same time, I have tried to incorporate into the analysis a broader sampling of expert and elite opinion from across the political spectrum in order to track more closely the development of new ideas in Soviet foreign and defense policies and to explore their impact on decision making.

Finally, to a much greater extent than in any of my earlier writings, the analysis is informed by a series of informal discussions with Soviet scholars and former policymakers interested in or involved with the development of Gorbachev's "new political thinking." These have been ongoing since the mid-1980s. I have found these discussions to be of enormous (and continuing) value, particularly in providing a degree of thematic coherence to the analysis as a whole. I am especially grateful to scholars at the Institute of Far Eastern Studies, the Institute of World Economy and International Relations, and the Institute of U.S.A. and Canada Studies, now of the Russian Academy of Sciences, and to officials once attached to the Soviet ministries of Defense and Foreign Affairs and, most especially, to the CPSU Central Committee. They have been more than generous with their time. I have not always taken their analyses to heart, but I have listened carefully and done my best to do justice to their often penetrating and always interesting observations on the transformation of Soviet politics and society.

In almost all cases the Russian-language sources used in the text are translations from the original. The only exceptions are those that appear in transliterated Russian; these I have used in the original. Unless otherwise indicated, the translated works are from the U.S. Department of Commerce series, *Foreign Broadcast Information Service* (Soviet Union).

Chapter 1

The Brezhnev Legacy

ON NOVEMBER 10, 1982, LEONID ILYCH BREZHNEV, GENERAL secretary of the Communist Party of the Soviet Union and chairman of the Presidium of the Supreme Soviet, succumbed to the combined effects of heart disease, circulatory failure, and respiratory collapse. At the dignified, if leaden, Kremlin ceremony staged to commemorate his life and times, Brezhnev's closest associates eulogized the fallen leader as a veritable titan of Soviet history, who through his many accomplishments in both domestic and foreign policy had earned for himself a place of honor in the pantheon of Bolshevik heroes. At 75, Brezhnev had outlived most of the individuals, including Nikolai Podgorny, Aleksei Kosygin, and Mikhail Suslov, with whom he had come to power some eighteen years before in the bloodless coup that forced Nikita Khrushchev into retirement. Within another twenty-eight months, Brezhnev's two immediate successors, Yuri Andropov and Konstantin Chernenko, also would be dead, opening the way for the election of Mikhail Gorbachev who, at 53, was to became the youngest CPSU general secretary since Stalin.

The two decades separating the fall of Khrushchev and the death of Chernenko constitute a distinct and largely self-contained period in the history of the Soviet Union that may properly be considered the Brezhnev era, despite the absence from the scene after November 1982 of the man for whom the period is named. It was during these years, particularly from the late 1960s to the mid-1970s, that the Soviet Union, in the confident judgment of much of its leadership, seemed poised to assume the elusive mantle of world leadership. Notwithstanding the many ailments even then plaguing the Soviet system, the middle Brezhnev years were a time of considerable optimism, as senior Kremlin leaders celebrated what they termed "the worldwide shift in the correlation of forces"—the eagerly awaited, though long-delayed, point at which the socialist community of states would attain decisive material, as well as political, advantage over the forces of "militarism and reaction" led by the United States.

By 1985 the optimism that had once informed Soviet policy was nowhere to be found. A decade earlier Soviet leaders had looked to the future with a mixture of hope and anxiety. Their heirs, by contrast, could visualize only disaster. Rather than a socialist utopia in the making, Gorbachev and those elevated to power with him confronted a country in extremis, a society virtually immobilized by an interlocking series of crises of unprecedented scale and intensity. Brezhnev, so recently celebrated for his many contributions to the task of "socialist construction," was soon vilified as both symbol and architect of the Kremlin's precipitous decline.

While Brezhnev and those who ruled with him may be assigned much of the responsibility for the calamities that eventually over-took the Soviet Union, it was also through their efforts, misguided though they may have been, that the USSR first attained superpower status. And to no single manifestation of Moscow's rise to globalism during the 1960s and 1970s did this leadership assign greater importance than to the acquisition and deployment of military capabilities, especially strategic nuclear forces, roughly equal to those of the United States. In a period of less than ten years—from the removal of Khrushchev in October 1964 to the signing of the first strategic arms limitation (SALT) agreements in May 1972—senior Kremlin leaders engineered what can only be described as a spectacular turnabout in Moscow's military fortunes, creating a posture of nuclear plenty from a base of abject inferiority. If, in the words of one well-placed Soviet military official, the United States had once enjoyed a degree of strategic nuclear advantage sufficient to enable it to deliver a "disarming" first strike against the Soviet

Union,[1] by the mid-1970s such was no longer the case. Were the imperialists foolish enough to unleash the dogs of war, Moscow warned, under any and all conditions the aggressors would be dealt "an annihilating retaliatory strike."[2]

In addition to the dramatic expansion in the *size* of their strategic nuclear arsenal during these years, the Soviets also undertook major *qualitative* improvements through the introduction and application of such advanced technologies as multiple independently targetable reentry vehicles (MIRVs), mobile missile launchers, and sophisticated stellar-navigational systems. Moreover, they did so at a rate that U.S. and other Western defense officials found both surprising and profoundly disturbing. Nor were these impressive strides limited to Moscow's nuclear forces. Beginning in the first half of the 1970s, the Soviet Union embarked on an ambitious and costly program to increase the number and improve the quality of its non-nuclear forces, including weapon systems earmarked for possible use in the theater, such as tactical aircraft, tanks, armored fighting vehicles, armored personnel carriers, and artillery. Even the Soviet navy, long the most neglected of the country's five military services, grew in important ways during these years of budgetary bounty.

For a number of reasons Soviet leaders attached enormous significance to their country's military buildup. With its realization, they detected, for example, indisputable evidence of the truly advanced standing of the national economy and of the robust state of Soviet science and technology, both basic and applied. For Brezhnev and his colleagues, raised to political maturity during the years when senior Soviet officials, including Stalin, held out the American economy as the model of industrial efficiency and technological prowess, the attainment of essential military equality with Washington must have been a source of immense satisfaction.

The military buildup also affirmed the Kremlin's standing as a global power, lending new authority to Moscow's claim that with the dramatic growth in the "material positions of socialism" had come the right to be consulted on virtually every issue of consequence then confronting the international community.[3] At a more practical level, the development of "survivable" strategic nuclear forces—intercontinental-range ballistic missiles (ICBMs) housed in blast-resistant concrete and steel silos and shorter-range systems deployed on difficult-to-detect ballistic-missile submarines—provided critically important and long-sought insurance against any U.S. strategic military "bolt out of the blue," while also bringing to an end what Soviet officials characterized as Washington's persistent efforts to extract political advantage at the expense of the socialist community through what they derisively termed "nuclear blackmail."

Detailing seriatim the specific implications of the changing military balance between East and West during these years, while useful analytically, both understates and distorts the true significance from the Soviet perspective of the ongoing shift in "the correlation of forces." To a much greater degree than their counterparts in the West, the Soviets consistently sought to place ongoing political, military, economic, and social trends and developments within a larger and, to them, more satisfying context. As heirs to the intellectual traditions of Karl Marx and Friedrich Engels, many Soviets—some consciously, some through ignorance of alternative methods—labored during the 1960s and 1970s to understand events in such a way as to reveal their purposiveness, or "progressive" character, consistent with the notion of historical determinism that constituted the bedrock of Marxist philosophy. They did so in the belief that adherence to this method ensured a degree of analytical rigor, of "objectivity," missing in Western "bourgeois" thought, which they considered not only subjective but also ahistorical. And from superior analyses, this logic implied, could only come superior policies.[4]

The contention that such mental processes influenced both the formation and the conduct of Soviet security policies during the Brezhnev era is itself contentious. To some Western observers, it *overstated* the role of ideology in Soviet policy, suggesting a fealty or sensitivity to Marxist-Leninist teachings on the part of the leadership that is difficult to substantiate, given the historical record. According to this interpretation, since Stalin's triumph over his political rivals in the late 1920s, Soviet international behavior is best understood in terms of realpolitik, and not by reference to the sterile precepts of a nineteenth-century ideology long since overtaken by events.[5] To others, it *understated* the reality, ignoring the extent to which ideology not only shaped the way Soviet leaders, from Lenin to Brezhnev, interpreted the world around them, but also guided their actions. For these analysts, at least through the early 1980s, a deep familiarity with Marxism-Leninism is the key to an informed, persuasive understanding of Soviet policy.[6]

The argument presented here departs from both interpretations. The teachings of Marx and Lenin, while a less than reliable guide to Soviet action, influenced the way in which senior Soviet leaders thought about and made sense of the phenomena they observed—much as the ideas of Thomas Jefferson, Andrew Jackson, Franklin Roosevelt, and others have influenced, and continue to influence, the beliefs and attitudes of American leaders. Especially in the way that information is gathered, processed, and put to work, belief systems matter, leaving their mark in subtle ways that are, nonetheless, critically important.[7] That Brezhnev and his cohort would not have internalized particularly the methodological tenets of the official ideology of the Soviet Union is absurd on the face of it. It is in this sense, above all others, that Marxism-Leninism may be said to have played an important role in the formation and implementation of Soviet security policies in the years under review.

It was, moreover, by reference to such processes that Soviet analysts, military and civilian, succeeded in constructing an explanation for the Kremlin's rise to globalism that was holistic, diagnostic, and prescriptive. At the apex of this construct was a series of observations about the character of the contemporary international political system and the relationship between war and politics in the nuclear age. These beliefs also shaped 1) the development of military doctrine and strategy; 2) nuclear and conventional force postures; 3) arms control policies; and 4) civil-military relations.

THE INTERNATIONAL SYSTEM

Brezhnev, Podgorny, and Kosygin came to power with a collection of ideas about international politics that were consistent, for the most part, with the canons of modern-day Marxism-Leninism, especially as these had been formulated and enunciated by Khrushchev. Two of these ideas—the notion of an international system organized along class lines and belief in the fundamental irreconcilability of the interests of world socialism and world capitalism—were to have particular impact on the development of Soviet foreign and military policies across much of the period under review, from the mid-1960s to the mid-1980s.

The more fundamental of the two ideas was the conviction that countries of the world could be divided into three groups: those controlled by *capitalist interests*, such as the United States and most of the countries of Western Europe; those led by representatives of the *working class*, such as the Soviet Union and its allies; and those at an *intermediate stage of economic and political development*, typically former colonies of Europe's metropolitan powers. In the 1960s the Soviets labeled this third group of countries either "revolutionary" or "national democracies," depending on the precise character of their leaderships. Both were seen, by definition, to be "progressive" in their domestic and foreign policies, making them natural, if unofficial, allies of the international socialist community. Khrushchev, never one to let reality stand in the way of a good propaganda thrust, went so far as to declare in the early 1960s that some two-thirds of the world's people, including most of those then living in Africa and Asia, had embarked on the "noncapitalist path of development," thereby dealing a blow against world capitalism from which it was unlikely to recover.[8] More cautious by nature, Khrushchev's successors chose not to repeat this claim, which, even by the standards of the Kremlin's most ebullient leader, seemed to have gone too far. At least for a time, however, they did embrace the logic.

Soviet theorists went to considerable lengths during the middle decades of the twentieth century to elaborate a model of world politics in which the single most important feature of contemporary international relations was said to be the division of states along class lines, rather than, as Western scholars tended to argue, the struggle of each state, acting on its own or in alliance with others, to secure its national interests. In other words, whereas most Western theorizing emphasized the individual state's pursuit of power within a global system that was at best indifferent to its survival, Soviet authors drew attention to an alleged identity of interests between and among countries organized along similar socio-economic lines.[9]

In most Western models, the domestic structure of a state—be it socialist or capitalist—is essentially irrelevant to an understanding of or an ability to predict its external behavior; under normal conditions, states will act to maximize their power. In the Soviet model, a country's internal economic, political, and social relations largely determined its place, role, and conduct within the international system. From this analytical device emerged Moscow's fascination with the concept of "the correlation of forces," or the evolving balance of human and material resources between the world socialist system (including countries pursuing a "noncapitalist path"), which was seen to be gaining strength, and its imperialist counterpart, said to be in decline.

The second idea, the irreconcilability of interests between socialism and imperialism, derived from the first. As a regressive mode of production, capitalism not only exploited human labor but also gave rise to political institutions that reflected the interests of the dominant classes—those in possession of the means of production—while repressing those of the proletariat. Within developed capitalist societies, therefore, class conflict was inevitable. Socialism, by contrast, served the economic and political interests of the working classes through the public, rather than the private, ownership of the means of production. And since the proletariat, coupled with its natural allies, the impoverished peasantry, constituted the vast majority of the Russian population at the time of the Great October Revolution, the Bolsheviks could claim that with the defeat of capitalism inside the empire would come an eventual end to class strife and the creation, under socialist auspices, of a kind of social nirvana: "From each according to his abilities, to each according to his needs."

With the establishment in 1917 of the "world's first socialist state," the class struggle acquired an important international dimension. Henceforth, the irreconcilability of interests that typified class relations within capitalist societies would be reproduced at an international level, as the imperialists sought to destroy the government led by representatives of the Russian working class.[10] Given the threat to imperialism latent in the Bolshevik seizure of power, Lenin and his colleagues simply assumed that the capitalist states would seek to dislodge them, which the Allied military intervention of 1918–1919 only seemed to confirm.

Even if the young Soviet state could withstand the attempts by its class enemies—both foreign and domestic—to topple it, the dangers inherent in imperialism would persist. Imperialism, in the Soviet estimate, was both repressive domestically and aggressive internationally, always seeking new markets to absorb its excess productive capacities. Competition between and among imperialist states was, therefore, inevitable. Interstate violence, or war, was often the result. In the Kremlin's view, the great danger was that such conflicts could spread, even to countries, like the Soviet Union, that had opted out of the imperial system, as the combatants sought to acquire new resources with which to wage their military campaigns. Either directly or indirectly, in other words, the imperialist system constituted a continuing and deadly serious threat to the security of the Soviet state.

By the 1970s, Soviet views about the international system and the conflict between socialism and imperialism had evolved considerably. In important ways, however, the original constructs continued to undergird Moscow's approach to the world beyond its borders. For example, at four successive CPSU congresses, convened at five-year intervals between 1966 and 1981, Brezhnev began each report on the international situation with a stout defense of the analytical utility of class as the most powerful tool for understanding the character of contemporary international politics, the clearest evidence of which, he argued, was the manifest solidarity of interests linking all the world's working classes, or "proletarian internationalism."[11] Theoretical treatments of these and related themes, generated by scholars of the Soviet Academy of Sciences, began the same way. On the ineluctability of conflict between the two world systems, the Soviets also succeeded in retaining the formula, even as they abandoned much of its content—thanks in large part to the *deus ex machina* provided by Khrushchev, who, in his address to the twentieth CPSU congress in 1956, had pronounced a new world war possible, though no longer inevitable.[12] In its essence, however, the dangerous, predatory nature of imperialism was said to remain unaltered.

WAR, POLITICAL CHANGE, AND NUCLEAR WEAPONS

From the beginning, Soviet leaders were ambivalent about war. On the one hand, as few others they knew its terrors firsthand, having weathered at great cost both a civil war (1917–1920) and an international conflict of unprecedented ferocity (1941–1945). Particularly in a world dominated by capitalist countries, the Soviets appeared to conclude, the threat of war was a real and ever-present danger. On the other hand, the establishment of the Soviet state was itself a consequence, at least in part, of the upheavals attending Russian participation in World War I, just as the creation of a community of socialist states was a direct outgrowth of the Kremlin's feat of arms in World War II.

This is not to suggest that the Soviet leadership ever welcomed a major war, let alone that they sought one, at any point after the initial Bolshevik seizure of power in 1917. This was particularly true for the period after 1945, when Moscow's most likely adversary had demonstrated an ability to manufacture atomic weapons and a willingness to use them. It is to suggest, however, that in the judgment of those responsible for the country's fate, until the mid-1980s a war involving the Soviet Union and the West remained a distinct possibility, the results of which could be either good or bad from the Kremlin's perspective, depending on the character and timing of the conflict, material conditions, and, of course, the outcome. This conviction was to have a profound and not altogether positive impact on Soviet thinking during the roughly two decades of the Brezhnev regime.

Of the many changes wrought by World War II, none was more important than the appearance of nuclear weapons. To most of those who studied their effects, the bombings of Hiroshima and Nagasaki signaled a quantum leap in the destructiveness of modern weaponry, precipitating one of the few genuine revolutions in military affairs. Initially, the Soviets resisted such logic. Under Stalin, Soviet military science downplayed the importance of the bomb, pointing instead to the continuing validity of what were termed "the five permanently operating factors" of war, first enumerated by the Soviet dictator in the closing months of the war.[13]

Stalin's refusal to accord nuclear weapons any special status was based both on military and on political considerations. The operational significance of the weapons was as yet unclear, according to Soviet military theorists, owing to the circumstances of their initial use. Attacking the defenseless cities of an exhausted adversary, smaller and more densely populated than the state of California, was hardly the same as carrying out an effective air offensive, atomic or otherwise, against a country as large and as well-defended as the Soviet Union—a point, incidentally, not lost on U.S. military planners in the early postwar years.[14] At a political level, Stalin could not afford to manifest anxiety at the appearance of these weapons; were he to do so, he must have reasoned, the Americans could seek to deprive the Kremlin of the fruits of its hard-fought military victory, especially in Europe, where Soviet forces were now firmly installed, from Germany in the north to Bulgaria in the south. Looking to the future, to cower before the bomb could also provide the United States with a valuable new tool to threaten and coerce the Soviet Union in the struggle for power and influence that was likely to develop between East and West in the postwar period. Such considerations, however, did not prevent what amounted to a crash Soviet program to acquire the weapons. The first Soviet test of an atomic (or fission) weapon took place in August 1949, followed four years later by the detonation of a mixed, fission-fusion device.

With Stalin's death in 1953, the Soviet military was at last free to investigate the impact of nuclear weapons on doctrine, strategy, and tactics. There ensued a lively series of debates, conducted for the most part on the pages of *Voennaya mysl'* (*Military Thought*), the limited-circulation journal of the Soviet General Staff.[15] In 1960 the first stage of the debate drew to a close with the promulgation of a new military doctrine, in which senior Soviet officials, civilian as well as military, acknowledged the primacy of nuclear weapons. Their use in war, the Soviets now admitted, would prove "decisive" to the outcome, most notably in any conflict involving the United States and the Soviet Union.

DOCTRINE AND STRATEGY: 1964–1985

In its broad outlines, this doctrinal reformulation was to inform the development of Soviet military policies for more than 25 years, supplying the intellectual justification for the expansion of nuclear capabilities that began in earnest in the last several years of Khrushchev's tenure and continued, more or less without interruption, until Chernenko's death in 1985. During these years, those charged with safeguarding Soviet security interests focused much of their attention on resolving two interconnected problems associated with the acquisition by Washington and Moscow of large and extraordinarily destructive nuclear weapons arsenals.

Deterring the Americans

The first and most immediate task was to forestall any U.S. preemptive nuclear strike against the USSR and to complicate any American plans for possible recourse to nuclear weapons in the event of a local conflict with the potential to escalate. Given Soviet assessments of the inherently aggressive nature of imperialism, as well as the reality of U.S. strategic superiority throughout the 1950s and early 1960s, the problem was a real one from the Kremlin's perspective, and one that the Soviet leadership moved quickly to address. An important catalyst in this regard was the Cuban missile crisis, which had exposed the underlying weakness of Moscow's nuclear posture.

To a degree, of course, the problem was of Soviet making. In an effort to extract political mileage from the early successes of the Soviet space and ballistic missile programs, Khrushchev had resorted to a kind of nuclear saber-rattling, in which on at least one occasion he directed his premier to threaten London and Paris with thermonuclear incineration;[16] other incidents involving the great powers, over Berlin for example, sensitized the West to the Kremlin's growing nuclear might. Rather than making the West more pliant, the technique only accelerated Washington's nuclear buildup; the result was a strategic balance by the early 1960s at least as precarious from the Soviet perspective as any that had existed during the postwar period.

Two other responses were rather more effective in buttressing Moscow's deterrent. The first was the decision by the post-Stalin leadership to communicate to the West the essentials of Soviet military doctrine in the form of a General Staff publication, edited by Marshal V. D. Sokolovskii.[17] Three versions of the text appeared between 1962 and 1968; in each edition, the authors described the basic elements of contemporary Soviet military thought. Most important in this context was the depiction of Soviet political-military purposes as profoundly *defensive* in nature—the protection of the USSR and the socialist community against unprovoked attack—rather than offensive or aggressive, as often portrayed in the West, and the claim that any war involving the Soviet Union and the United States would likely eventuate in a strategic nuclear exchange, regardless of how it began.

The first assertion was designed to reassure the West that it had nothing to fear from the growth in Soviet military capabilities; the second was to disabuse American military planners of any illusions they might have had about keeping a war between Washington and Moscow "limited," either in its intensity or geographic scope. The Soviets also sought to convince the imperialists that while a world war waged with nuclear weapons would wreak untold havoc on the combatants, the superiority of socialism, moral as well as material, would enable the Soviet Union and its allies to prevail. In light of the conditions then obtaining, it is extremely unlikely that any responsible official in Moscow put much faith in this claim—but, then again, such was not its central purpose.

The second response was the decision to emplace "survivable" nuclear forces in sufficient numbers and of sufficient range to pose a credible retaliatory threat to the United States, following any American first strike. The Soviets had been the first to test and to deploy a land-based intercontinental-range ballistic missile in the second half of the 1950s, but this first-generation system was never procured in any numbers, a fact known to the American intelligence community within several years of its appearance.[18] The missile itself was extremely vulnerable to preemption: not only did it require fueling immediately before launch, thereby reducing its operational readiness, but it was also deployed above ground. Such exposed basing made the missiles tempting targets for American weaponeers, who, assuming they could locate the missiles, could disable them by nuclear detonations in the general vicinity of the launch sites. Their only possible military utility was in a first strike, which only served to heighten existing American anxieties and to increase the probability that the United States might attack first in a crisis. In other words, rather than enhancing deterrence, as Moscow doubtless intended, the first Soviet ICBMs had the perverse effect of undermining it.

To remedy the situation and to provide additional assurance against attack, between the early 1960s and the early 1970s the Soviets procured hundreds of second- and third-generation long-range missile systems that they deployed in silos, significantly reducing their vulnerability. The missiles were powered by storable liquid fuel, which guaranteed a much higher degree of readiness than had heretofore been the case. By the late 1960s, the Soviets were also building ballistic missile submarines, the most "survivable" launch platforms for nuclear weapons, given the difficulty in detecting their whereabouts—a necessary first step in their elimination (for a more detailed discussion of these issues, see below). Moscow further augmented its deterrent stance during the decade by accelerating warhead production, improving command-and-control arrangemen.●, and expanding and upgrading the country's early-warning systems.

In short, by the time the first SALT negotiations convened in 1969, the Soviet Union had put in place a reliable capacity to retaliate with devastating effectiveness for any American preemptive strike, a key requirement of a stable deterrent balance. Only slightly less significant, given the importance of appearances in world politics, Moscow was also beginning to close the gap with Washington quantitatively, as the number of deployed Soviet missiles and heavy bombers topped 1,500—versus approximately 2,200 for the United States. Moreover, the Soviets were building new strategic systems at the rate of several hundred per year; U.S. deployments, by contrast, had leveled off at the end of 1967.[19]

What If Deterrence Fails?

Having solved at least for a time this first-order problem associated with the advent of nuclear weapons, the Soviets were able to concentrate on a second, more vexing, problem. Granted that these weapons had vastly complicated military thought, not to mention the development, design, and execution of military operations. Could they also be said to have disrupted the traditional relationship between war and politics, as many in the West were arguing?

Were they in fact "absolute" weapons, in the sense that their reciprocal use could well eliminate the distinction between victor and vanquished?

Moscow's answer, which evolved across the twenty years of the Brezhnev era, was always equivocal, the result of crosscurrents generated by ideology, military experience, economic considerations, informed observation, common sense, and self-interest.[20] At the outset of the period, the Soviets seemed drawn to the logic of victory, despite the manifold obstacles to the realization of such a goal under conditions of nuclear plenty. To suggest otherwise was to open to question the final triumph of socialism over capitalism which was, after all, historically determined. The ultimate victory of socialism did not require the defeat of capitalism by force of arms; the latter, rent by ever-more intense "contradictions," would eventually collapse of its own accord. On the other hand, in their desperation the imperialists might well resort to war in a misguided effort to arrest the forces of history; should they do so, the Soviet Union and its allies must be in a position to respond decisively to deny the aggressors their war aims. Given a failure of deterrence, in other words, the purpose of military strategy would shift, from the prevention of war to the attainment of victory.

How, precisely, to ensure such a favorable outcome, however, was a policy conundrum of the first rank. Assuming a contest between relative equals, the key to military victory had always been the ability to destroy the enemy's armed forces. By so doing, the adversary's power to coerce, its capacity to inflict pain for political purposes, is at least attenuated, if not eliminated altogether. In the nuclear age, neutralizing the enemy's ability to inflict pain could be accomplished in two ways, most likely in combination: through the preemptive use of one's own offensive weapons to destroy as much of the enemy's striking power as possible; and through the ability to shield one's territory and population from the effects of direct attack. By the early 1970s the ability of the United States and the Soviet Union to destroy at least a fraction of the other side's offensive forces through preemptive strikes was impressive, and getting better all the time. The capacity to defend against the enemy's inevitable retaliatory strike, however, was poor, and getting worse. The predictable consequences of even a relatively small return volley—representing, for example, no more than 20 percent of each side's prewar arsenal—were sufficient, in U.S. calculations, to dissuade any sane leader from initiating a nuclear conflict.

Under Brezhnev, the Soviets devoted significant resources to the acquisition of an assured retaliatory capability. They also invested tens of billions of rubles in the development of weapons deemed by U.S. analysts to be "counterforce"-capable—that is, weapons configured for possible first use against stationary or fixed military assets, especially silo-based long-range ballistic missiles, ballistic missile submarines not on patrol, and important command-and-control installations. From this development, above all others, arose the concerns expressed in the 1970s by many in the United States about Soviet military intentions and the alleged commitment of the Kremlin to the development of a nuclear warfighting strategy.

At the same time, the Soviets were investing heavily (how heavily remains a matter of dispute) in strategic defensive measures, presumably to lessen the consequences of any American *second* strike. Western observers pointed with particular alarm to the construction of an antiballistic missile (ABM) system around Moscow, to the existence of a nationwide air-defense network, and to the Kremlin's persistent interest in civil defense, all of which were seen to underscore the Soviet Union's determination to erect an effective damage-limiting posture.

The readiness of Soviet leaders to conclude an agreement with the United States severely limiting antiballistic missiles strongly suggests, however, that the Kremlin's commitment to a nuclear war–fighting strategy remained tentative and problematic. Despite the clear emphasis in Soviet policy on the procurement of active and passive measures designed to limit damage in the event of war, the fact remains that in signing the ABM Treaty in 1972, the Soviets deprived themselves of the single most promising near-term technology for alleviating the destructive consequences of any large-scale nuclear exchange between the superpowers. That they probably did so out of narrow self-interest—the Americans were in a better position to exploit the technology at this time—should not obscure the larger point: only through the aggressive pursuit of ABM and ABM-related technologies could the Kremlin hope to implement a credible strategy for waging and winning a nuclear war. In closing off that option, they resigned themselves, in practice and at least for a time, to a "deterrence-through-punishment," rather than a "deterrence-through-denial," strategy.

As Raymond Garthoff convincingly argues, the Kremlin's doubts about the utility of victory as the organizing principle of contemporary Soviet military strategy were already well advanced by the time that the U.S. and Soviet SALT negotiators began their deliberations in 1969. Among the evidence in support of this contention were high-level military discussions, conducted during the late 1960s and throughout the 1970s, in which the resort to nuclear weapons in a war involving the West was equated with national suicide. Senior civilian officials expressed similar sentiments, but their pronouncements were often confused and capable of being interpreted in different ways.[21]

It was against this backdrop that Soviet military authorities worked to develop plans for keeping a possible East-West conflict in Europe non-nuclear by devising various "withhold" strategies (thereby placing the onus on NATO for any first use of nuclear weapons) and by targeting with conventional forces the alliance's tactical and theater nuclear assets. Creating a viable "conventional option," as this strategy was termed in the West, also helps to explain the extensive upgrading of Soviet and other Warsaw Pact theater military forces that began in the mid-1970s.[22] These efforts notwithstanding, senior Soviet officials appear to have had relatively little confidence at this or any other juncture that a major military engagement between the forces of NATO and the Warsaw Pact could remain non-nuclear for long. Certainly any *strategic* exchange between the United States and the Soviet Union would very likely begin—and end—with nuclear strikes.

The Soviet dilemma was clear. Though perhaps unlikely, a nuclear war between socialist and capitalist states could not be ruled out. Both the weight of ideology and simple military logic suggested that in the event, the Soviet Union should seek to prevail. However, the irreducibility of the U.S. nuclear deterrent, coupled with the inadequacy of defensive measures, rendered that goal unattainable, at least for a time. What to do?

Accommodating the Nuclear Revolution

By the mid-1970s the leadership had settled on a three-part strategy that combined elements of traditional military thought with the emerging logic of nuclear deterrence. It was an uneasy fit. The first part of the strategy, which operated somewhat at cross-purposes with the other two, was the decision to maintain a high degree of operational military readiness, which Moscow linked to the undiminished threat posed by imperialism, both to deter the West and to communicate Moscow's resolve to safeguard and, if possible, extend the boundaries of the international socialist community. While understandable, the Kremlin's heavy reliance on military power to establish and maintain its status as Washington's equal was in the final analysis counterproductive; the United States, observing the steady growth in Soviet military capabilities across the preceding decade, eventually took fright and initiated a corresponding buildup that largely offset whatever political and military advantages the Kremlin might have been seeking through the expansion of its armed forces.

The second element was the willingness to conclude arms control agreements with the United States, a tactic that yielded rather better results. In addition to the modest military benefits that might have accrued from the process, arms control treaties, particularly those limiting or otherwise constraining central strategic systems, eased the threat of war, or so Moscow seemed to believe. In the Kremlin's judgment, successful arms control weakened American reactionaries and strengthened the hand of what Soviet observers called the "realists" within U.S. "ruling circles," diminishing the likelihood of conflict.[23] To the extent that an American president could negotiate with his Soviet counterparts on sensitive military issues and still secure reelection, Soviet interests could be served. Such in fact was the case during the Nixon years, although by the end of President Gerald Ford's tenure in office in 1977 the strategy had already started to unravel for a complex of reasons, some under Moscow's control, some not, but all of which the Soviets professed not to understand.

By 1981 the arms control process had ceased to generate any rewards worth mentioning from the Soviet perspective, and while the leadership continued to emphasize its value—and to bemoan its demise—the endorsement had a hollow ring. Besides, the Americans had just elected as president Ronald Reagan, who, as one of SALT's most forceful critics, was unlikely to rush to conclude any new agreements with Moscow. For the time being, substantial arms control was at an end. With its disappearance, the Kremlin lost a useful tool, not only for gauging U.S. military intentions, but also for influencing American defense policy more generally.

The third element in Moscow's strategy was in many ways the most interesting. In a series of very high-level statements, beginning in earnest with Brezhnev's January 1977 address in the city of Tula (for centuries a center of Russian and later Soviet arms manufacture), the leadership sought to rearticulate important provisions of the country's military doctrine. Coming at the very outset of the Carter administration, one clear purpose was to set a more positive tone for U.S.–Soviet relations in the wake of what had been a difficult several years. A second purpose, however, was to enunciate a change in doctrine, or, more precisely, to draw out certain emendations to doctrine, some of recent vintage, that U.S. policymakers could not have known about, had failed to detect, or had misconstrued. In his remarks, Brezhnev explicitly rejected military superiority as a goal of Soviet policy, endorsed the concepts of strategic parity and a stable deterrent balance, and reaffirmed Moscow's interest in nuclear arms control.[24]

In what came to be known in the West as the "Tula line," other senior Soviet authorities, including Defense Minister Dmitri Ustinov and chief of the General Staff Nikolai Ogarkov, echoed and, in some cases, amplified the general secretary's remarks, both then and later.[25] In July 1982, Ustinov, for example, explained the government's decision to undertake a commitment not to be the first to use nuclear weapons, announced the previous May, as Moscow's response to the spiraling arms race; he also linked the decision to what he termed the inadmissibility of the resort to war, especially nuclear war, as a means for resolving international differences.[26] Brezhnev himself returned to these themes on several occasions, most notably at the twenty-sixth CPSU congress in February 1981 and in a *Pravda* statement, released over his signature, in October of the same year.[27] In each instance, the overarching goal, it appears, was to reassure the United States that while the Soviet Union had taken, and would continue to take, reasonable precautions to provide for its security and to maintain rough strategic parity with the United States, the Kremlin had not and would not attempt to upset the existing military balance and did not subscribe to the thesis that a nuclear war could be fought and won. The Soviets also reiterated their willingness to reduce their nuclear forces on a reciprocal basis with Washington to the lowest possible level.

When, however, in March 1977 the Soviet leadership rejected the Carter administration's proposal for "deep cuts" in central strategic systems, Washington's skepticism about the sincerity of Moscow's new line, already substantial, deepened. Foreign Minister Andrei Gromyko's efforts to justify the Soviet action—in which he asserted that the proposals constituted an abrupt and unwarranted departure from what had been achieved in the SALT II negotiations *and*, if implemented, would redound to Washington's advantage— did little to ease U.S. suspicions.[28]

The task of sorting out Soviet intentions grew more difficult during the remaining years of the Brezhnev leadership, as Moscow, responding to the perceived need to maintain military vigilance and to keep up with the Americans, pressed ahead with several high-visibility strategic nuclear programs, including yet another generation of land-based ballistic missiles, a new class of ballistic missile submarine, and development of a long-range strategic bomber (see below). The fact that, overall, Soviet military procurements remained constant (actually declining in some areas) between 1977 and 1982, was not apparent at the time and was only revealed by U.S. intelligence at mid-decade. Soviet military spending, which had grown at an annual rate of approximately 5 percent between 1966 and the early 1970s, also slowed during the second half of the Brezhnev era, averaging roughly a 2 percent increase each year.[29]

In reviewing the development of Soviet military thinking from the mid-1960s to the mid-1980s, the analyst is struck by the relative orderliness with which the period began and the confusion with which it ended. Upon their assumption of power in 1964, the new Soviet leaders, acting in concert with the uniformed military, sanctioned a number of important revisions to doctrine, reactivated certain command arrangements that had been discarded in earlier years, accelerated weapons production, and sought to rationalize procurement practices. They did so in order to eliminate or to correct for the many distortions in military affairs which, in their judgment, had been introduced by Khrushchev. They moved with particular alacrity, for example, to do away with the so-called one-variant strategy for a war between East and West, in which an exchange of nuclear-tipped ballistic missiles would begin the conflict and determine its outcome. In its place they substituted a less rigid formula, one which would allow for a range of military contingencies—from an engagement featuring conventional weapons only, at one end of the spectrum, to an all-out nuclear war, at the other.

In keeping with these reforms, in 1967 the leadership also restored an independent ground-forces command, which Khrushchev had seen fit to abolish some five years before.[30] The regime increased spending on weapons of all types and pressed Soviet research and development facilities with renewed vigor to exploit emerging technological opportunities of possible utility to the armed forces. In short, within several years of its arrival, the post-Khrushchev leadership had imparted a degree of purposiveness to Soviet military planning that had been lacking during much of the previous decade. Most notably in terms of output, the strategy paid off handsomely in the near term, impressing not only those responsible for the expansion, but Western observers as well.

By the early part of the 1980s, the environment had changed considerably. While the drive to attain essential military equality with the United States had produced a strategic posture every bit as menacing as Washington's, the Kremlin had discovered that this remarkable achievement did not matter all that much. The political rewards, such as they were, hardly seemed to justify the expense. Expressive of the irony in this situation was an *Economist* cover in 1981: an aged Brezhnev, his marshal's uniform ablaze with medals, stared uncertainly off into the distance; at the bottom of the page, the caption read, "All Dressed Up and No Place to Go."[31]

After almost two decades of unremitting effort, in other words, the Soviet Union had become a military colossus, only to find that its political power within the international community—its power to effect outcomes advantageous to Soviet interests—had not kept pace; if anything, it had declined relative to that of the West, which was beginning to emerge from the economic recession and accompanying political malaise of the late 1970s. To make matters worse, Moscow's global ambitions had all but bankrupted the country, leaving the Soviet people materially worse off relative to their counterparts in neighboring capitalist states than at the outset of Brezhnev's tenure.

As it slowly absorbed the implications of this disturbing reality, the exhausted leadership struggled to respond. In the narrow area of doctrine, it introduced important modifications that it hoped would convey to the West the fundamentally defensive character of Soviet military power. It proclaimed its adherence to American-style deterrence, denounced the pursuit of military superiority, and rejected the notion of victory in a nuclear war. It did so, however, in a vocabulary that was arcane, obscure, and open to interpretation. Most importantly, Brezhnev and his two immediate successors refused to sanction the two actions that might have generated a positive response from their Western interlocutors: unilateral cuts in the country's bloated military establishment, followed by good-faith proposals for deep, bilateral reductions in U.S. and Soviet nuclear and conventional forces. Absent these steps, the leadership's dogged efforts to convince the West of the fundamentally benign purposes of Soviet military power rang hollow. It would take a veritable revolution in Kremlin foreign and security policies to accomplish that objective, which in 1985 was still several years away.

THE DEVELOPMENT OF SOVIET MILITARY CAPABILITIES

In 1965 the argument that the expansion of Soviet military power could prove dysfunctional would have struck Kremlin leaders as incredible. It was the perceived weakness of the country's military posture, at least in part, that had emboldened Brezhnev and his co-conspirators to retire Khrushchev in the first place. So serious had the situation become that by the time of the October 1962 Cuban missile crisis Soviet leaders had reason to fear a disarming American first strike. At the time, the United States possessed something on the order of a 4:1 advantage over the Soviet Union in the number of deployed strategic systems; measured in terms of deliverable weapons, the margin of superiority might have been two to three times as high, particularly if the Americans had chosen to strike first.[32] By any calculation, Moscow's plight was a desperate one.

Strategic Nuclear Forces

In order to improve the Soviet Union's relative military standing, within months of its assumption to power the new leadership embarked upon a broadly based program to expand and diversify the country's nuclear and conventional capabilities. As noted, the results were remarkable, especially in the area of long-range, land-based missile development. In 1964 the Soviets had approximately 200 deployed ICBMs, predominantly the second-generation SS-7, which, while a marked improvement over its predecessor, suffered from a number of technical and operational shortcomings. Five years later the Kremlin maintained well over 1,000 operational ICBMs, mostly third-generation weapons, including some 700 SS-11s and 200 SS-9s, to that point the largest missile system (for military purposes) ever produced.[33] In contrast to earlier Soviet weapons, the latter two systems were deployed in vertical underground silos, affording them a higher degree of readiness, as well as greater protection against attack. The SS-9 provoked no small alarm among American defense officials. Not only was the missile's payload immense, enabling it deliver an extremely large warhead across great distances, but it could also be refitted at some future date with MIRV technology. With multiple warheads, these missiles could pose a major threat to U.S. Minuteman and Titan missiles, the land-based leg of Washington's nuclear triad.

In 1975 the Soviets began to phase in three additional systems—the SS-17, SS-18, and SS-19—to supplement and replace those deployed between the mid-1960s and the early 1970s. Each was equipped with MIRV warheads, their accuracy approaching those of the best American weapons. The SS-18 force alone grew to contain some 3,000 warheads, or half again as many as had been deployed with the U.S. Minuteman and Titan ICBMs. When Presidents Carter and Brezhnev signed the SALT II treaty in June 1979, the Kremlin's arsenal of long-range silo-based missiles had grown to some 1,400 (down from a high of 1,618 in 1975), outfitted with roughly 6,000 warheads. During the first half of the 1980s, the pace of modernization slackened, although it did not stop. Two new systems, the ten-warhead SS-24 and the single-warhead SS-25, were introduced as one-for-one replacements for the SS-17 (in the former case) and for the SS-11 and SS-13 (in the latter case); both were paired with mobile launchers.

A similar momentum characterized the ballistic missile submarine (SSBN) program, which between 1968 and 1985 turned out 50 boats, as well as some 800 missiles. In all, the Soviets produced three classes of SSBN—Yankee, Delta, and Typhoon—and six distinct missile types, with ranges of up to 9,000 kilometers. In 1978 the first Soviet submarine-launched ballistic missile (SLBM) equipped with MIRV became operational, ten years after the United States had begun to introduce such systems. By 1985 the Soviets were maintaining 62 modern ballistic missile submarines, armed with 950 SLBMs and approximately 3,000 warheads.

In contrast to the United States, which devoted enormous resources to the procurement of intercontinental-range bombers in the postwar period, the Soviets all but ignored the development of strategic airpower, focusing instead on missile production. Following an initial flirtation with long-range bombers during the 1950s, which resulted in the production of several hundred Mya-4 Bison and Tu-20 Bear bombers, the Soviets drew back. In 1986 they began flight-testing the Tu-160, or Blackjack bomber, the first such Soviet venture in 25 years. The aircraft, which is similar to, though larger than, the American B1-B, endured an abnormally long developmental cycle. Begun under Brezhnev, the Blackjack never entered serial production.

No such reticence marked Soviet efforts in the area of strategic defenses. While the ABM treaty prevented any significant quantitative expansion of the Moscow-based *Galosh* system, the agreement permitted extensive qualitative improvements. The leadership sanctioned several costly upgrades of the system from the early 1970s to the mid-1980s. It also undertook an expensive program to enhance the country's early warning capabilities, particularly against the short-flight-time SLBMs. One part of this effort resulted in the construction of a large phased-array radar in central Siberia, near the city of Krasnoyarsk, that contravened a key provision of the

ABM treaty; the radar constituted a minor, if persistent, irritant in relations between Washington and Moscow during the early 1980s that was not resolved until late in the decade. No arms control agreements limited work on the Soviet Union's nationwide system of air defenses, which continued to expand, both in terms of coverage and sophistication.

The U.S. Defense Department has estimated that for the entire postwar period total Soviet expenditures on the strategic defensive mission (including air-defense systems) equaled or surpassed the Kremlin's spending on offensive forces; for the years 1965 to 1985, the latter is likely to have absorbed proportionately greater resources than the former, though by how much is probably impossible to determine. By any measure, however, the leadership's drive to provide Soviet society with at least some degree of protection against nuclear attack can only be described as prodigious.

Precisely what in operational military terms the Soviets were trying to accomplish with their strategic nuclear buildup remains something of a mystery. The argument that they sought to deter the outbreak of nuclear war is correct, of course, but insufficient; it does not explain, for example, the Kremlin's heavy investment in counterforce-capable weapon systems and its persistent fascination with active and passive measures designed to limit damage in the event of a nuclear exchange. An alternative explanation, that Moscow aimed at nothing less than the potential to fight and win a nuclear war is equally unsatisfying, unless one assumes a degree of technological ignorance on the part of the leadership that is almost willful in its dimensions. Especially with an adversary as well-armed as the United States, it is difficult to imagine senior Soviet leaders holding faithfully to a vision of military strategy with "victory" as its centerpiece.

The most compelling explanation is that beyond an ability to deter, Moscow sought against ever-increasing odds to mitigate the predictable consequences of war. To paraphrase analyst Michael MccGwire, the overarching Soviet purpose during these years was not to prevail in a nuclear war with Washington, but to survive it; not to win, in other words, but also not to lose.[34] Even this relatively modest goal, however, was to prove elusive as time went on. Owing to the peculiar dynamics of the nuclear competition between the superpowers, each Soviet move to enhance its relative military standing—which the leadership routinely characterized as "defensive" in nature—only seemed to provoke the Americans (if not at the time, then later), resulting in some action or combination of actions that either devalued Moscow's initial move or actually made matters worse from a military perspective.

By the mid-1980s, the strategic military balance was no more favorable to the Soviet Union than it had been ten years before, despite expenditures totaling several hundred billion rubles. In an effort both to deny and to accommodate the nuclear revolution, the Soviets failed to do either. In the mistaken belief that the acquisition of more and better nuclear weapons would generate tangible military rewards and greater security, Moscow pressed ahead, oblivious to the mounting evidence that such was not the case; too late in the process to have much of an impact on the Soviet Union's declining political and economic fortunes, the leadership was to discover that the weapons did neither.

Theater Military Forces

A similar confidence in the utility of military power influenced the Brezhnev leadership's stance toward the development of the Soviet Union's theater nuclear and conventional capabilities, particularly in Europe, where the formidable armies of the Warsaw Pact confronted well-armed NATO forces. At 31 divisions, 20 of them concentrated within immediate striking distance of the inter-German border, Moscow's European military presence constituted a powerful reminder to the West of the Soviet Union's seemingly unshakable commitment to safeguard the "postwar gains of socialism." In the 1970s most Western observers attached special weight to the rapid growth of the Soviet Union's strategic nuclear arsenal in detailing the Kremlin's rise to superpower status. Less often the focus of analysis was the development of the country's theater military capabilities, a task to which the Soviets appear to have devoted at least as much attention and even greater resources.

In rejecting the Khrushchev formula for war with the West (the one-variant strategy), the political leadership made it possible for senior officials within the Ministry of Defense and the General Staff to undertake a wide-ranging assessment of Soviet theater military requirements in light of the evolving nature of Western capabilities and, after 1967, of changes in NATO strategy. A principal conclusion of this reappraisal was that a war in Europe could well begin with a prolonged conventional phase, as each side resisted the temptation to employ nuclear weapons for fear of escalation. Given NATO's explicit threat to resort to the use of such weapons, however, Western restraint could end abruptly and without warning, especially if the war were going badly for the United States and its allies. Keeping the nuclear threshold in Europe as high as possible became, therefore, an important objective under Brezhnev. In service of that goal, senior Soviet military authorities with responsibility for the defense of the Warsaw Pact enacted a number of far-reaching reforms, organizational as well as operational, specifically designed to enhance the ability of the alliance both to wage a non-nuclear military campaign in Europe and to conclude hostilities on terms favorable to the East.

An exhaustive review of the Kremlin's decade-long undertaking to enhance the ability of Soviet (and Warsaw Pact) forces to conduct sustained, large-scale, and effective military operations in Europe lies beyond the scope of this chapter.[35] For purposes of the present analysis, a brief review of three developments should suffice to illustrate not only the scale of the effort, but also its underlying intent.

Paradoxically, given the emphasis in Soviet writings on the military inutility of nuclear weapons in the theater, the most visible change in the Kremlin's posture toward Europe was the appearance beginning in 1977 of the SS-20 intermediate-range ballistic missile. Deployment of two "operational-tactical" missile systems, the SS-21 and SS-23, followed in 1978 and 1979, respectively. To reduce the likelihood of NATO counterdeployments, the Kremlin characterized all three weapons as "modernizations" of or "replacements" for existing systems.[36] Whatever the merits of Soviet claims, the West reacted poorly to the new missiles. NATO established a high-level group in 1977 to examine the problem of Soviet nuclear modernization and to issue recommendations. The "Dual Track" decision followed two years later, by which alliance members agreed to seek reductions in Soviet long-range theater nuclear forces through negotiations and, failing such a venture, to begin the deployment of some 572 American Pershing II and ground-launched cruise missiles on the territory of five NATO states.

In retrospect, the Kremlin's decision to press ahead with the procurement of advanced, intermediate- and medium-range nuclear systems was a mistake, arousing a determined Western response that was to place at risk important elements of the Soviet Union's strategic, as well as theater, nuclear posture. That this should have been the case was not without irony. The West saw the Soviet deployments as a Kremlin attempt to secure a position of manifest nuclear dominance in Europe. While such thinking might have played a part in Moscow's calculations, at least as central to Soviet decision-makers was the perceived need to *restore* a reliable deterrent balance of theater nuclear forces in Europe, which in their judgment had deteriorated markedly since the mid-1960s.[37] In other words, whatever ambitions the Soviets might have had regarding the provision of forces suitable for waging an effective nuclear campaign against NATO were secondary to enhancing the deterrent posture of the Warsaw Pact. Lending credibility to this interpretation was Moscow's unwavering rejection of limited nuclear war as a viable military option, particularly in the European context, which they routinely condemned as a dangerous chimera;[38] in fact, it was the West's persistent fascination with the concept, in the Kremlin's view, that made all too real the possibility of a major war in Europe.

Western defense officials also reacted with deepening alarm to the continuous introduction during the mid-to-late 1970s of new or improved weapons systems designed to enhance the offensive firepower and sustainability of Soviet conventional forces. Areas long accorded special weight in Moscow's military planning, such as armor (tanks, armored fighting vehicles, and armored personnel carriers) and artillery, fared well during these years. It was, however, developments in tactical air power, or what the Soviets termed frontal aviation, that made perhaps the greatest impression on Western military experts.

In the 1970s the Soviets introduced a number of aircraft whose primary mission was to operate in tandem with advancing Warsaw Pact ground forces in order to facilitate realization of the alliance's ambitious military objectives (such as the prompt seizure of as much NATO terrain as possible). In contrast to earlier generations of

Soviet fighters that had been built largely for purposes of air defense, the newer aircraft—such as the MiG-27J Flogger, Su-17H/K Fitter, Su-24 Fencer, and Su-25 Frogfoot—could perform a much wider range of military missions, including close air support, ground attack, and deep strike. This shift in emphasis gave rise to fresh fears in the West about the ability of the Warsaw Pact to make good on its threat to carry a war to the territory of its adversary from the very outset of hostilities, thereby vastly complicating NATO's plans for a "forward defense." Longer-range bombers, such as the Tu-22 Backfire, which, like the Su-24, could deliver nuclear as well as conventional ordnance, further complicated Western military planning and contributed to the widely held belief that the Soviet Union was bent on nothing less than the attainment of usable military superiority in Europe.

At about the same time, the Soviets undertook a third set of activities that seemed to confirm the malevolence of the Kremlin's intentions. At the urging of Marshal Ogarkov, chief of the Soviet General Staff from 1977 to 1984, the military proposed and the civilian leadership sanctioned the establishment of so-called theaters of military operations (or TVD, for Teatr Voennykh Deistvii), an intermediate level of command intended to function between the various fronts and supreme military headquarters in Moscow. The announced purpose of the reform was to rationalize Soviet military planning and to streamline preparations for war. Western observers reacted sharply, noting that the only precedent for such an action was Moscow's experience in World War II, during which Stalin had instituted a similar command structure to correct the glaring deficiencies that characterized Soviet military operations during the opening phases of the war. It certainly did not relieve Western anxieties when senior Soviet military spokesmen, including Ogarkov, began to draw explicit parallels between international conditions obtaining in the early 1980s and those of 1938–1939.[39]

As with the considerable expansion in Soviet strategic forces under Brezhnev, the leadership's decision to allocate precious resources to modernize and expand Warsaw Pact theater capabilities is difficult to explain by simple reference to the logic of deterrence and defense. By these standards, the buildup must be considered excessive, if not provocative. The growth in the Soviet navy during these years, as well as the ongoing improvements to theater forces deployed elsewhere along the Soviet periphery, such as the border with China, fall into the same category.

Perhaps senior Soviet leaders, military and civilian, believed that war with the West remained a distinct possibility, if not a near-term prospect, despite some thirty years of peace, making the provision of robust military capabilities not just desirable, but a national imperative. Perhaps others within the national security decision-making apparatus clung to a belief in the attainability of at least a negotiated victory over the West in the event of conventional military hostilities. Perhaps it was a case of bureaucratic inertia, attributable to the influence of a Soviet "military-industrial complex," that made it difficult to arrest the process of expansion, absent decisive and sustained intervention by high-ranking political leaders. Or perhaps the steady growth in capabilities was the price of the military's support for détente and arms control with the West, extracted from a reluctant political leadership either too preoccupied or too exhausted to resist the demands of the armed forces.

The answer, probably, lies in a combination of these and other motives and pressures that even the leadership might have had a hard time articulating. At base, however, it was the strongly held conviction that in a world divided along class lines—a world in which the clash of interests between East and West could turn violent at any moment—the most reliable guarantee of peace was the deployment of forces adequate to deter any imperialist military adventure directed against the Soviet Union or its allies. The armed forces of the state, Brezhnev frequently reminded his listeners, must be sufficient to dissuade a would-be opponent from any and all attempts to disturb "the peaceful labor of the Soviet people."[40] And for much of 1960s and 1970s, Soviet leaders were drawn to a military formula that in answer to the question, How much is enough? could supply but one response: more.

ARMS CONTROL

Few issues in connection with the Soviet Union were more thoroughly scrutinized by U.S. Kremlin watchers than Moscow's arms control policies. In this the Kremlinologists were joined by members of the U.S. defense and strategic studies communities. That this should have been the case is hardly surprising. Apart from the occasional crisis, for a period of some twenty years, stretching from the late 1960s to the late 1980s, superpower arms control was the principal output—much of the process and most of the substance— of U.S.–Soviet relations. With negotiations underway, pundits were inclined to describe relations as "good," or at least improving; when there were no talks, or when discussions had broken down, these same observers often pronounced relations "tense," or in decline. For better than two decades, arms control functioned as a bell-wether of the superpower relationship. In part, this reflected a lack of movement in other dimensions of the U.S.–Soviet dialogue; little else of real importance seemed to be happening. At a second level, however, the preoccupation made sense: arms control negotiations were very serious business, an apparently earnest attempt by U.S. and Soviet leaders to reduce the burden of nuclear and conventional armaments and to prevent the outbreak of war. Little wonder, then, that many of the best-known Soviet specialists in the United States either made or enhanced their reputations by commenting on developments in arms control.

A precise rendering of Soviet positions in the major arms control negotiations of the period—SALT I, SALT II, the Central European force reduction negotiations, INF, and START—is neither necessary to nor appropriate for this analysis. A number of excellent studies have been written on these and related topics, many of which recount, in exquisite detail, the evolution of Soviet objectives, attitudes, positions, and negotiating strategies.[41] The story of Soviet arms control under Brezhnev has been told often and well, in other words. (It should be noted, however, that as good as these accounts are, they are also flawed, inasmuch as they rely almost exclusively on Western, rather than Soviet sources; with better access to Soviet materials, our knowledge of and interpretations regarding Moscow's motivations and conduct in this and other areas should improve significantly.)

A more useful approach is to address a number of questions about the Soviet Union and arms control that shed light on the Kremlin's experience at a more general level. What motivated Soviet leaders to enter into this process in the first place? Did their motives change over time and with experience? In Moscow's estimate, what, if anything of lasting value did the negotiations produce? And why, prior to Gorbachev, did the two sides fail to achieve greater progress in this sensitive and vital area?

The answer to the first question is deceptively simple. Kremlin leaders believed that by engaging the United States in a process of negotiation, initially focused on the limitation of strategic offensive and defense forces, they could enhance the international political standing, as well as the military security, of the Soviet state. The first of these two ambitions, enhanced prestige, appears to have been at the center of Soviet calculations, and strong, albeit circumstantial evidence exists in support of this contention.

The most telling evidence is that the Soviets said as much. In explaining (and justifying) the SALT process to its population, the leadership invariably took note of the profound political significance of the negotiations, insisting that they demonstrated the spectacular improvement in recent years in the "positions" of the socialist community, relative to those of the Western camp. In presenting the SALT I accords to the public, Soviet commentators typically began with a review of the Basic Principles of Relations Agreement, which Nixon and Brezhnev signed at the May 1972 summit in Moscow. In the agreement the two countries were treated as political actors of equal stature, with equal rights and responsibilities within the international system. The ABM Treaty and the Interim Agreement on Offensive Weapons, concluded at the same time, were also discussed in these analyses, often at considerable length, but in a way that suggested that the two accords were secondary to, and derivative of, the Basic Principles Agreement.

A second piece of evidence is Soviet conduct during the first phase of the SALT II negotiations (1972–1974). While the Americans lobbied hard to initiate discussions on a long-term treaty to regulate strategic offensive forces in anticipation of the expiration of the Interim Agreement in 1977, the Kremlin pressed for yet another political declaration (this one on the prevention of nuclear war) and for an intensification of economic and trade relations. The Soviet leadership seemed unprepared for, if not bewildered by, the American sense of urgency regarding the conclusion of a follow-on agreement to limit strategic nuclear forces, an urgency that had developed in the wake of the controversy surrounding the submission to Congress of the Interim Agreement. Only when the future of détente appeared to be at stake, during the spring and summer of 1974, did the Soviets at last become energized about SALT, enabling the two sides to agree in November 1974 at Vladivostok on a framework for a new treaty.[42]

In the first half of the 1970s, it was the political aspect of the arms control process, more than the concrete military ramifications, to which the Soviet leadership returned, again and again, in its discussions with representatives of the Nixon and Ford administrations. Although not insensitive to the symbolic significance of détente, the Americans became impatient with this Soviet posture, which delayed the negotiations and frustrated U.S. efforts to employ SALT as a device to constrain the growth in Soviet nuclear might.

Military considerations were not entirely absent, of course, in Moscow's arms control policies. In the strategic context, Soviet goals were of two kinds. The first was fundamentally defensive in character. The Kremlin's stance toward the ABM Treaty negotiations illustrates the point. In signing the treaty, the leadership agreed to the imposition of severe restrictions on a number of activities necessary to provide a measure of protection against nuclear-tipped ballistic missiles. The major incentive, it seems, was Moscow's estimate of the likely implications of an unregulated competition in the development and deployment of ABM systems, a competition the Soviets had begun but which the Americans had recently joined. Given U.S. technological strengths, the Kremlin appears to have determined that the United States could quickly overtake the Soviet lead in this area and attain for itself an important and, from Moscow's perspective, dangerous military advantage. Better to choke off the competition at an early stage, the Soviets seem to have reasoned, than to run the risk of falling behind, which could result in a serious deterioration of the country's military position, should the Americans ever succeed in deploying effective ABM systems.[43]

A second Soviet military goal in arms control was rather more ambitious, although not without a defensive element. As noted, in the 1970s the Soviets had yet to abandon the objective of "not losing" a nuclear war with the United States. In keeping with that objective, they insisted on terms in SALT that allowed them to continue with programs to improve the performance characteristics and operational readiness of their central strategic forces. The introduction of the so-called fourth-generation systems discussed earlier in this chapter was but the most visible manifestation of Moscow's determination to persist in such "modernization" efforts, within the qualitative and quantitative restrictions contained in SALT I and SALT II. Much to their chagrin, however, the Soviets were to discover that in demanding, and obtaining, such latitude for themselves, they also secured it for the United States, which shortly after the conclusion of SALT I announced its intention to press ahead with the development of a new, multiple-warhead land-based ballistic missile (the MX), the Trident submarine system, and the B-1 bomber. As the Kremlin moved to round out its strategic capabilities, in other words, Washington did the same.

A similar motivation—to preserve or to improve Moscow's relative military standing—inspired the Soviet negotiating strategy at the long-running (and ultimately unsuccessful) Mutual and Balanced Force Reduction negotiations (MBFR), in which some eleven NATO and Warsaw Pact countries took part, including the two superpowers. The negotiations, which convened in Vienna in 1973, were soon at an impasse, as each alliance advanced proposals intended to place severe restrictions on the forces it deemed most destabilizing (which invariably were those in abundance on the other side), while leaving its own capabilities as unfettered as possible. Western MBFR proposals were patently self-serving in this regard. Even so, they paled in comparison to the plans offered by the East, which relied on some of the most tortured reasoning ever employed in the history of U.S.–Soviet arms control negotiations.[44] A comparable set of goals heavily influenced Soviet positions in other forums, such as the negotiations on intermediate-range nuclear forces (INF), especially from their inception in 1981 to the Kremlin's walkout in 1983, and the START talks, during their initial phase (1982–1983).

It is unlikely that the Brezhnev leadership ever expected to extract usable military advantages at U.S. expense through arms control. At no point did Moscow anticipate that the agreements concluded with Washington, whatever their content, would eventuate in a clear shift in the military balance of power. To believe that the SALT negotiations, for example, could produce such an outcome, Soviet leaders would have had to assume that their American counterparts were either stupid or weak-willed. The evidence suggests that they assumed neither. They could, and probably did, assume that within the restraints imposed by SALT enough freedom would remain to complete the modernization cycle then underway, to compensate for steps the Americans might take to augment their own capabilities, and to position themselves for a rapid military "breakout" should the agreements already in place collapse or future negotiations end in failure. They also appear to have believed, at least during the first half of the 1970s, that by restricting some U.S. military programs, even at the cost of limiting several of their own, they could obstruct what they saw as residual American ambitions to acquire forces, sufficient in number and quality, to enable the United States to prevail in the event of a nuclear war. By complicating that task, arms control could contribute to the realization of Moscow's goal if not to win, then at least not to lose, a U.S.–Soviet strategic exchange.

Did Soviet purposes in pursuing arms control agreements with the West change over time? In one sense the answer is clearly no. Affirming Moscow's status as the "other" superpower, reducing political tensions with the United States, and placing limits on some of the most threatening aspects of the strategic military competition were as central to the Brezhnev leadership in the early 1980s as they had been a decade before.

In a second sense, however, Moscow's motivations did change, largely as a result of shifting U.S. policies and interests. The Soviets began the arms control process with considerable self-confidence; particularly in the international context, Moscow's fortunes appeared to be on the rise. The Americans, it seemed, were prepared at last to accommodate the expansion of Soviet power and influence, and prospects looked good for a sustained improvement in superpower relations. By the very end of the 1970s, that optimism had started to fade. Among other unwelcome developments, Moscow's domestic problems were proliferating rapidly and the international environment had turned decidedly less friendly (witness the rise of Solidarity in Poland and the sharply negative reaction worldwide to the Kremlin's military intervention in Afghanistan). The United

States, responding to Moscow's sustained military buildup and to the Soviet Union's apparent willingness to employ some of that power in service of new-found interests abroad, began to rearm. The situation soon went from bad to worse with the NATO Dual Track decision, followed by the demise of SALT II in the aftermath of the invasion of Afghanistan. In 1980 the electoral landslide that brought Ronald Reagan to power in the United States effectively buried détente.

With the dramatic downturn in East-West relations, the role assigned to arms control in Soviet diplomacy shifted, from one of several initiatives to anchor and propel the relaxation of tensions to special, elevated status as the veritable engine of détente—or what remained of it. At precisely the time when Western governments, led by the United States, were deciding that the reach of arms control had exceeded its grasp, the Soviets became its most ardent disciples. As late as February 1981, Brezhnev was insisting on the inevitability of détente and on the need to supplement the arms control agreements of the past with new and more far-reaching accords.[45] The Soviets were either unwilling or unable, however, to depart significantly from the logic that actually determined their negotiating positions at this late juncture in Brezhnev's leadership, which undercut the effectiveness of Moscow's appeal, doubtless a sincere one, to return to the bargaining table with all deliberate speed.

The manifest optimism, often mixed with an almost smug self-satisfaction, that had found its way into most Soviet treatments of superpower arms control during the early to mid-1970s had yielded by the time of Brezhnev's death to an equally palpable sense of mystification and disbelief. How, the Soviets seemed to be asking, could something that had started so well have ended so poorly? From an initial reading of the potential utility of arms control, in which the leadership had concluded that the negotiations could be employed to complete the Kremlin's passage from second- to first-class status within the international system, conditions had so deteriorated by 1982 that the true value of the process was seen to reside in its ability to neutralize, or at a minimum complicate, Washington's grab for military superiority.

In the period after 1980 but before 1985, the Soviet evaluation of SALT (and of the other arms control negotiations of the 1970s to which the Kremlin was a party) was equivocal, and heavily influenced by the circumstances of its demise. On the one hand, both the agreements and the process that produced them were exempt from criticism: the leadership was correct to have committed the country to this course and the results, such as they were, were favorable to the interests of both sides. On the other hand, much more could and should have been achieved. Predictably, it was successive U.S. administrations, Moscow alleged, that had made greater progress impossible, first by seeking unilateral advantages and, later, by surrendering the political initiative at home to "the forces of reaction and militarism." (The notion that Soviet leaders might not have been immune to similar pressures was, of course, never addressed.) From Moscow's vantage point, the shortcomings of SALT were in the execution, not in the design.

On balance, the Soviets judged their experience with arms control to have been positive and beneficial, inasmuch as the process generated accords of marginal military value, as well as providing incontrovertible evidence that the two countries could work together on sensitive security issues when they deemed it in their national interest to do so. The obstacles to further movement were political or, more precisely, human in character, rather than structural; as such, they were capable of being overcome, either through education and experience or with a change in leadership. When Soviet analysts advanced this argument in the early 1980s, they had no way of knowing just how prescient their observations would turn out to be. Within several years, a new generation of Soviet leaders was preparing to act on this and related insights. When they did, however, the locus was Moscow, not Washington.

CIVIL-MILITARY RELATIONS

Understanding the pattern of relations between ranking civilian and military leaders in the Soviet Union in the period after Stalin's death has been a central concern of a number of respected Western scholars. Various models were developed in an effort to replicate reality. Roman Kolkowicz, writing about the Khrushchev years, saw the relationship as essentially conflictual in nature, with the military frequently at odds with the political leadership over questions of doctrine, strategy, procurement, and budget.[46] Timothy Colton, focusing on the first half of the Brezhnev era, characterized relations as more consensual than adversarial, with the two groups in broad agreement on objectives, if not always on the proper methods to achieve them.[47] Others, including Condoleezza Rice, Matthew Evangelista, and Dale Herspring, advanced interpretations that both reinforced and departed from the explanations offered by Kolkowicz and Colton.[48]

Most Western observers would now agree that civil-military relations under Brezhnev cannot be fully explained by reference to any single model; both conflictual and consensual, depending on the issue and its timing, they were complex, subtle, and dynamic. At the outset of the period, relations were harmonious for the most part, the result of a strong coincidence of views among the country's leaders, political and military, on the need to amend the dangerous doctrinal pronouncements of Khrushchev and to allocate additional resources to assure the development of a more balanced military posture. In the judgment of the leadership, each step was indispensable, both to restrain the imperialists and to facilitate the assumption by the Kremlin of its rightful place as Washington's equal on the world stage.

By the end of Brezhnev's tenure, serious fissures had begun to emerge, despite the realization of these goals. On the one hand, civilian leaders, confronted with indisputable evidence of an economy in decline, sought ways to hold the line on military expenditures and instructed the armed forces to make do with the existing level of resources; responsible military officials, on the other hand, warned of a growing Western threat and pleaded for the maintenance of, if not an actual increase in, defense spending. A diffuse and obscure debate on the future of the armed forces ensued on the pages of important Soviet publications, including *Pravda* and *Krasnaya zvezda*, the organ of the Ministry of Defense. By 1985 there was even speculation that relations between the country's senior political and military leaders had deteriorated to the point that an attempt by the armed forces to seize power could not be ruled out.

In looking back over the period, such concerns seem wildly off the mark. No reliable evidence has yet surfaced to suggest that ranking members of the Soviet high command ever set out to enhance their role in political decision making at the expense of their civilian superiors—let alone that they might have been prepared under certain conditions to seek the latter's removal. On the contrary, it would appear that the military, whatever the intensity of its displeasure toward the end of the Brezhnev era, was content to respect the "leading role" of the party in national security decision making, having learned in earlier episodes the high costs of incurring the displeasure of the politicians.[49]

Moreover, on most of the issues that mattered most to the General Staff and the five services—popular respect for the armed forces, a large and guaranteed manpower pool, either access to or control over the best of Soviet industry, and, until late in the period, significant and predictable increases in the defense budget—the political and military leaderships were of a single mind. Until the money began to run out, in other words, such tensions as might have existed between the two communities were resolved through a quiet process of bargaining and accommodation that left each side satisfied, for the most part, with the outcome.

One area in which real differences did emerge was the likelihood and probable character of a future war involving NATO and the Warsaw Pact. The issue, which had important budgetary and allocative implications, not only set elements within the military against the political leadership, but also and more interestingly precipitated a split between the General Staff, or at least its leading voice, and other organizations within the armed forces, including the premier Soviet service, the Strategic Rocket Forces.

On one side of the issue stood Marshal Ogarkov, the gifted and forceful chief of the General Staff. In his writings and public statements, Ogarkov was a tireless advocate for the Soviet armed forces, advising, and at time cajoling, Kremlin leaders to provide everything necessary to meet the expanding needs of the military. Among other causes, he championed the closest possible synchronization of the civilian and military economies in order to maximize efficiency and to facilitate the country's transition to a wartime footing, should the need arise. He stressed greater rigor in military training programs, many of which he deemed inadequate and inferior to those in the West.[50]

In promoting these and other goals, most of which would require additional expenditures, Ogarkov could not have been unaware of the fact that his advocacy placed him increasingly at odds with political leaders who were struggling to constrain the growth in military spending, particularly during the second half of his tenure as chief. In the early 1980s, Ogarkov's urgings that the government do more to ensure the country's security grew, if anything, more strident, as he detected the emergence of a powerful new threat to Soviet security interests.

As he analyzed the introduction and application of various advanced weapons technologies within NATO, Ogarkov warned of a potentially calamitous deterioration in the military position of the Warsaw Pact, an erosion of strength so severe, in his view, that in the event of war with the West a Soviet defeat could not be ruled out. To prevent such a catastrophe, he proposed increases in military spending, coupled with a substantial reallocation of resources within the military budget. Only by so doing, Ogarkov seemed to believe, could the Soviet Union hope to develop and deploy conventional capabilities of comparable sophistication and utility to those being produced in the West.[51]

It was at this juncture that Ogarkov appears to have run afoul of important interests, both within the political leadership and within his own military. Given the slowdown in defense spending toward the end of the 1970s, the Kremlin was extremely unlikely to appropriate additional funds in support of *any* military mission; in suggesting that his superiors reverse themselves on this point, Ogarkov was, at a minimum, rowing against the tide. He also, however, alienated many of his fellow officers. In laying out his case, Ogarkov contended that the threat to the Soviet Union posed by U.S. strategic nuclear forces had been successfully contained; through heroic Soviet efforts, a stable deterrent balance had been created that could not be undone by the Americans, whatever their ambitions. Logically, then, a further expansion of Soviet strategic forces was unnecessary, even wasteful. In an environment of fiscal austerity, Ogarkov contended, difficult choices had to be made; what he seemed to be proposing was that a portion of the monies previously earmarked for strategic modernization be redirected to areas where the need was greatest—investment in advanced conventional weaponry and in associated high-technology industries.[52]

Predictably, the Ogarkov thesis generated opposition. Spokesmen for the Strategic Rocket Forces, including Commander-in-Chief Vladimir Tolubko, rising to the defense of the service and its mission, took strong exception to the thrust of Ogarkov's argument. Dire warnings were issued about the direction of U.S. strategic policy under the Reagan administration, the fundamental purpose of which, in these estimates, was to restore American military superiority and to provide the United States with the requisite forces to fight and win a nuclear war. Existing conditions, Tolubko argued, demanded an undiminished flow of resources to the Strategic Rocket Forces, which constituted the bedrock of Soviet power and the principal bulwark against American military aggression. The early 1980s, in Tolubko's view, was no time to relax military vigilance, least of all by choking off appropriations essential to the preservation of Moscow's nuclear deterrent.[53] Other military authorities, not all of them representatives of the Strategic Rocket Forces, echoed the Tolubko line.[54]

Eventually, selected civilian leaders joined the anti-Ogarkov chorus, focusing, however, less on the issues that divided the chief of the General Staff from his uniformed adversaries than on the question of military expenditures. Several weeks before his death in November 1982, Brezhnev, addressing a gathering of the country's senior commanders, underscored the party's commitment to satisfy the legitimate needs of the military. At the same time, he counseled the armed forces to make better, more efficient use of the resources allocated to them—clearly implying that an increase in appropriations, however justified, was not in the offing.[55]

Relations between Ogarkov and his opponents, military and political, did not improve substantially during the Andropov-Chernenko interregnum, and in September 1984 the marshal was relieved of his duties. Ogarkov's principal deputy at the General Staff, Sergei Akhromeyev, was named to replace him. For several years following his dismissal, Ogarkov headed the Western Theater of Military Operations, the establishment of which he had made a major focus of his activities while chief. Subsequently, he was reassigned to the Main Inspectorate, typically the last stop for a Soviet officer of Ogarkov's rank, prior to retirement.

The Ogarkov episode was interesting on several counts. First, the debate itself was unusually accessible to readers of the Soviet press. Ogarkov, in particular, employed language that was anything but obscure; he declined, for example, to disguise his real concerns by expressing his points of view elliptically, so as to diminish the appearance of conflict with the senior leadership. In the years before glasnost, such bluntness was, to understate the point, atypical. Second, the disagreements between Ogarkov and his opponents, both in and out of the armed forces, were about important operational military issues; only indirectly were they also about the distribution of political power within the Soviet system and the role of the military in Soviet society. However unhappy the political leaders might have been with Ogarkov, in other words, he was not dismissed because the Kremlin feared a military coup d'état.

As Herspring has suggested, the Chernenko leadership might have demoted Ogarkov in order to render his words less significant, perhaps even to silence him; it also might have acted to make it easier to elevate some other candidate to the post of minister of defense, when the time finally came to replace the ailing Dmitri Ustinov.[56]

Whatever the precise reasons, the apparent ease with which the Kremlin relieved Ogarkov of his responsibilities in 1984 probably said as much about the state of Soviet civil-military relations at this juncture as did any other event during the twenty-year period under review.[57]

Finally, to a degree not always recognized in Western treatments of this fascinating episode, Ogarkov was vindicated in his contention that only the enactment of emergency measures could preserve Soviet security interests during the last two decades of the twentieth century. Upon its assumption to power in March 1985, the new leadership began a comprehensive review of Soviet foreign and military policies. What Gorbachev and his colleagues found must have troubled them deeply. Rather than sanction a crash program to expand the country's theater military capabilities, however, as Ogarkov had proposed, they eventually settled on a much more radical plan of action: a professed willingness to reduce Soviet military power to its lowest level in forty years in exchange for corresponding (if smaller) reductions in Western capabilities. It was a solution that Ogarkov would doubtless have resisted, given both his professional experience and his profound suspicion of the West. At the same time, the logic of the position would have been clear to him, unlike the reasoning that had informed the arguments of his opponents earlier in the decade.

The relatively few instances of deep or sustained conflict between the civilian and military sectors of Soviet society from the mid-1960s to the mid-1980s did not mean that relations were consensual. There were disagreements, some of which surfaced on occasion, though seldom with the visibility that attended the Ogarkov affair. Moreover, many of the problems that were later to confront Gorbachev in his dealings with the military—from the resistance to change within the high command to the nationalities question—had been present for years in nascent form. Most of these problems were kept out of the public domain because to reveal them was to expose the shortcomings of the system and, perhaps, to endanger the security of the Soviet state. With the passage of time, it also became easier to defer consideration of or to ignore contentious issues than it was to confront them. Such escapism suited the interests and, just as importantly, the temperaments of those in power.

THE BREZHNEV YEARS: ASSESSING THE COSTS OF STAGNATION

Assessing the Brezhnev era in the areas of military policy and arms control is difficult, complicated by the emergence of a nearly universal consensus that, while the period was not without its high points, overall it was one of stagnation and torpor for the Soviet Union. There is, of course, much truth to this statement. Soviet economic performance declined sharply during the second half of Brezhnev's stewardship; from 1975 to 1982 infant mortality rates increased, living standards dropped, and the average life expectancy of the ordinary citizen fell by several years. The manifest decay of Soviet civil society—the increasingly lifeless character of many of the country's official and quasi-official institutions, from the Young

Communist League to the Moscow Writers' Union—had its origins in the repressive and regressive social policies pursued by Brezhnev and his confederates. So severe was the all-round Soviet malaise that by 1990–1991 Western concerns about the USSR had shifted from fears centering on the country's alleged aggressive intent and expansionist tendencies to anxieties about its capacity to weather a new "Time of Troubles" and to survive as a coherent political entity.

In these evaluations it is sometimes overlooked that within their own frames of reference, those who had come to power in the Kremlin in October 1964 had attained by the early 1980s many of the goals they had set for themselves and for their country. Foremost among these was the dramatic growth in the Soviet Union's nuclear and conventional military capabilities, realized at great cost over the preceding twenty years. From a position of abject strategic inferiority, not only had Soviet leaders succeeded in catching up with the United States, but they had gone on to acquire forces more numerous and at least as potent as those in American possession. In Europe many Western analysts judged the Warsaw Pact threat to NATO to be greater by an order of magnitude at the start of the 1980s than at any previous juncture in the forty-year history of the East-West military confrontation. The ability of the Soviet Union to project military power to such distant and diverse locations as southern Africa and Southeast Asia, made possible by the expansion of the country's naval forces, provoked similar Western assessments.

The long list of arms control agreements concluded with Washington at several high-profile summit meetings during the 1970s seemed to confirm the fundamental wisdom of the leadership's investment strategies, lending important substantiation to the claim that the growth in Soviet military power had compelled the United States to accord the Kremlin new respect; together with other factors, it appeared, the development of Moscow's strategic and conventional military potential had contributed measurably to the manifest shift in "the correlation of forces" during the 1970s, in a direction favorable to the interests of the socialist community.

The leadership's assertions were correct, but also shortsighted. At the time they were undertaken, the steps to expand the country's military capabilities seemed to promise payoffs of sufficient weight to justify the considerable expense involved. Moreover, from the mid-1960s to the early 1970s the economy was growing at a fast enough rate to support a policy of guns *and* butter, or so it appeared at the time. Only later did it become apparent that the demands placed on the economy as a result of the military buildup had introduced serious, and in fact fatal, distortions and dislocations, depriving central planners of desperately needed resources to engineer the country's transition from "extensive" to "intensive" economic growth—a transition that was never accomplished. As a consequence, as Soviet military assets proliferated, the growth in the economy that supported that expansion first slowed and then stopped altogether. At precisely the point at which the Soviet Union became secure against any and all external threats, the system that had produced this highly desirable condition lost the ability to provide for the minimal material needs of its own people.

A second problem with the leadership's strategy was that it misdiagnosed the true nature of the Western threat to the Soviet Union and its allies. The entire basis of Soviet security policy under Brezhnev was the conviction that the overarching danger to the Kremlin was military in character; in fact, the threat was economic and, as it turned out, socio-political. A more sophisticated appraisal of the true challenge confronting Moscow during the 1960s and 1970s might have produced very different policies, with fewer resources earmarked for military purposes and more for the enrichment and empowerment of the society that Soviet armed forces were pledged to defend.

A related failing was the belief that in a world of hostile states, the larger the armed forces and the more weapons a country maintained the better off it was likely to be. While true under some conditions, particularly before the advent of nuclear deterrence, the adage had lost much of its significance by the last quarter of the twentieth century. Moscow's unleavened faith in the utility of military power led, in turn, to a version of what Western game theorists call "the fallacy of the last move." Soviet leaders appear to have convinced themselves that reductions in defense spending could and would be undertaken at some future date—once the programs to offset the latest American military innovation had been funded and new deployments assured.

The only problem with this analysis was that "someday" never came. Just as one set of problems was being resolved, new ones appeared, necessitating a fresh round of appropriations to the military. The threat, it seemed, was ever-new, ever-changing, and ever-expanding.

U.S. policymakers shared much the same perspective; a key difference, however, was that the American economy was perhaps three times the size of its Soviet counterpart, thus better able to absorb such expenditures, and much more efficient. In an open-ended arms race with Washington, therefore, Moscow's victory was anything but assured; under these conditions, for the Soviets even to hold their own against the Americans, the United States would have to tire of the game, opt out, and give up. It did none of the three. By 1985 the profound, elemental bankruptcy of Moscow's military and security policies could no longer be disguised. The time had come for thoroughgoing reform.

Chapter 2

Military Doctrine and the Restructuring of the Armed Forces

N O INSTITUTION OF SOVIET RULE AND NO SECTOR OF SOVIET society escaped the shock waves of change generated by the reformist policies of Mikhail Gorbachev. In the almost seven years that he served as the Soviet Union's supreme political leader, Gorbachev struck at virtually every aspect of the administrative-command system in a determined effort to halt the precipitous decline in the country's material fortunes and to make good on the failed promises of the October Revolution. In his quest to renew Soviet society, Gorbachev himself grew progressively, if reluctantly, more radical, eschewing many of the half measures and mild palliatives with which he began his tenure. Ultimately, the embattled Soviet leader embraced a program that aimed at nothing less than the eradication of the economically stagnant, politically moribund, and socially ossified collection of institutions bequeathed to him by Stalin's heirs.

The Gorbachev revolution had a major impact on all dimensions of Soviet life, but in few areas were the effects of change more visible and far-reaching than in the military sphere. From the formation of doctrine and strategy at the "high" end of the spectrum, to such operational issues as the sizing and equipping of the armed forces, the Soviet defense establishment was forced to accommodate an extensive series of reforms mandated by an impatient political leadership, eager to shift national priorities and to reallocate resources accordingly. This process, which generated considerable tension between senior civilians and their military counterparts, was never completed.

Throughout the Gorbachev era, and for understandable reasons, the projected reforms were a matter of extreme political sensitivity and great practical complexity. In perhaps no other policy domain were the consequences of a mistake in judgment potentially so profound. Despite the risks, the essential contours of the reformist vision were apparent by the late 1980s: in the Soviet Union of the 1990s, according to Gorbachev and those allied with ·him, defense spending was to be curtailed, military capabilities reduced, and the use of the armed forces for any purpose other than defense of the country's most vital interests prohibited.

The investigation of three issues, related but distinct, guides the analysis that follows: how the political leadership came to adopt this radical agenda; the specific content of the proposed reforms; and what did, and did not, change in the Soviet military in the areas of doctrine, strategy, and force posture in the six and a half years that separated Gorbachev's political rise and fall.

THE SOURCES OF CHANGE

The single most important catalyst for change within the Soviet system was the country's dismal and declining economic performance. It was the abject failure of the economy to provide a level of goods and services sufficient to satisfy even the minimal needs and wants of the Soviet population—with worse, perhaps, yet to come—that compelled the leadership to break with the policies of the past and commit itself to a reform program of unprecedented scope and intensity. As an integral part of the system, the Soviet military establishment was both a victim of the country's broadly based decline, as well as one of its most important agents.

The existing system victimized the military in at least two ways. First, as the economy stagnated during the first half of the 1980s, the political leadership placed the military services on notice that henceforth they would have to make do with fewer resources. The yearly increases in defense spending, which in happier times had ranged from between 4 and 5 percent, were cut in half. At the end of decade, the economy was unable to sustain even this smaller increment, and military appropriations actually declined for the first time in almost thirty years. In January 1989 Gorbachev announced a cutback in military spending totaling 14.2 percent (from 1987 levels), as well as a 19.2 percent drop in military production, to be carried out over a two-year period.[1] For an institution long accustomed to privileged treatment, the budgetary constraints imposed by the government must have come as an unpleasant surprise.

Second, as Gorbachev and others repeatedly explained to party and government officials responsible for Soviet economic development, the critical shortcoming of the administrative-command system was its manifest inability to promote patterns of intensive, as opposed to extensive, economic growth.[2] The central direction of the economy had enabled the Soviet Union to post impressive rates of growth from the late 1920s to the mid-1960s, during the years of the first to the seventh five-year plans. Officials of the State Planning Commission (Gosplan) could, and did, measure the success of the system by reference to various statistical indicators. Underscoring the annual increases in steel production was perhaps the most familiar, though hardly the only way in which Soviet authorities sought to convince themselves (and others) of the superiority of the state-run economy. As proficient as the system became in producing at least some goods, however, it did so with enormous inefficiencies. Moreover, Soviet goods, military and civilian, seldom equaled the quality of the equipment generated by the Western market economies, with their demonstrated capacity to make effective and innovative use of advanced civilian, military, and dual-use technologies.

During his years as chief of the General Staff, Marshal Ogarkov had made the failure of the Soviet economy to stay abreast of the West technologically and to produce military goods of comparable quality an important part of his campaign to force needed changes in the country's system of military procurement. Despite dire warnings about the West overtaking the Soviet Union militarily in the absence of profound systemic reform, Ogarkov's civilian superiors largely ignored his advice. In the years following Ogarkov's ouster as chief, the frightful vision first sketched out by the indomitable marshal—of a Soviet Union less and less able to compete with the United States and its allies in the production and deployment of sophisticated and highly destructive non-nuclear military capabilities—become all too real. Far from narrowing, the gap between East and West in military and militarily related technologies continued to widen.

In a second sense, however, the military was also an agent—a central cause—of Moscow's long economic slide. With its large budget share, its priority claim on scarce resources, and its ability to commandeer goods and services in the name of national security, the Soviet defense establishment deprived the civilian economy of its due. In providing the armed forces with the best the Soviet economy had to offer in terms of human talent, industrial and technological assets, and research and development facilities, the Brezhnev leadership crippled the development of the nonmilitary sector. As a result, growth rates sagged, the industrial infrastructure began to erode, the transport and distribution systems crumbled, and agricultural production either stagnated or grew by increments too small to satisfy the requirements of Soviet consumers.

In his opening address to the Twenty-eighth Congress of the Communist Party of the Soviet Union in July 1990, Gorbachev, willing at last to break with the political tradition of never speaking ill of the country's armed forces, pointedly condemned the practice of according the military special economic treatment. The "militarization of the Soviet economy," the president bluntly advised the assembled delegates, had "swallowed colossal material and intellectual resources, the best that there were."[3] Gorbachev's message could not have been more explicit: the military, in demanding and receiving goods and services far in excess of those required to satisfy its legitimate needs, had contributed directly to the pervasive crisis, the "grim legacy," now confronting Kremlin leaders and Soviet society as a whole.[4]

Predating the depiction of the military as an economic parasite, selected political leaders, including Gorbachev, had taken aim at the armed forces by impugning the utility of military power—or, more correctly, the relentless expansion of military power—in safeguarding Soviet national interests. Distinct from and less direct than the economic critique, this line of attack was, if anything, potentially more damaging to the interests of the military. Being accused of practicing a kind of economic larceny was one thing; having the very core of one's social mission called into question was quite another.

In suggesting that Brezhnev-era leaders, including senior representatives of the armed forces, were partly to blame for the worsening of the country's military and geopolitical position during the early 1980s (for example, by provoking the Reagan defense buildup), Gorbachev and the others who made this charge were sounding a new theme in the history of Soviet civil-military relations.[5] Later discussions, in which predominantly "new thinking" civilians (official and non-official alike) criticized the decisions to proceed with the deployment of the SS-20 missile in the mid-1970s and to invade Afghanistan at the end of the decade, could hardly have been seen as anything other than veiled attacks on the military, notwithstanding the authors' tendency to indict by name ranking political figures only—most typically Brezhnev, Mikhail Suslov, and Defense Minister Dmitri Ustinov.[6]

At issue in these critiques was less the use of force, per se, than the relationship in Soviet foreign policy between military power and political purpose, more generally, throughout the postwar period. In a nearly complete reversal of the prevailing wisdom in Moscow, the new leadership alleged that rather than advancing and securing Soviet interests, the previous regime's excessive reliance on the military as an instrument of policy had done the country irreparable harm, by exacerbating tensions with adversaries, straining relations with allies, and frightening virtually everyone else. Moreover, by arousing countervailing steps on the part of the West, the expansion in Soviet military capabilities had failed to produce the one outcome that might have enabled the leadership to justify to its own population the enormity of the postwar defense burden—namely, decisive, usable military superiority.

This two-pronged indictment of the military, as economically dysfunctional and politically counterproductive, was to a degree an exercise in scapegoating on the part of the new political leadership, which as time went on became increasingly frustrated at the agonizingly slow pace of reform. As a key architect of the now discredited policies of the past, the Soviet defense establishment could not hope to escape censure at the hands of Brezhnev's successors.

At the same time, the leadership's highly critical treatment of the military was part and parcel of a much larger process of reflection and reform which, in its playing out, led to an important branch point in Soviet thinking regarding national and international security. Among its other consequences, it symbolized the *de facto* rejection of some forty years of Soviet history, a history in which military power—the raw capacity to inflict incalculable pain and suffering on the Kremlin's potential enemies—was seen to constitute the central source of Soviet security in a world dominated by predatory and unpredictable imperialist countries led by the United States. It was also a belated recognition of the fact that in the four decades following the conclusion of the Second World War, economic power and technological clout had attained a degree of importance in the international system equal to or greater than that accorded to military might, and that in sealing itself off from the increasingly interdependent world beyond its borders, the Soviet Union had fallen years behind its capitalist rivals. Without an immediate redirection of the country's energies, the leadership warned, away from militarism and toward economic and technological regeneration, any hopes of maintaining the Soviet Union's precarious hold on its superpower status were illusory.[7]

Kremlin leaders were not insensitive to the potential ramifications, both at home and abroad, of this proposed shift in emphasis. They were careful to underscore, for example, the Soviet Union's undisputed right as a sovereign state to deploy whatever forces the leadership deemed necessary for purposes of self-defense. The need for reliable, effective armed forces sufficient to deter outright aggression against the USSR, they assured the country, was not open to question. What was at issue, however, was how best to determine the country's *legitimate* military requirements—not by reference to some imagined set of circumstances conjured up by disciples of the "old thinking," but in response to the actual conditions and real problems then confronting the Soviet Union in its dealings with the outside world.[8]

ANALYSIS AND PRESCRIPTION

Two irreducible convictions appear to have guided Kremlin decision-makers in their efforts to remake Soviet security policy. The first was that Soviet society had to adopt, implement, and make irreversible the full array of economic and political reforms advanced by the Gorbachev leadership. The second, and more important for this discussion, was that Soviet foreign policy had positively to assist the realization of this ambitious domestic agenda. Although long described in precisely these terms, in reality the historical relationship between Soviet foreign and domestic policies had been considerably more complex and, from the perspective of the Gorbachev leadership, less than satisfactory.

In the view of this new (and last) generation of Soviet leaders, the militarization of Soviet foreign policy that had been allowed to occur in the 1960s and 1970s had prevented the attainment of even the modest economic goals repeatedly articulated but then abandoned by Brezhnev and his colleagues. This disjunction between vision and reality had an extremely potent and altogether negative effect on the population, simultaneously stifling individual initiative and undermining the sense of collective responsibility that for seventy years formed the bedrock of the Soviet social contract. Whatever feelings of pride the Soviet people might once have felt in their country's attainment of political and military equality with the United States was more than offset, in this construction, by the steady decline in their standard of living.

To restore faith in the Soviet social contract, life had to improve for the average citizen. For life to improve, the system had to change. A necessary first step was to redirect at least a portion of the resources heretofore earmarked for the military's use to more socially beneficial ends, such as the modernization of the industrial base and the acceleration of production, and to seek an end to the ruinous military competition with the United States. A second and more momentous step was to overcome the Soviet Union's hostility toward and isolation from the Western-led international economic order so that the country could begin to reap substantial material rewards. Both required that Moscow adopt a fundamentally new conception of the international system and the Soviet Union's place within it.

This the leadership sought to do in essentially three phases, each a departure from the hoary traditions of Marxism-Leninism. The first, and least provocative, was built around a sharp denunciation of the existing system of domestic economic, political, and social relations. While this assault was continuous—witness the speeches of Gorbachev, Foreign Minister Eduard Shevardnadze, and presidential counselor Aleksandr Yakovlev at the twenty-eighth CPSU congress in 1990—much of its force had been spent by the end of the 1980s. The second phase was the attempt to educate the Soviet people about the world around them and to demythologize the ideas, institutions, and processes that dominate human relations and drive economic activity in the industrialized West. Gorbachev's campaign to "democratize" the Soviet political system by shifting the locus of sovereignty from the Communist party to popularly elected bodies at the local, regional, and federal levels, and to revalidate the concept of the economic marketplace were but two examples of this strategy, albeit the most important and certainly the most dramatic. While at base this effort was designed to spur the renewal of Soviet domestic society, the link, on the one hand, between "democracy" and "perestroika," and, on the other, Moscow's attempts to fashion a fundamentally new set of relationships with the noncommunist international community, was apparent.[9]

The leadership's attempts to articulate a new set of conceptions to guide the formation and conduct of Soviet foreign policy represented the third phase of this effort. Here Soviet leaders, principally Gorbachev, Shevardnadze, and Vadim Medvedev (until July 1990 the party's chief ideologist) had to walk a political and conceptual tightrope, at one and the same time propounding an interpretation of international politics that departed in absolutely vital ways from the ideologically driven vision passed to them by their predecessors, while also remaining true (more in form than in substance) to the allegedly timeless teachings of Marx and Lenin. The fit between the old and the new was less than perfect and, at times, a source of considerable confusion, not only to Western observers, but also to the Soviets.

To compound the problem, the new foreign policy line emerged piecemeal, requiring the senior leadership to engage in a continuous process of explanation, modification, emendation, and correction. A comparison of Gorbachev's 1986 report to the twenty-seventh CPSU congress, in which he described in comparatively traditional terms both the sources and the purposes of Soviet foreign policy, and his July 1989 address to the Council of Europe in Strasbourg (by which time he had dispensed entirely with the logic, and much of the vocabulary, of Marxism-Leninism) reveals the remarkable evolution of his own thinking and the extraordinary degree of change in the Soviet depiction of world politics and international relations in a period of little more than three years.[10]

At the apex of this conceptual revolution, or what the Soviet preferred to call "the new political thinking," was *the subordination of the "international class struggle"*—that is, the global competition between imperialism and its reactionary allies and the progressive forces of world socialism—*to what Gorbachev characterized as the "supremacy of the common human idea."*[11] In his nearly seven years in office, the Soviet president worked relentlessly to establish the intellectual and ideological validity of this idea, taking care to emphasize, largely for the benefit of his Communist colleagues, "the interconnection of the proletarian and class interest with that common to all mankind."[12] This universality of human values, according to Gorbachev, mandated a different approach to the resolution of international conflicts, most especially agreement among political leaders everywhere on the inadmissibility of war as a means of settling outstanding differences between opposing states. Given the destructive capabilities at their disposal, countries armed with nuclear weapons were enjoined to take the lead in this effort.

In a July 1988 speech to a Foreign Ministry–sponsored conference on the changing nature of Soviet foreign policy interests, Shevardnadze made much the same point, though more concisely, when he posited that "the new political thinking views peaceful coexistence in the context of the realities of the nuclear century. We are fully justified in refusing to see in it a special form of the class struggle. One must not identify coexistence . . . with the class struggle." To eliminate any possible ambiguity on this score, the foreign minister declared that "the struggle between the two opposing [world] systems is no longer a determining tendency of the present-day era."[13] Gorbachev, employing similar but less charged language, had conveyed the identical message a month before in his opening remarks to the nineteenth CPSU conference, and would do so again, six months later, in his address to the United Nations General Assembly.

At least one ranking Soviet official, then Politburo member Yegor Ligachev, took strong exception to the new formula, although he failed to generate much overt support for his position among well-placed Soviet officials. He never did embrace the "new political thinking" in its entirety—an indication of the deep suspicion with which at least some important constituencies within the Soviet polity viewed these departures—and during the most active phase of his opposition consistently staked out a more orthodox position than either Gorbachev or Shevardnadze on most foreign policy issues.[14]

Equally provocative, and of far greater consequence, was Gorbachev's affirmation of the right of every country, without exception, to chart its own political and economic destiny, safe from outside interference. In endorsing what he termed *"the freedom of choice,"* the Soviet leader removed a second key pillar of Soviet foreign policy, known in the West as the "Brezhnev doctrine," or the putative right of one communist country (e.g., the Soviet Union) to intervene in the internal affairs of another in order ostensibly to preserve the gains of socialism and to crush, if need be, counterrevolutionary forces.[15] It was by reference to such logic, of course, that Moscow had justified for over twenty years the 1968 Warsaw Pact invasion of Czechoslovakia and its own intervention in Afghanistan eleven years later.

The impact of Gorbachev's edict on the "freedom of choice" is difficult to exaggerate. In advancing this argument, the Soviet leader may be said to have precipitated—and to have lent powerful sanction to—the political upheavals that were soon to engulf Eastern Europe, which began in the wake of the successful conclusion of the Polish Roundtable negotiations in April 1989 and ended, some eight months later, with the executions of Romanian dictator Nicolae Ceauşescu and his wife at the hands of their own people. In part because of Gorbachev's fealty to the concept of noninterference in the internal affairs of other countries, by 1990 the Kremlin's Eastern European *glacis* had collapsed, the two Germanys had begun their march toward unification, and East-West relations had entered a period of change no less profound than that which attended the creation of the postwar international system in the years immediately following World War II.

A third element in the "new political thinking," and the one with the most tangible military implications, was the proposition that *in the nuclear age security between states could only be mutual.* First expressed by Gorbachev at the twenty-seventh CPSU congress (and refined in numerous statements thereafter), the concept created dramatic new possibilities in bilateral, as well as multilateral, arms control negotiations to which the Kremlin was a party (for a more detailed discussion of Gorbachev's arms control strategy, see chapter 3).

In advancing this view, Gorbachev abandoned the position—a veritable article of faith among earlier generations of Kremlin leaders—that the steady accumulation of military capabilities on Moscow's part added in an almost linear way to the security of the Soviet state by incrementally reducing the likelihood of unprovoked attack. It also constituted acceptance of what Western international relations theorists term "the security dilemma"—the unpleasant realization that at least some steps a country takes to enhance its defensive military position can be, and often are, interpreted by an actual or potential adversary as threatening, rather than reassuring, in nature.[16] One result of this dynamic, the Soviets finally acknowledged, was the arms race, a phenomenon that often left the participants less secure than before. In accepting the fundamentally reciprocal character, in particular, of the superpower military competition, the Kremlin removed a key obstacle to the gradual ratcheting down of that competition; depending on the degree to which Moscow was prepared to act on this realization, the same logic also provided a seemingly compelling rationale for the reduction of Soviet armed forces, as well as for their eventual reconfiguration for the performance of predominantly defensive military missions.

A number of Western analysts tended to dismiss the new Soviet line on foreign and security policy as more cosmetic than real, a clever and artful repackaging of positions and objectives long at the heart of the Kremlin's diplomacy. Moscow's underlying purposes, they warned, as well as its capacity for military mischief, remained much as before. Others contended that however sincere Gorbachev might have been in seeking to redirect Soviet policies, words were not the same as deeds. His ability to implement the directives issued in his name, they argued, was severely constrained by a host of factors, from the opposition he confronted in the party, state, and military apparatuses to the capacity of the Soviet bureaucracy to defeat even the most ardent and persistent of reformers. A third group seemed prepared to take the Gorbachev revolution more at face value, detecting in the Soviet president's rhetoric a rejection of previous policies so complete as to render impossible any return to the status quo ante. Whatever might happen in the future, they alleged, the system of beliefs that from 1945 to 1985 so strongly influenced the Kremlin's international behavior could never be reconstituted.[17]

The concrete steps that Soviet leaders took in the areas of military and security policy to conform to the "new political thinking" are examined in detail in the succeeding sections of this chapter. It is a central contention of this study that the radical shifts in the expression of Soviet policy described above—explicit subordination of class interests to those of humankind, insistence on the inadmissibility of war, support of the right of every sovereign state to determine its own political and economic makeup, and recognition of the "security dilemma"—when taken together, constituted far more than a mere tactical adjustment, a bending of traditional rhetoric, in the service of ancient goals.

Although incomplete, and not without the occasional contradiction, the architecture of policy that Soviet leaders sketched out between 1985 and 1991 constituted a genuine revolution in the country's approach to military and security affairs. For the first time in Soviet history the Kremlin sought self-consciously to reconcile the pursuit of Soviet national security interests with the those of the international community. No less for Gorbachev than for earlier Soviet leaders then, words—the ideas, themes, and constructs that he employed to frame and to inform the conduct of policy—did matter.

DOCTRINE AND STRATEGY

For the Gorbachev leadership, the reconceptualization of Soviet foreign policy represented a vitally important, if long overdue, first step in a much larger process designed to arrest the visible erosion of the Kremlin's international political position. The second and more difficult task was to devise, and to ensure the implementation of, policy initiatives consistent with this objective and with the new conception of Moscow's relationship to, and place within, the contemporary international system.

In the area of security policy, this second step proved to be a problem of significant proportions, requiring the country's top political leaders to assume a central and continuing role in the recasting of Soviet and Warsaw Pact military doctrine.[18] The reasons were twofold. First, in the judgment of the leadership, it was precisely the failure of Brezhnev and his civilian associates to exercise meaningful oversight of the military establishment, particularly the former's disinclination to challenge the latter's requests for ever greater resources, that had led to the militarization of Soviet foreign policy in the first place; to correct the situation (and to prevent a recurrence), Gorbachev moved aggressively to reestablish the primacy of the political leadership in national security decision making (see chapter 4 for a more detailed discussion of the development of civil-military relations under Gorbachev). Second, it was only through such direct intervention that senior civilian authorities could hope to overcome the resistance they anticipated from *within* the military to the far-reaching changes in doctrine and strategy that they proposed.

The struggle over doctrinal reform proceeded on three distinct levels after 1985, expressed here in the manner preferred by Soviet officials and analysts of military affairs. At the most general level, the political leadership directed that Soviet doctrine be reformulated in such a way as to convey its profoundly *defensive* character; at an intermediate level of analysis, military planners and theoreticians were instructed to reconcile what the Soviets termed the "political-military" and the "military-technical" aspects of doctrine in order, primarily, to bring the latter into line with the new emphasis on defense and defensive missions; finally, and at a more basic level, the country's military specialists were told to develop reliable and realistic plans to guide the conduct of Soviet (and Warsaw Pact) military operations, featuring fewer and less heavily armed forces.

Recasting the Political-Military Aspect of Doctrine

The least controversial part of this campaign was the revision of the manifestly political dimension of military doctrine. That this should have been the case is hardly surprising, given the Kremlin's long-standing depiction of Soviet military purposes as exclusively defensive in nature (and its description of the Warsaw Pact as a purely defensive alliance). In an effort to dispel the appearance of business as usual, Moscow seized on the May 1986 meeting of the pact's Political Consultative Committee (PCC) to reaffirm the alliance's sincere dedication to peace in Europe and to underscore its commitment to a negotiated drawdown in NATO and Warsaw Pact military forces "from the Atlantic to the Urals." Especially intriguing was the pronouncement in the fifth and final part of the declaration that, in the interest of promoting security in Europe, "the military concepts and doctrines of the military alliances must be based on defensive principles" and on "the reduction of military potentials to the limits necessary for defense."[19]

The Kremlin engineered a more elaborate, and much better organized, statement on Warsaw Pact (and by implication Soviet) military doctrine at the June 1987 session of the PCC, held in Berlin. On this occasion, the Soviets made certain that the conferees issued a separate document on Warsaw Pact military policy, which began with a carefully formulated expression of its political foundation. "The military doctrine of the Warsaw Treaty member states," the declaration read, was "strictly a defensive one" and "subjugated to the task of preventing war, both nuclear and conventional." The political essence of alliance doctrine, the statement continued, could be summed up in four principles: that the Warsaw Pact allies would never, "under any circumstances," undertake military action against any country or alliance of countries (unless they themselves were to become the target of attack); that they would never be the first to use nuclear weapons; that they had no territorial claims against any state "either in Europe or outside it"; and that they did not view any people or any state as their enemy.[20]

Little in the declaration was actually new; most of the commitments, such as the no-first-use pledge and the rejection of territorial ambitions, could be found in earlier pronouncements of the PCC.

The one clear innovation was the rather curious construction regarding the subordination of military doctrine to the maintenance of peace. Although it was initially dismissed by the West as vacuous rhetoric, Soviet spokesmen, including prominent representatives of the military, were to return to this expression repeatedly in the months and years to come, attaching to it great importance.

The point, it seemed, was that heretofore the overarching purpose of Soviet and Warsaw Pact military doctrine had been to *prepare* the alliance for war; in this sense, it may be said to have operated at cross purposes with the consistent political directive to avoid an East-West military conflagration at all costs. Now, for the first time, the primary goal of military policy must be to *prevent* the outbreak of hostilities. How, over time, this change in emphasis might have affected Soviet and Warsaw Pact operational plans and military capabilities remains unclear. The Soviets did supply a clue of sorts later in the same document, when the Eastern allies reiterated their support for reductions in troops and armaments "down to the level where neither side, in ensuring its defense, would have means for a sudden attack on the other side, for starting offensive operations in general."[21]

Reconciling the Political-Military and the Military-Technical Parts of Doctrine

The emergence of a sharp debate among high-ranking Soviet military officials over the direction of doctrinal development in the months after the issuance of the June 1987 Warsaw Pact statement offers strong prima facie evidence that key issues were seen to be at stake. The debate's ostensible focus was the degree to which the two components of military doctrine—the political-military and the military-technical—could, or could not, be said to operate in conformity. In actuality, at issue was the future shape of Soviet armed forces, since the outcome of the debate would likely determine such sensitive issues as manning levels, the optimal and most stabilizing balance between "offensive" and "defensive" military means, and the tradeoffs in procurement policy between reliance on quality and quantity.

Those arguing if favor of conformity, such as General Makhmut Gareyev, deputy chief of the General Staff, alleged that there was not, nor had there ever been, any real inconsistency between the two halves of doctrine. In other words, and appearances to the contrary notwithstanding, the military-technical component of doctrine was just as "defensive" as its political-military counterpart. Consequently, the doctrinal shift that had been previewed in Budapest in 1986 and confirmed in Berlin a year later could be accommodated *without* extensive changes in either the makeup or the capabilities of Soviet forces. According to those espousing this viewpoint, the existing Soviet (and Warsaw Pact) military posture in Europe constituted "a reliable bulwark for peace," whatever the precise correlation of forces between East and West, thereby obviating the need for any large-scale, unilateral adjustments in either the number of deployed troops or the performance characteristics of their weapons.[22]

Those who took exception to this argument stopped short, at least in their public pronouncements, of describing the two parts of doctrine as inconsistent; notwithstanding the reluctance to make explicit what Western military authorities had long suspected, their underlying purpose—the core message of their remarks—was difficult to miss. The leading spokesmen of this view were the late Marshal Sergei Akhromeyev, until December 1988 chief of the General Staff, and General Dmitri Yazov, whom Gorbachev had plucked out of relative obscurity in 1987 to head the Ministry of Defense. In the course of a tightly worded piece on the current state of Soviet military thinking, published in February 1988, Akhromeyev made his position clear. After affirming the "defensive thrust" of the country's military policy, the marshal went on to declare that "politically, this has always been the nature of our military doctrine . . . since the very first days of Great October. But now its defensive thrust *is also being further developed and clarified in the military-technical sphere* (emphasis added).[23] The implication—that important work remained to be done in the development and "clarification" of the second and more substantial part of doctrine—was unmistakable.

Six months later, in remarks to the party faithful at the General Staff, Akhromeyev was more direct, noting that the "restructuring" of the Soviet military was proceeding "in a contradictory fashion and with difficulty." Denouncing what he termed various "errors" on the part of the General Staff in assessing the current military situation, as well as the organization's attachment to "old ideas," Akhromeyev advised his audience:

> We must continue to work to improve military building in accordance with the principles of balance and defense sufficiency and in light of the activity of the United States and the NATO bloc. This is the main and the most complex question in the practical implementation of military doctrine . . . . There is some clarity on this issue in theory, but when it comes to practice many directorates are elaborating new decisions slowly and timidly.[24]

In January 1989, one month after his resignation as chief of the General Staff, Akhromeyev all but admitted that in determining the kinds of forces the Soviet Union needed to safeguard its security—one of three cardinal tasks he ascribed to those responsible for the development of the military-technical aspect of doctrine—the Kremlin had procured and deployed forces in excess of those required for defensive purposes.[25] Using similar, if less graphic language, Yazov had implied much the same thing on two occasions during 1988 (both times to representatives of the foreign media).[26] In the wake of these high-level interventions, particularly Akhromeyev's forthright statement of August 1988, testimonials in support of the "defensive" character of the existing military-technical component of doctrine rapidly declined in number.

The controversy surrounding the adoption of the new military doctrine unfolded along other dimensions, as well. As indicated, among the points in contention were proposed changes in the methods of military procurement. Some officials, it appears, were less than enthusiastic at the prospect of having to substitute quality for quantity as the major determinant of weapons production. Again, Akhromeyev and Yazov led the charge against such "old thinking." The issue, they argued, had been thoroughly considered by responsible officials, both military and civilian. The duty of the Soviet defense establishment was not to second-guess the wisdom of the decision, but to embrace it. The problem had arisen in the first place, according to Yazov, because "purely localistic, short-term, and sometimes simply careerist considerations" had blocked the road to military innovation. As a result, "flaws occurred in determining the prospects of developing armaments, in the operational-tactical substantiation of particular models, and in ensuring that

their quality and reliability conformed with modern requirements."[27] To correct the situation, the defense minister called for a
change in methods, "from an extensive, cost-driven track to an
intensive, economical track."[28] Excessive reliance on quantitative
parameters was not only expensive, Yazov wrote, but increasingly
ineffective "from both military-political and actual military point[s]
of view."[29]

Akhromeyev linked the proposed shift to larger trends at work
in Soviet society (especially the looming economic crisis) and to
anticipated reductions in the size of Soviet armed forces. Perestroika, he noted, requires the General Staff "to review many positions and to resolve many questions in a new way."

> With regard to arms and equipment this means that the troops and
> fleets will probably receive less, but the combat effectiveness and
> quality must be higher, so that it is possible to resolve tasks with fewer
> combat resources, yet more effectively.
>
> [W]e must find new methods of maintaining combat potential at
> a proper level guaranteeing reliable security for the country under
> conditions of possible reductions in both nuclear and conventional
> arms.[30]

Akhromeyev, never one to mince words, had framed the issue
in precisely the right way: in an era of extensive social and political
reform, budgetary contraction, and substantial arms control, the
military had to adapt and learn to make more efficient use of a
declining share of the country's material and human resources. The
message was a painful one to those on the receiving end, and certain
to arouse the most deeply seated anxieties of the professional Soviet
military.

Operational Considerations

Those responsible for the planning of military operations felt the
trauma associated with doctrinal reform more keenly, perhaps, than
any other group within the Soviet defense hierarchy. It was, after all,
at the operational level that the changes in doctrine, once implemented, would have had the greatest impact. Considerable controversy attended discussion of these issues. Moreover, it was a
controversy in which not only the uniformed military took part, but
also civilians—ranging from such senior officials as Gorbachev and
Shevardnadze, to a host of less consequential figures attached to

various academic institutes in and around Moscow and to the Soviet media.

At the center of the debate were two issues: the significance and utility of the concept of *sufficiency* in determining both the size and the combat potential of Soviet military forces, and the definition of *defensive* military operations. The two were related, of course. Gorbachev introduced the first of these ideas in his report to the twenty-seventh CPSU congress, delivered in February 1986. "Our country," Gorbachev announced, "is in favor of withdrawing weapons of mass destruction from circulation and confining military potential to the bounds of reasonable sufficiency."[31] He did not at this juncture explain what this might mean for the posturing of Soviet forces, either nuclear or conventional. Whatever drama Gorbachev had sought to generate with this statement was largely lost, in any event, as a result of his repetition two sentences later of a phrase first coined by Brezhnev. While the Soviet Union would lay no claim to greater security for itself, he intoned, "it will not settle for less."[32]

Predictably, given the character of its unveiling, the concept of sufficiency did not immediately revolutionize Soviet military thought. In his remarks to the party congress, for example, then Defense Minister Sergei Sokolov avoided use of the term altogether. Instead, he advised the delegates that Soviet general purpose forces were being developed "within the limits necessary for defense"—a more neutral, if equally vague, formula that raised at least as many questions as it answered.[33]

"Sufficiency" acquired a measure of substance, as well as a powerful political boost, at the June 1986 meeting of the Warsaw Pact Political Consultative Committee; more details were forthcoming when alliance officials reconvened in Berlin the following year. Soviet spokesmen also hosted a number of background briefings, particularly in the period after the Berlin meeting, that provided further insights.[34]

Regarding *strategic nuclear forces*, the definition of "reasonable sufficiency" was relatively straightforward, at least as ranking nonmilitary Soviets described it beginning in 1987. Taking nuclear deterrence as a military given—by which these spokesmen meant the continuing dominance of offensive (as opposed to defensive) military capabilities in the U.S.–Soviet strategic relationship—sufficiency was defined as the capacity to inflict "unacceptable damage" on an aggressor in response to any preemptive nuclear strike.[35] Estimates as to what that might entail in terms of the number of weapons ranged from several hundred (a "minimum deterrence" posture) to several thousand.[36] More than the quantity of weapons, what mattered most in this context was the possession of a reliable, secure nuclear reserve, able to retaliate under any and all circumstances with devastating effectiveness. Obviously, in a strategic environment dominated by second-strike forces, potent defensive capabilities—whether conventional antiballistic missile systems or exotic space-based weapons—would have no place.

While not without its detractors, support for "stabilizing" reductions in strategic offensive forces had become well enough established in Soviet arms control policy by the time of Gorbachev's election as general secretary that logical extensions of that position were unlikely to provoke much of a reaction on the part of the military, one way or another. Whatever faith Soviet leaders once might have had in the Kremlin's ability to wage and win a nuclear war seems to have all but evaporated by the mid-1980s.[37] Certainly, the Gorbachev generation of leaders, military as well as civilian, seemed convinced that the pursuit of meaningful strategic superiority was a dangerous and wasteful chimera. The one issue concerning the limitation of strategic forces around which representatives of the military *did* tend to rally was the perceived need to undertake such reductions with the United States on a reciprocal and symmetrical basis. Even on this subject, however, opinions differed and the military spoke with more than one voice.[38]

An obvious disconnect existed between what Soviet authorities said they supported in the area of strategic nuclear force reductions (and in the concepts to guide their possible use in war) and the character and composition of the Kremlin's nuclear arsenal. The forces then at Moscow's command enjoyed considerable counterforce capabilities, for example, a reality that called into question the sincerity of their interest in "minimum deterrence." Moreover, improvements to system performance, such as the attainment of better and better missile accuracies, were ongoing throughout the

Gorbachev years. The same could be said, of course, about U.S. strategic forces.

Important changes will take place in the structure of the U.S. and (now) Russian nuclear postures, as a result of the July 1991 START agreement and of developments in U.S.–Russian strategic relations in the period since the Soviet collapse. Meaningful operational constraints on the capabilities of these weapons, however, will have to await the actual implementation of these accords, especially those negotiated by Presidents George Bush and Boris Yeltsin during the latter's visit to the United States in June 1992.[39]

Far deeper divisions attended the discussion of what constituted sufficiency in *conventional military power*—the acquisition and deployment of armed forces and armaments for possible use in theater operations. Suggestive of the differences in opinion on this sensitive issue was the tendency of the political leadership to speak in terms of "reasonable sufficiency" as the most appropriate yardstick for determining theater military potential, while senior military officials preferred the phrases "defense sufficiency," or "sufficiency for defense." The two concepts were not mutually exclusive. They were not, however, identical, and the differences were significant.

The analytical basis of the political rendering had two parts: that the military capabilities of East and West far exceeded those necessary for the defense of their vital interests; and that the United States and its NATO allies had sought, as a matter of conscious policy, to exhaust the economies of the Warsaw Pact states through a ruinous military competition.[40] Given these assumptions, the most useful and cost-effective way for the socialist countries, including the Soviet Union, to organize their defense efforts was by reference to the concept of "reasonable sufficiency."

But sufficient for what? In response to this key question, government and academic representatives offered a three-part answer: that Soviet (and Warsaw Pact) capabilities should be sufficient both in number and in kind to deny the West military superiority; that the forces of each alliance in Europe should be so constituted as to rule out the possibility of a successful surprise attack; and that each side, while reliably able to "repulse aggression," should be deprived of the capacity to mount "offensive" military operations.[41] In deciding how best to satisfy these goals, advocates also underscored the importance of casting aside old habits of thinking and outdated methods. As one military academic wrote in June 1988, "the response to the other side's military-technical initiatives must be not so much a symmetrical or asymmetrical response as the optimum response . . . based on the political, combat, and economic effectiveness of the arms chosen."[42]

But should the necessary changes be instituted unilaterally, or through a process of negotiation involving adversary states? The most typical response was that a combination of initiatives, some unilateral, others bi- or multilateral, should be relied upon, depending on the circumstances. The most important variable in making these decisions was not how they might appear to the other side, but how such steps would effect national, regional, and international security. If the reforms, including reductions, could be safely implemented without obtaining concessions from the other side, there was little reason to delay.[43] If the proposed actions might endanger the well-being of the USSR, then they should only be undertaken collectively and in the context of a mutually binding agreement to enhance the security of all concerned.

Some proponents of "reasonable sufficiency" advocated a more radical course, calling for the adoption of a minimum deterrence posture in the theater—necessitating deep, asymmetrical reductions in troop levels and most kinds of military equipment, particularly weapon systems most closely associated with the conduct of offensive operations, such as tanks, armored fighting vehicles, and longer-range, heavily armed tactical aircraft.[44] Even within the community seeking major reforms, however, those championing this point of view constituted a distinct minority and none occupied positions of authority during the early years of the Gorbachev era.

By and large, the Soviet military accommodated and adopted without dissent the first two articles of the political leadership's reform agenda regarding theater doctrine—the rejection of superiority as a goal of policy and the desirability of depriving either side of the ability to execute a surprise attack. It was the third provision, the injunction against offensive military operations, that became a source of contention and debate.

Five months after the adoption in Berlin of the Warsaw Pact's new military doctrine in May 1987, for example, Defense Minister Yazov defined the military objectives of the Warsaw Pact states in terms that suggested a less than resounding endorsement of this principle. "The whole defense readiness system of the Warsaw Treaty," Yazov stated, "is built in such a way as to halt the aggressor, wrest his criminal plans and, if aggression against any of the Treaty participants does become a fact through the imperialist's fault, *decisively repulse it* (emphasis added)."[45] Deputy chief of the General Staff Gareyev had employed a very similar construction several months earlier: "The armed forces of the allied countries are maintained in sufficient combat readiness to prevent themselves from being taken unawares, and if they are nonetheless attacked, *they will issue a crushing rebuff to the aggressor* (emphasis added)."[46]

Historically, the use by Kremlin officials of the phrases "decisively repulse" and "crushing rebuff" in reference to military operations had been quite deliberate—to convey Moscow's determination to seize the initiative from the adversary, to defeat his armed forces, and to secure the combat victory of the Soviet Union and its allies. None of these goals was to be found on the list of approved military objectives developed and expressed by the new political leadership. Their appearance in such high-level statements, particularly Yazov's, as late as the fall of 1987, was curious, to say the least.

Eighteen months later, in March 1989, General Mikhail A. Moiseyev, Akhromeyev's successor as chief of the General Staff, tried his hand at crafting a similar statement. The general's effort, which bore the mark of heavy civilian input, began well enough, but at the critical juncture retreated into evasion. "Today," Moiseyev wrote,

> defensive operations will be the Soviet Armed Forces' main form of action at the beginning of the war. In training our Armed Forces, defense on a strategic, operational, and tactical scale has been moved to the fore. This, of course, does not mean behaving passively or handing the initiative wholly to the aggressor. If he attacks he must be not only stopped but brought to his senses."[47]

As RAND Corporation analysts John G. Hines and Donald Mahoney suggest in their excellent study on the development of

Soviet military art in the 1980s, the delegitimation of offensive operations placed the uniformed military in an extremely difficult—indeed, what some might term an impossible—position.[48] Once Soviet forces had met and contained the aggressive thrusts of the adversary, what then? According to the new military doctrine, it seemed, the fighting was to stop, the enemy having either realized the error of his ways or exhausted himself. But what if the fighting didn't end? What if the enemy were to resume his assault? Were Soviet forces to be on the defensive perpetually? Were they never to take the war to the aggressor?

In an obvious effort to close the logical lacunae in the new doctrine, Soviet military officials drew a distinction between what they termed "offensive" and "counteroffensive" operations (and, as indicated in Moiseyev's statement, between the beginning and ensuing stages of conflict). The former, they alleged, were characteristic of aggressive intent and, therefore, illegitimate; the latter, the justifiable province of the defender who, following the successful blunting of the enemy's attack, had every right to undertake offensive action in the interest of bringing the war to a prompt conclusion and on favorable terms.[49] *When* one chose to take the military initiative (and *how* it was described) assumed in this context singular importance.

This shift in emphasis and in planning from an "offensive" posture to one designed to support strictly "counteroffensive" operations raised a host of nettlesome issues for the Soviets concerning manning levels, equipment needs, mobilization schedules, and the like. What level of deployed forces would be adequate for the latter purpose but insufficient to mount an offensive at the outset of hostilities? What was the correct balance during peacetime between tank and motorized infantry divisions? Should the number of tanks, armored fighting vehicles, and armored personnel carriers in either or both types of divisions be reduced, and if so, by how much? And how could Soviet armed forces be reconfigured in such a way as to curtail their numbers when the two alliances were at peace, while also providing for their rapid expansion, should the shooting start?[50]

The answers to these and related questions were still being formulated when the Soviet flag was lowered over the Kremlin for the last time in December 1991. In 1990 Soviet plans called for reductions in active duty forces of between 6 and 20 percent (10 to 12 percent for the ground forces), with reductions on a similar scale projected for armor, artillery, and tactical aircraft.[51]

Concerning its forces deployed in or oriented toward Europe, Moscow clearly hoped to coordinate the anticipated drawdown in troop and equipment levels with corresponding, if smaller, reductions in comparable Western forces. The Soviets also communicated their willingness to negotiate the withdrawal of all land-based, short-range nuclear systems from Europe left undisturbed by the December 1987 INF Treaty—a step they eventually took, in concert with Washington, late in 1991.

Deciding how and what to cut was made infinitely more complex by the sudden collapse in 1989 of orthodox communist regimes in Eastern Europe, particularly those in East Germany, Poland, Czechoslovakia, and Hungary—the first three representing the Warsaw Pact's Northern Tier (see chapter 3 for a discussion of the security implications of the collapse of Soviet power in Europe). The liberation and democratization of its former satellites utterly transformed the Soviet Union's political position on the continent, while simultaneously eviscerating its traditional theater military strategy. Whether, and for how long, *any* Soviet troops would have remained in Eastern Europe had the USSR not collapsed is impossible to know. The conclusion of agreements between Moscow, on the one hand, and Prague and Budapest, on the other, requiring the withdrawal by mid-1991 of all Soviet forces (some 135,000 troops in all) turned out to be but the first scene of a multi-act play—a play, moreover, performed by a cast of characters on the Russian side that Gorbachev could only have imagined.

How far the Soviets had come along the path of military reform before they began to lose control of the process—and how much further they still had to go—emerged clearly in the course of a long interview with General Moiseyev, which ran in the Soviet periodical *Nedelya* in May 1989. In answer to a question concerning the reorganization of Soviet armed forces, Moiseyev stated that the General Staff had defined its task as

> the practical implementation of the demands of the defensive military doctrine, which involves giving the armed forces an unequivocally

defensive structure, amending the theory of military art, and developing fundamentally new theses for training and using Armed Forces in line with new views.[52]

This work, he declared, was being "stepped up." "The structure of the General Staff is being improved in order to ensure that each of its organs promptly resolves all the tasks facing it. This work is still not completed . . . but the results are already visible." He concluded with an admission that "old habits and "stereotypes" die hard, complicating and obstructing the process of reform.[53] To overcome the legacy of the past, he insisted,

> we must all learn to think and work in a new way, take a bolder look ahead, and take the new atmosphere and the new demands into account. The General Staff also must more vigorously restructure itself, more promptly join in the practical work of restructuring . . . and devote greater efforts to overcoming elements of stagnation once and for all . . . .[54]

THE RESTRUCTURING OF THE ARMED FORCES

Of the many tasks confronting General Moiseyev and his General Staff colleagues during the years of reform, one of the most difficult was how to implement the unilateral force reductions announced by Gorbachev in his UN General Assembly speech of December 7, 1988, and to do so in such a way as not to endanger the security of the Soviet state. In that address, Gorbachev promised to reduce the numerical strength of the armed forces by 500,000 within two years and to withdraw from service and destroy 10,000 tanks, 8,500 artillery systems, and 800 combat aircraft.[55] As part of the reduction plan, he pledged to remove (and to demobilize) six Soviet tank divisions, containing some 50,000 troops and 5,000 tanks, from Czechoslovakia, Hungary, and what was then the German Democratic Republic (GDR).[56] Also to be withdrawn were assault landing and river-crossing forces "with their armaments and combat equipment." "All remaining Soviet divisions on the territory of our allies," Gorbachev declared, "will be reorganized. They will be given a different structure from today's, which will become unambiguously defensive after the removal of a large number of their tanks."[57]

Shortly after Gorbachev's speech, the Soviets indicated that the manpower reductions would be divided among three theaters: the

European USSR and Eastern Europe (240,000); the Far East (200,000); and Central Asia (60,000). When Shevardnadze visited Beijing in February 1989, the foreign minister further stipulated that of the 200,000 troops to be demobilized in the Far East, some 60 percent would be drawn from the forces then deployed along the Sino-Soviet frontier. At the same time, he revealed that 50,000 troops stationed in Mongolia—some two-thirds of the Soviet to-tal—would soon be returning to the territory of the USSR.

In the period after the December 1988 initiative, the political context within which Gorbachev developed and presented his plan for the remaking of Soviet power in Europe changed radically, in ways neither he nor anyone else could have anticipated. Events notwithstanding, the Soviet leader kept to his timetable; the 50,000 Soviet troops he said would depart the GDR, Czechoslovakia, and Hungary by the end of 1990 did so, and on schedule; the demobiliz-ation of the 450,000 stationed within the USSR also was completed. Approximately three-fifths of the Kremlin's forces that remained in Eastern Europe would have followed suit, it seems, in keeping with the terms of the bilateral agreements struck with the governments in Prague and Budapest and the terms of the November 1990 treaty on the reduction of conventional forces in Europe (CFE).

With the completion of the reductions announced in December 1988, the number of active-duty Soviet military personnel declined from approximately 4,250,000 to 3,750,000; the army shrank from 1.6 to 1.3 million.[58] Reports also surfaced of discussions within the government on the desirability of additional cuts in military man-power on the order of a million, or more, by the mid-1990s, which, if implemented, would have resulted in an effective 40 percent reduction in Soviet armed forces from 1988 levels.

Reductions in weapon systems demanded by the CFE Treaty also would have had a far-reaching impact on the Soviet Union's conventional military posture, especially in the European USSR, where most of the cuts would have fallen. Soviet tank holdings in the region, for example, would have declined by two-thirds, from ap-proximately 40,000 in 1988 to 13,150; reductions in the number of deployed armored personnel carriers (32 percent) and artillery sys-tems (5 percent) would also have been significant. Cuts in tactical aircraft would have totaled approximately 1,300 systems, or 20 percent of the total Soviet inventory.[59]

(With the collapse of the Soviet Union in December 1991, the task of implementing the reductions mandated in the CFE Treaty fell to seven of the USSR's fifteen successor states: Russia, Belarus, Ukraine, Armenia, Georgia, Azerbaijan, and Moldova. In May 1992, following a series of bilateral and multilateral discussions involving Western as well as Commonwealth of Independent States (CIS) governments, these countries informed the other signatories to CFE that they had agreed on a formula to apportion the seven kinds of military equipment limited by the agreement; they also declared that they would submit the accord to their respective parliaments for ratification in the nearest future.)

In accommodating the directives of the political leadership to restructure Soviet conventional forces, the General Staff sought to resolve three sets of issues that operated at different levels (a fourth and wholly separate set of questions, taken up in chapter 4, concerned the Defense Ministry's role in facilitating the process of demilitarization and in easing the very real domestic economic and social strains generated by the downsizing of Soviet armed forces):

- What was the character of the theater military threat likely to face the Soviet Union in future years, and against which the country's armed forces would have to be prepared to offer stout resistance?

- What principles should guide the use of Soviet forces in war?

- And how, within the quantitative parameters set by the leadership and confirmed by various international agreements, was the Soviet military to be equipped and organized?

The answer to the first question reflected the fact that while much had changed in Soviet policy, some key elements had endured. According to the General Staff, the armed forces of the NATO allies constituted Moscow's foremost military challenge. The threat, wrote Akhromeyev in January 1989, "is not all that difficult to define: the military leadership of the United States and the North Atlantic alliance itself names the Soviet Union as its main, probable adversary."[60] The principal danger posed by the West was seen to reside in its ability to conduct highly destructive military operations employing conventional, as well as nuclear, means. All U.S. plans, Moiseyev alleged in March 1989, are based on conducting military operations on someone else's territory, and allow for preemptive strikes "on suspicion," and massive strikes, at that, in order to suppress resistance in the initial stages of a war. The armed forces of the United States and its allies are trained and equipped accordingly.[61]

This assessment—for almost forty years the touchstone of Soviet military planning—underwent significant modification as a consequence of the rapidly changing face of East-West relations. At the July 1990 NATO Summit session in London, the Western allies, following the lead of their Eastern counterparts, declared the Cold War at an end. They also, and more to the point from the Soviet perspective, previewed plans to thin out alliance forces deployed along the central front, abandoned their commitment to "forward defense," characterized their nuclear arms as "weapons of last resort," and proposed a series of nonaggression pacts between NATO and individual Warsaw Treaty states. The Soviet response to the NATO communiqué was both quick and enthusiastic, Gorbachev, for one, pronouncing it an "important impulse" toward peace.[62] Later the same month, Chancellor Helmut Kohl, at the end of two days of meetings with Gorbachev in the Russian city of Stavropol, agreed to limit the size of the *Bundeswehr* to 370,000 following the unification of the two Germanys, and not immediately to deploy German forces committed to NATO on the territory of the GDR. It was an important concession to Moscow, which, in combination with other inducements, enabled Kohl to extract from the Soviets their consent to a united Germany entering NATO.[63]

In answer to the second question—what principles might guide the use of Soviet forces in the event of war—the military had long since received its marching orders. As discussed in the preceding section, however, the adoption of new military doctrine, with its emphasis on "defensive" operations, created significant problems of both a definitional and a practical nature. In reference to the latter, Soviet military planners concentrated on three major tasks: adjusting to the anticipated recall of forward-deployed units (and to reductions in manpower, more generally); reducing the weight of armor, and armored forces, within front-line units; and determining the most appropriate basis for the organization of the armed forces.

On the first of these issues, the military had precious little room to maneuver, the withdrawal of forces from Eastern Europe and the downsizing of the army having been decreed by the political leadership. By 1990 the primary job of the General Staff was simply to carry out these directives as expeditiously as possible and in a manner likely to preserve essential Soviet security interests.

The military, as befitted their role within the Soviet system, seemed to have had a significantly greater voice in the debates surrounding the second and third of these issues. On the disposition of armored forces, for example, it was Moiseyev, in his capacity as chief of the General Staff, who announced in 1989 that the 14 Soviet tank divisions scheduled to remain in Eastern Europe (following the withdrawal of the six divisions announced in December 1988) would be reconfigured along "defensive" lines. Some 20 percent of the tanks assigned to these units, Moiseyev stated, were to be withdrawn from service; for motorized infantry divisions, the corresponding figure was 40 percent.[64]

Despite their penchant for intervening in the military's affairs, it was highly unlikely that civilian leaders would have descended to this level of operational detail, lacking both the expertise and, one presumes, the inclination to do so. To allay any such concerns, both Moiseyev and Akhromeyev were quick to insist that responsible military authorities had been centrally involved in these deliberations from the outset.[65]

Military representatives also took the lead in deciding how best to organize the country's armed forces under conditions of radical economic and social reform, a sensitive issue in Soviet politics; they conveyed their recommendations in the form of a draft plan for comprehensive reform of the armed forces, formally submitted to the Supreme Soviet in November 1990. The proposals, signed by Defense Minister Yazov, envisaged a three-stage process—1990 to 1994, 1994 to 1995, and 1995 to 2000—at the end of which the five Soviet military services would have completed the steps deemed necessary by the General Staff to bring the armed forces into compliance with the dictates of "the new political thinking," "reasonable sufficiency," and "defensive defense."[66] The draft program of military reform was still under discussion when the union came apart barely a year later; it was, of course, never implemented.

Just how consequential the changes in Moscow's conventional military posture were between Gorbachev's December 1988 UN initiative and the collapse of the union three years later was at the time a matter of some contention among Western military analysts.

On two points, however, the community was in substantial accord. Virtually all Western experts were of the opinion that the reduction in Soviet forces and equipment, when combined with the collapse of the Warsaw Pact, effectively eliminated the threat of an Eastern "standing-start" military offensive against NATO. Warning times for such an attack now extended to months (rather than days or weeks) in the judgment of most observers. They also agreed, however, that even after the completion of "restructuring," Soviet forces oriented toward Europe were likely to enjoy considerable "punch"—sufficient, certainly, for the conduct of effective and sustained defensive military operations and, with augmentation, of formidable "counteroffensive" missions—assuming that the country itself did not disintegrate and descend into political chaos.[67]

The impact of the doctrinal reforms on the character and composition of the Soviet strategic arsenal was far more modest. Offensive forces, in fact, were still being modernized in the first half of 1991, although at a slower rate than they had been during the preceding five-year period. Deployments of the SS-24 and SS-25 ICBMs, for example, continued until the very end. A fifth variant of the SS-18 was being readied for testing even as Gorbachev was cleaning out his Kremlin office. Until mid-1991 new ballistic missile submarines were entering service at the rate of one per year. At least one Western source reported that the Blackjack bomber, following years of delay, was about to enter serial production (it never did).[68]

The Soviet naval shipbuilding program also seemed immune, at least for a time, to the changes in military doctrine. Through 1989 the pace of construction neither increased nor decreased. A second Tbilisi-class aircraft carrier began sea trials in 1990 and a third such ship, also displacing 65,000 tons, was under construction when the country ceased to exist.[69] In 1991 the Soviets announced reductions in the absolute number of deployed vessels, but these appeared to have come about largely as the result of an effort to substitute quality for quantity, rather than as the consequence of a decision to reduce capabilities, per se.

THE FAILURE OF MILITARY REFORM

In forcing the adoption of the new military doctrine, and in demanding the enactment of measures to bring Soviet capabilities into line with the twin dictates of "defensive defense" and "reasonable sufficiency," the Gorbachev leadership took dead aim at the very foundation of Soviet power in the modern world. For over four decades the Kremlin's military muscle had protected the USSR from attack and invasion, helped to maintain order within its sphere of influence, and garnered the respect, if not the affection, of the Western community of states. With the country's attainment of a vast potential to destroy, the generation of leaders preceding Gorbachev took manifest pride in proclaiming the Soviet Union's arrival as the "other" superpower.

The heart of the Gorbachev indictment against the military policies of the Brezhnev leadership was that the latter's claims, while true in a narrow sense, were fundamentally fraudulent: as powerful as the Soviet Union had become militarily, it had lost precious ground to the developed world economically and, as a consequence, been forced to cede the initiative politically. The more Gorbachev and those gathered about him learned about the rate and extent of the country's domestic deterioration, the more alarmed they became. To remedy the situation, they advanced a truly radical program to reverse Soviet priorities—to discard the emphasis on military prowess in favor of an ambitious and expensive effort to restore the economic (and hence the political) vitality of Soviet society.

The plan, which continued to develop even as the country careened toward collapse, was an audacious one. It was also fraught with risk. What if the reforms were to fail? What if the Soviet Union, rather than recovering economically, persisted along its downward spiral? Political and interethnic relations within and between the fifteen constituent republics were already strained to the breaking point and were likely to erode further, vastly complicating efforts to restructure them, and Soviet society, on a more democratic and voluntaristic basis. Under such conditions, the dissolution of the union, once the stuff of right-wing, anti-Soviet fantasies, was distinctly possible. Even assuming partial success, and a modest economic recovery over the near-to-medium term, the weight of the Soviet Union within the international system, especially as measured by its capacity to influence political outcomes in both proximate and more distant environments, would be demonstrably less than at any time since the period between the two world wars.

How, then, to safeguard Soviet security interests during this time of transition? The great irony (and one that could not have escaped the attention of the leadership) was that Moscow's traditional response to such challenges—the maintenance of sufficient military power to ward off the aggressive designs of any would-be adversary or combination of adversaries—was precisely the response that had precipitated the broader systemic crisis to begin with. Part of Gorbachev's strategy, then, was to turn this ancient wisdom on its head. His central premise was that the international environment was, or could be made, fundamentally benign and nonthreatening from Moscow's perspective.

On the correctness of this judgment hinged not only Gorbachev's fate as a political leader, but the future of the Soviet Union. The Gorbachev reform program constituted, therefore, an enormous gamble that by end of 1990 had already resulted in a cascade of foreign and security policy concessions—from the INF treaty in 1987 to the loss of Eastern Europe in 1989–1990—quite without precedent in the Soviet experience.

In the end, of course, Gorbachev's high-risk strategy did not pay off. It failed, however, not because Moscow's adversaries rushed to exploit the Soviet Union's manifest weakness, but because the domestic political terrain under Gorbachev's feet turned to quicksand. The intensification of the economic and political crises—which were themselves the root causes of the effort to transform the character and conduct of Soviet security policy—deprived Gorbachev, and all those who had worked with him, of the opportunity to press ahead with his military reform program. In this area, as in so many others, the Soviet leader was forced to settle for what might have been.

The two chapters that follow investigate several of the most important dimensions of change—the content and conduct between 1985 and 1991 of Moscow's East-West and arms control diplomacy and the development of civil-military relations under Gorbachev—along which the reformers struggled both to transform Soviet society and to recast the foundation of the country's relationship with the world beyond its borders.

Chapter 3

Arms Control and Regional Security

FROM THE LATE 1960S TO THE LATE 1980S, THE ATTEMPT TO REGU-
late the East-West military competition through a process of
formal negotiation constituted the highest of high politics. No other
issue on the international agenda attracted as much attention or
consumed as much political energy as the effort to produce agreements limiting U.S. and Soviet (and NATO and Warsaw Pact)
military capabilities. Most important to Washington and Moscow
were negotiations to curtail strategic nuclear forces. With the capacity to annihilate one another's societies in less time than it takes
most Americans to commute to work, leaders in both countries
went to great lengths to underscore their sensitivity to this unprecedented situation and to convey their determination to safeguard the
peace. The most concrete expression of this commitment was the
institutionalization of the arms control process itself. From the
opening session of the Strategic Arms Limitation Talks in November
1969 to the signing of the Strategic Arms Reduction Treaty in July
1991, U.S. and Soviet negotiators convened at some point, if only
briefly, during 20 of these 23 years.[1]

Beyond their objective importance, U.S.–Soviet arms control
efforts also came to possess considerable symbolic significance.
From the late 1960s to the mid-1980s—when Washington and
Moscow seemed either unwilling or unable to make real progress in
resolving the deep differences that divided them—the negotiations

served as a kind of substitute political discourse, generating just enough by way of agreements to justify the enterprise and to sustain the hope of better things to come. With little else to guide them, U.S. political observers fastened on the often arcane developments in nuclear and conventional arms control in an attempt to gauge the precise state of relations between Washington and Moscow and to anticipate future developments.

Relations between the superpowers were at something of a low point when Gorbachev succeeded Konstantin Chernenko as CPSU general secretary in March 1985. While marginally better than they had been earlier in the decade, relations had yet to recover from the September 1983 downing of Korean Airlines Flight 007 off the Kamchatka Peninsula by Soviet air defense forces attached to the Far Eastern military command. Two months later, in November 1983, the Andropov leadership, in a deliberate move to sow dissension between the United States and its NATO allies, broke off negotiations to limit U.S. and Soviet intermediate-range nuclear forces, allegedly in response to the arrival in Europe of the first contingent of U.S. Pershing II missiles. The following week the Kremlin declined to set a date for the resumption of the START talks. For fourteen months, from the Soviet INF walkout to the January 1985 meeting in Geneva between Secretary of State George Shultz and Foreign Minister Andrei Gromyko, superpower relations were at a virtual standstill. Seldom had the linkage between superpower arms control and the larger fabric of U.S.–Soviet relations—the clear dependence of the former on the latter—been more explicit.

By the end of the decade, the political impasse between the United States and the Soviet Union had given way to the most extensive and broadly based détente in the troubled fifty-year history of the relationship. In five short years, Gorbachev, with the active assistance of Presidents Reagan and Bush, engineered a truly remarkable turnabout in relations, a dramatic shift from enmity to amity that may well constitute one of the most impressive diplomatic and political feats of the twentieth century.

To move relations off dead center and to lay the groundwork for a new, more cooperative era between East and West, Gorbachev turned first to arms control. The decision could not have come easily to the Soviet leader who, despite his obvious impatience with the status quo, in 1985 had yet to express the full extent of his displeasure with existing Soviet policies (and with the system responsible for their generation). The Kremlin's reluctance to endorse, let alone propose, dramatic departures in security policy had been a characteristic feature of Soviet diplomacy since the ouster of Nikita Khrushchev in the mid-1960s. As a consequence, Gorbachev's stratagem caught most Western governments by surprise. It also, it seems, sent shock waves through much of the Soviet bureaucracy, stunned Moscow's conservative Eastern European allies, and contributed to the most important series of changes in international politics since the conclusion of the Second World War.

In resurrecting arms control, Gorbachev sought to revitalize East-West relations in the shortest possible time, principally by eliciting a prompt and positive U.S. response. Combined with other gestures, such as his willingness to meet with President Reagan barely six months after assuming office, Gorbachev hoped to utilize progress in the START and INF negotiations to free himself, and Soviet diplomacy, of the disastrous legacy of Brezhnev-era policies—policies that had done so much in his judgment to erode Moscow's power and standing within the international community over the preceding decade. Later in the 1980s Gorbachev sought to employ much the same strategy in an arena closer to home—the NATO–Warsaw Pact negotiations on conventional forces in Europe (CFE).

As he distanced himself from the failures of the past, however, Gorbachev soon discovered that decisive change along any single dimension of policy, in this instance the Soviet approach to arms control, created pressures for change along other dimensions, as well. As Soviet officials affirmed their commitment to "the new political thinking," countries both within and beyond Moscow's orbit began, warily at first, to put Soviet words to the test. When the leadership persisted in its support of change, the result was an extraordinary degree of volatility, both in Moscow's state-to-state relations and in international politics more generally. In seeking reform, Gorbachev ended up precipitating a revolution.

The chapter begins with a discussion of the factors that induced Gorbachev and his government to abandon existing Soviet positions in the START and INF negotiations. It continues with a depiction of

the apparent connection in Soviet thinking between the larger foreign and security policy agenda of the new leadership and the "new
look" in arms control during Gorbachev's first five years at the helm
(1985–1990). The next three sections of the chapter examine in
detail the content and evolution of the Soviet Union's strategic and
regional (Europe and Asia) arms control policies across the same
time frame. The chapter concludes with a brief analysis of developments during Gorbachev's final year in office.

STARTING OVER

Moscow's arms control policies, like Washington's, were very much
a product of the extraordinary stresses and strains generated by the
nuclear revolution. A political response to the obvious dangers
associated with the spectacular growth during the postwar period of
U.S. and Soviet strategic weapons arsenals, Moscow's arms control
policies constituted a subset of national security policy, at once
connected to and distinct from both foreign and military policy
considerations. The fact that such diplomacy (and the attendant
negotiations) had to serve two masters simultaneously was a manageable problem for the Soviets so long as the country's international political and military objectives coincided.

From the mid-1940s to the mid-1980s, such was indeed the case.
Moscow looked to the development and expansion of its military
capabilities to underwrite its status as a great power and, later, to
bolster its claims to world leadership. For the most part, Soviet leaders
designed their arms control policies to comport with these objectives.
One would be hard pressed, for example, to discern in the Soviet
Union's SALT positions during the 1970s a political agenda that
departed in important ways from that which informed the leadership's conduct of foreign and military policy, more generally.

Prior to the advent of Gorbachev, Kremlin leaders adhered to
what can only be considered a manifestly self-interested conception
of arms control, one designed, first and foremost, to denote the
Soviet Union's arrival on the world scene as Washington's political
equal and to advantage the USSR militarily at the expense of its
principal rival. Only secondarily, and relatively late in the process,
did the Brezhnev leadership begin to evince a seemingly sincere

interest in utilizing the arms control process to regulate the strategic military competition, chiefly to render the relationship more predictable and to help contain the economic costs of the competition. By that time, however, American policymakers had started to lose faith in the enterprise and to view Moscow's belated embrace of Western-style deterrence and arms control theory as opportunistic, equivocal, and subject to change without notice.

As the Soviets were to discover, arms control becomes a matter of far greater complexity when foreign policy goals begin to diverge from those in the military sphere. At such junctures, leaders must decide whether the pursuit of negotiated constraints on military forces is preeminently a *political instrument*, to be used in the service of broader diplomatic goals, or, more narrowly, an adjunct to *defense policy*. For Gorbachev, the need to resolve this question was a paramount consideration early on, given the emerging tension between the dictates of the "new political thinking," on the one hand, and the substance and trajectory of the country's military policies and programs, on the other.

In determining that the country's best hope of surmounting its myriad economic, political, and social problems lay in the direction of fundamental reform, as well as long-term assistance from and interdependence with the developed world, the new leadership found itself, in fact, with precious little room to maneuver in foreign policy. Substantial domestic reform is a high-risk venture under the best of circumstances; the dangers associated with change of this magnitude increase significantly when the external environment is unsettled, hostile, or threatening. Moreover, Moscow could hardly seek to enlist Western support in the rebuilding of Soviet society while, at the same time, pursuing a hard line toward the United States and NATO Europe.

In response to these realities, Gorbachev and his colleagues moved with alacrity to repair relations with the West. They did so by distancing themselves from the imperial ambitions of their predecessors, disavowing the use of force, proclaiming an end to the Cold War, and drawing attention to the largely untapped potential for international cooperation. Most importantly for purposes of this analysis, within eighteen months of attaining power, Gorbachev had all but abandoned existing Soviet positions in arms control, dropping, for instance, the Soviet Union's longstanding opposition to the so-called Zero Option in INF and expressing support for notional 50 percent reductions in strategic nuclear forces.

In directing that arms control policy serve the larger political purposes of the state, even at the possible expense of the country's military posture, Gorbachev took a critical first step in demonstrating the seriousness of his commitment to demilitarize Kremlin foreign policy and to impart much needed substance to the rhetoric of the "new political thinking." Ultimately, of course, the leadership would be required to translate words into deeds by authorizing consequential reductions in military power if Western policymakers were to set aside the deep skepticism with which they tended to greet each, allegedly new, Soviet foreign policy initiative.

At the outset, however, Gorbachev's most pressing task was to break the logjam in East-West relations. This he sought to do by articulating a new set of conceptions regarding the utility of force in international politics and, most especially, the role of military power in Soviet foreign policy. As detailed in chapter 2, conforming to this alternative paradigm necessitated a nearly complete recasting of Soviet military doctrine, as well as far-reaching changes in the character and composition of the country's armed forces. It was to arms control, however, that Gorbachev first turned to establish his *bona fides*, make meaningful contact with the West, and jump-start the stalled political discourse.

At the core of Gorbachev's critique of existing Soviet foreign and military policies was his conviction that while appropriate perhaps to an earlier age, by the mid-1980s they had lost all relevance to the real problems confronting the Soviet state. Particularly damaging had been the Brezhnev leadership's fixation with military power and its dogged pursuit of what even some Soviet analysts had begun to term a posture of "absolute security." By looking to the continuous expansion of nuclear and conventional capabilities to affirm Moscow's standing as the communist superpower, these leaders had in fact brought the country to the very edge of economic ruin, effectively destroying the material basis of its position within the international system. To make matters worse, in their determination to deploy military forces equal to or greater than those available to the Soviet Union's potential adversaries, they had committed a policy blunder of literally colossal proportions, in light of the remote possibility of *any* direct, large-scale military engagement between East and West—as a consequence, primarily, of the deployment by each side of reliable, second-strike nuclear forces.

But how to reverse course? How to begin the process of reducing armaments without endangering national security, which both the Soviet elite and the population in general had been taught to believe could only be guaranteed by the maintenance of military forces, to borrow a phrase from American politics, "second to none"? Gorbachev's response, as effective as it was simple, had always constituted the politician's first line of defense when seeking to redirect a country's military policy: redefine the threat.

Gorbachev, with the help most notably of Foreign Minister Shevardnadze, isolated two dangers that had either escaped notice in official Soviet depictions of the international security environment or been accorded scant attention. Only the first had to do with the United States in any direct sense. The Soviet Union, the leadership alleged, had allowed itself to be drawn into an expensive and open-ended arms race with Washington, the underlying purpose of which, from an American perspective, was not so much to establish effective military superiority(although that, too, would be welcome) as it was to exhaust the Kremlin economically. If allowed to proceed, this cynical ploy might enable the United States to prevail in the Cold War without firing a shot.[2]

The appropriate response, Gorbachev seemed to believe, was simply to opt out of the competition and to restructure Soviet military forces by reference to the logic of (nuclear) deterrence and (conventional) defense. The key to such a strategy, again according to senior Kremlin officials, was the ability to distinguish between vital, as distinct from peripheral, Soviet security interests—a task that Brezhnev and associates had been unwilling to perform.[3]

The second threat cited by Gorbachev was the ever-present danger of nuclear war, a staple of Soviet rhetoric since the late 1970s. Left to the likes of Brezhnev, Andropov, and Chernenko, however, the theme had failed to arouse much of a response on the part of audiences inside or outside the Soviet Union; in this instance, it appears, the messengers, none of whom had ever done much to ease the threat, compromised the message. In Gorbachev's far more capable hands, allusions to the dangers latent in the nuclear competition proved far more effective, not only in changing the terms of the debate on Soviet security policy but also in opening up new opportunities in arms control.

Gorbachev succeeded where others failed because, unlike those who had preceded him in office, he chose not to depict the United States as the sole culprit in this context; instead, he portrayed the nuclear threat as a kind of existential condition that, while very much a consequence of human action, had long since taken on a life of its own. In characterizing the situation in this way, Gorbachev also implied that the other nuclear-weapons states, including the Soviet Union, had to assume a degree of responsibility for the current state of affairs.[4] Along with other major issues confronting the international community, such as the degradation of the environment, economic inequality between developed and developing countries, and the persistence of highly destructive regional conflicts, Gorbachev used the nuclear danger to reinforce his appeal to overcome the division between East and West and to reconceive of relations between and among the countries of the world as "integral" and "interconnected."

The contrast between the old and the new political thinking could hardly have been more explicit. Under Brezhnev, the central threat to the security of the Soviet Union was seen to reside in the possibility of an unprovoked attack against the USSR by the United States, acting either alone or in concert with its imperialist allies. Under Gorbachev, the overarching military threat was that East and West might indeed come to blows—not, however, by design, as previous leaders had insisted, but through accident or miscalculation. A second and more imminent danger was that absent a respite from the calamitous military competition with the West, the Soviet Union would surely exhaust itself economically. According to Gorbachev, it was war itself, in combination with the extraordinarily costly measures that the Brezhnev regime had undertaken to prepare the country for such an eventuality, that constituted the most serious extant threats to the security of the Soviet state, rather than the more remote prospect of outright Western military aggression.

With war, rather than the West, identified as the real enemy, Gorbachev positioned himself and his government to cast aside existing Soviet positions in arms control and to reformulate policy in ways specifically designed to bring forth a positive response from the United States. The way was now clear, it seemed, to re-engage Washington on sensitive security matters and, ultimately, to conclude a new set of agreements with the United States (and NATO Europe) far more substantial than any signed during the checkered ten-year history of the SALT I and SALT II negotiations.

To underscore the respectability of his intentions, Gorbachev routinely coupled his appeals to broaden the scope and accelerate the pace of the negotiations with extended and well-developed arguments on the mutuality of U.S. and Soviet security interests, the inability of either side to prevail in the event of a nuclear war, and the urgent need to undertake asymmetrical reductions in NATO and Warsaw Pact conventional and theater nuclear forces so as to produce a situation of genuine military equality. Without question, arms control had moved to the top of Moscow's foreign policy agenda. But where, precisely, should Soviet energies be directed, and how much should the leadership be prepared to concede in order to secure a new round of agreements with the West?

GOING FOR BROKE: THE NUCLEAR AND SPACE TALKS, 1985–1989

During his first six months in office, Gorbachev seemed almost as uncertain as Chernenko and other senior Soviet officials had been during 1984 about how best to answer these questions. While the decision to resume negotiations with the United States on the reduction of strategic offensive and defensive forces and on the limitation of intermediate-range nuclear systems had been taken prior to Gorbachev's election to CPSU general secretary in March 1985, little else about Moscow's stance toward the negotiations had been resolved. As a consequence, the first several rounds of the Nuclear and Space Talks (NST) during the spring and early summer of 1985 came and went without noticeable drama. The Americans, for their part, seemed in no particular hurry to advance the dialogue, as evidenced by their submission of proposals similar in content to those under consideration when, late in 1983, Soviet negotiators broke off the START and INF talks and returned to Moscow.

Gorbachev's early arms control ventures were only slightly more imaginative. On April 7, 1985, the general secretary announced an unconditional moratorium on the deployment of Soviet intermediate-range nuclear missiles. Ten days later he proposed a second moratorium, to take effect immediately, on the underground testing of U.S. and Soviet nuclear weapons. The Reagan administration dismissed the first as an empty gesture (given the size of the existing Soviet INF arsenal), and the second as a propaganda ploy designed to divert attention from more pressing issues on the superpower arms control agenda. The White House also criticized the proposed ban on nuclear testing as unverifiable.

Four months later, in August 1985, Gorbachev announced that the Soviet Union would suspend nuclear weapons tests for a period of five months, beginning on August 6, the fortieth anniversary of the bombing of Hiroshima. He also pledged to extend the ban indefinitely, should the United States agree to take part. In sanctioning the moratorium on testing, Gorbachev took the first of several such unilateral gestures that would become his trademark in arms control. At the time, the initiative failed to arouse much of a reaction in the West, at least at an official level. Similar actions, undertaken later in his tenure, were to generate considerably more attention.

The cautious character of Gorbachev's early forays into arms control was attributable both to his relatively brief time in office and to his lack of familiarity with the subject matter. It also suggested, however, a more general failure on the part of the leadership to define at this juncture a firm set of objectives to inform the conduct of Soviet arms control policy; this, in turn, deprived the Soviets of an effective, coherent strategy by which they might attain their goals. In short, Moscow had yet to decide what it wanted and what price it was willing to pay.

By fall 1985, the leadership had sorted through its options and settled, at least tentatively, on a clear course of action. Between September and November, in particular, the essential features of the new Soviet line on arms control began to emerge. At the center of this vision was the decision to seek, through negotiations with Washington, the codification of the existing deterrence relationship—a military posture built around the undisputed preeminence of offensive nuclear forces—and, for the first time, to offer deep reductions in long-range systems to induce the Americans to go along. At its most elemental, it was a strategy to lock in the "assured destruction" model of nuclear deterrence and to eviscerate both the logic of, and domestic U.S. support for, the Reagan administration's Strategic Defense Initiative (SDI).

As late as June 1985, Moscow's official stance regarding the limitation of strategic offensive forces was that no such reductions were possible, pending a U.S. disavowal of SDI, including basic research activities heretofore permitted under terms of the 1972 ABM Treaty. With minor variations, this had been the consistent Soviet position since March 1983, when President Ronald Reagan, in a nationally televised address, first revealed his strong commitment to a research and development program to render nuclear weapons "impotent and obsolete."

By September 1985, the Kremlin line had changed dramatically. In his meeting with President Reagan at the White House at the end of that month, Foreign Minister Shevardnadze conveyed Moscow's interest in an agreement to reduce U.S. and Soviet nuclear weapon systems "capable of reaching each other's territory" by up to 50 percent, conditional on an American pledge to restrict research on and development of strategic defensive systems and to undertake a commitment not to test or to deploy what the Soviets termed "space-strike weapons." Three days later, in Geneva, Soviet negotiators formally submitted the proposal.[5]

In early October, in a speech before the French National Assembly and Senate, Gorbachev went beyond the public Soviet position on NST when he coupled the proposal to reduce strategic offensive forces by 50 percent with an offer to conclude an accord limiting intermediate-range nuclear missiles "separately, outside of direct connection with the problem of space and strategic arms." The Soviet leader also announced a reduction in SS-20 deployments to the level existing in June 1984, as well as the complete withdrawal from service of "the old, and very powerful" SS-5 missiles. "This means," Gorbachev asserted, "that taken as a whole, the number of medium-range missiles in the European zone of the USSR is now much smaller than ten or even fifteen years ago."[6]

U.S. officials welcomed both Soviet initiatives—on strategic offensive and intermediate-range nuclear forces—although they were quick to point out that important obstacles to agreement remained and that a quick consensus in either area was extremely unlikely. Among other problems, the Soviets were continuing to link progress on the limitation of strategic weapons to restrictions on SDI, a linkage the Reagan administration had steadfastly refused to consider. In addition, the gap separating the two sides in INF was as wide as ever, or so it seemed. Despite the U.S. insistence that the shift in the Soviet position was less sweeping than it seemed at first blush, the tone, if not yet the substance, of U.S.–Soviet relations clearly had changed for the better.

The Geneva Summit: November 1985

Doubtless, the announcement in midsummer that President Reagan and General Secretary Gorbachev would meet in Geneva, November 19–21, to review important bilateral and international issues did much to stimulate the Soviets to advance a new series of arms control proposals. The Geneva Summit would be the first encounter involving U.S. and Soviet leaders since the largely ceremonial meeting between Jimmy Carter and Leonid Brezhnev in June 1979 in Vienna at which the two presidents signed the SALT II treaty. As the date for the Geneva meeting drew near, speculation inevitably centered on a possible breakthrough in relations—speculation the Soviets encouraged and the Americans did their best to dampen.

The results of the Geneva Summit may well have exceeded even the Kremlin's expectations. According to both sides, the discussions between Reagan and Gorbachev, which touched on a wide range of bilateral and international issues, were "frank and useful." While important differences remained, the two leaders "confirmed the importance of an ongoing dialogue, reflecting their strong desire to seek common ground on existing problems." At Geneva, the governments also reaffirmed their determination to prevent the outbreak of war, insisting that "a nuclear war cannot be won and must never be fought." They promised not to seek military superiority. More concretely, the communiqué called for early progress in the Nuclear and Space Talks, "in particular in areas where there is common ground, including the principle of 50 percent reductions in the nuclear arms of the U.S. and the USSR appropriately applied, as well as the idea of an interim INF agreement."[7] The Kremlin could hardly have hoped for more.

At a briefing for the press on November 21, Gorbachev expressed general satisfaction with the results of the summit, noting that while the two sides had been unable to resolve their differences over SDI, each had a better understanding of the other's position. He seemed especially pleased that he had had an opportunity to outline Soviet objections to SDI directly to Reagan. The Soviet leader emphasized that he had done his best to convince the president of the program's potentially disastrous impact on strategic stability, in the context of which he underscored for the press that section of the communiqué (and of the January 1985 Shultz-Gromyko Statement) in which the two sides had committed themselves "to prevent an arms race in space and to terminate it on earth."[8]

Gorbachev's point was both interesting and subtle. The United States was on record as opposing any extension of the military competition to space; to the extent that the Strategic Defensive Initiative could be defined as offensive in character, the program could be said to contradict the stated U.S. position in the NST negotiations. The United States, of course, insisted that SDI was a "defensive shield," to deter, rather than to provoke, a conflict between the superpowers. The U.S. response notwithstanding, Gorbachev had begun to articulate an argument against SDI of considerably greater sophistication than that advanced by Andropov and Chernenko. Where his predecessors had simply denounced the program and refused to negotiate, Gorbachev chose instead to reframe the problem by drawing attention to the Soviet Union's readiness to conclude a far-reaching agreement on the reduction of long-range nuclear forces, if only the United States would recognize the inconsistency in its own negotiating stance and renounce its pursuit of "space-strike weapons" (advanced development and deployment of ground-based and conventional antiballistic missile systems were already severely constrained through the ABM Treaty). By depicting the situation in these terms, Gorbachev went a long way toward shifting the onus from Moscow to Washington for the relatively slow pace of the negotiations in the eight months that had elapsed since their resumption. If nothing else, the White House learned at Geneva that a far more skilled politician was now in charge of Moscow's arms control diplomacy than had been the case earlier in the decade.

A second major consequence of Geneva was the Kremlin's decision to consider the conclusion of an interim INF accord in advance of an agreement to limit strategic offensive and defensive capabilities. When Shultz and Gromyko agreed in January 1985 to resume the U.S.–Soviet arms control dialogue, they laid out a formula for the conduct of the negotiations in which discussions were to proceed on three distinct levels (strategic offensive systems, space and defensive weapons, and INF). According to that agreement, the discussions were to be conducted simultaneously, although progress in one area was not to be held hostage to progress in another. The Soviets also spoke vaguely about an "interrelationship" among the three elements of the NST talks, a connection the United States claimed not to recognize. In practice, the Kremlin had stalled in INF, awaiting, it seems, developments in the other two forums. At Geneva, Gorbachev reversed course and signaled his willingness to move forward with the negotiations on intermediate-range forces in the absence of a breakthrough on long-range, defensive, and space-based weapons.

In agreeing to separate INF from the other questions under active consideration in Geneva, Gorbachev and the Soviet leadership appear to have concluded that the military and political problems associated with recent changes in the balance of European theater nuclear forces were subordinate, if not peripheral, to the central security issue confronting Moscow and Washington—namely, how to attain effective regulation of the strategic military competition through a combination of deep reductions in offensive forces and meaningful constraints on SDI and related activities. In contrast to Brezhnev and Andropov, in particular, both of whom had refused to countenance any INF accord that would have sacrificed the Soviet Union's theater nuclear advantage in Europe, Gorbachev was prepared to cut just such a deal in order to overcome the deadlock in NST and to open the way for agreement in other, more vital areas.

But what kind of a deal, exactly? The two sides had been at loggerheads in INF since the outset of the negotiations in late 1981.

For its part, the United States was still holding fast to the Zero Option, or the proposal to cancel plans to deploy some 564 U.S. Pershing II and ground-launched cruise missiles in NATO Europe in exchange for the elimination of all medium-range ballistic missiles based on Soviet soil, including those deployed to the east of the Ural Mountains.[9] By 1984, the Soviets were offering to reduce their INF deployments by several hundred missiles, but only on the condition that NATO reverse its 1979 Dual Track decision and abandon its deployment plans.[10] Several efforts at compromise, including the infamous 1982 "Walk in the Woods" proposal, developed by U.S. and Soviet negotiators Paul Nitze and Yuli Kvitsinsky, had all come to naught.[11]

Suddenly, in January 1986, Gorbachev stunned the West by accepting, in effect, the Zero Option as the basis for agreement in INF. He did so in the context of a major address on Soviet arms control policy in which he sketched out an ambitious three-stage plan for the reduction and eventual elimination of all nuclear weapons by the year 2000. Relatively little in the plan was actually new; many of its provisions had surfaced in earlier Soviet statements, such as the proposal for a prompt, 50 percent reduction in the size of the U.S. and Soviet strategic arsenals, a formal ban on the development and testing of "space strike arms," and the cessation of all nuclear weapons testing. Beyond its ultimate goal, which U.S. officials dismissed as either insincere or a flight of fancy, the most remarkable feature of the plan was the explicit call for "the complete liquidation of Soviet and U.S. medium-range missiles in the European zone" (in exchange for which, Gorbachev stipulated, the United Kingdom and France must agree not to augment their nuclear forces).[12] At last, it appeared, the road was now open for the conclusion of the first major U.S.–Soviet arms control accord since the signing of the SALT II treaty some five and a half years before.

Almost two years would elapse before the superpowers would come to terms in INF, notwithstanding the significance of Gorbachev's dramatic concession. A host of issues, some real and some contrived, had to be resolved before a joint draft text could be readied for signing. Reaching consensus on the limitation of intermediate-range nuclear weapons, however, was only one of the Soviet leader's arms control objectives at this juncture.

The true value of an INF agreement, from Gorbachev's perspective, was in providing a much-needed boost to the negotiations on central strategic systems. In accommodating the American position in INF, Gorbachev hoped to demonstrate to the U.S. administration that he, unlike previous Soviet leaders, was willing to set aside the pursuit of near-term military and political advantage in the interests of securing a broader set of understandings to guide the development of U.S.–Soviet political and military relations during the remainder of the 1980s and beyond.

It was, characteristically, a bold scheme, requiring constant attention to detail and a readiness to adjust Soviet policy on short notice and in response to changing conditions. More to the point, it also assumed either the existence of, or the capacity to create, sufficient common ground between the superpowers on security-related matters to produce a number of interconnected agreements, affecting the most sensitive issues in the relationship. In 1986 it was far from self-evident that such a foundation either existed or could be established.

Drama in Reykjavik

During 1986, Gorbachev set out to prove that the deadlock between Washington and Moscow in the Nuclear and Space Talks could be overcome. He did so by placing—and then keeping—the question of the future of U.S.–Soviet security relations at the very top of the superpower agenda. Eager to build on the modest momentum generated by his discussions with President Reagan in Geneva, Gorbachev initiated (or approved) a host of important revisions to the Soviet negotiating position in NST at midyear that the American administration found difficult to ignore and, more importantly, that appeared to pique President Reagan's personal interest.

For example, six months after his January 1986 statement on the prospective abolition of all nuclear weapons by the year 2000, Gorbachev instructed Soviet negotiators in Geneva to present to their U.S. counterparts a new proposal, linking 50 percent reductions in central strategic systems to a commitment not to withdraw from the ABM Treaty for a period of fifteen to twenty years. What made the proposal significant was Moscow's apparent readiness to enter into an agreement that would have allowed SDI-related research, development, and testing to proceed, so long as such activities were confined to the laboratory. Previous Soviet proposals had always tied Moscow's acceptance of deep reductions in offensive forces to a U.S. pledge to renounce SDI and to halt work on the program at each and every stage, including preliminary research and development. Two weeks later, in a letter to Reagan, Gorbachev also signaled new flexibility in the Soviet INF position and invited the administration to test his sincerity.

The United States responded in July 1986 by affirming its commitment to 50 percent reductions in strategic offensive forces over five years. Concerning SDI, it advanced an interesting, if somewhat complex, three-part proposal. During the first phase, to last for seven and a half years, the two sides would agree to confine research, development, and testing efforts associated with strategic defenses to those permitted under the terms of the ABM Treaty. Over the succeeding two years, the sides would attempt to negotiate a new agreement to regulate the introduction of strategic defensive systems, while continuing with reductions in strategic offensive forces. Should, however, the parties fail to reach consensus by the end of that time, each would be free to proceed with full-scale defensive deployments after another six months. On INF, the U.S. administration reaffirmed its support for a global ban on intermediate-range systems (later modified to permit the maintenance on an interim basis of some 200 INF warheads, with a subceiling of 100 such weapons within range of Europe).

U.S. and Soviet negotiators formally submitted the revised proposals when the talks resumed in Geneva on September 18, 1986. The following day, in a letter to Reagan, Gorbachev suggested that the two men meet later in the fall, in London or Reykjavik, to discuss arms control issues and to prepare for a full-fledged summit in 1987. The administration responded positively to the Soviet initiative and on September 30, in Washington and Moscow, spokesmen for the two governments announced that Reagan and Gorbachev would come together in Iceland on October 11 and 12 for a "presummit" session.

Thus began preparations for what was to become one of the most unusual and intense rounds of negotiations between U.S. and Soviet leaders in the history of superpower relations. Since the

Geneva meeting in November 1985, the distance separating the U.S. and Soviet positions in NST had narrowed appreciably, although the differences yet to be overcome were anything but trivial. As had been the case all along, the central problem was how to reconcile the two sides' very different proposals regarding space and defensive weapons, without which no agreement seemed possible on reductions in central strategic forces.

The administration's three-part plan to finesse the problems created by SDI held little attraction for Moscow, as the United States had already stipulated that it would respect the terms of the ABM Treaty (broadly interpreted) through at least the early 1990s. The Soviets also recognized that neither side, whatever its preferences, would be in a position during the next seven and a half years to begin actual deployment of space-based strategic defensive systems. Similarly, Moscow's going-in position—that both sides would agree to abide by the ABM Treaty, in its narrow construction, for a period of ten to fifteen years—left Washington unmoved. Only with regard to INF, in other words, did an accord seem within reach as Reagan and Gorbachev set out for Reykjavik.

A second factor further complicated the meetings. The Americans, it seemed, were traveling to Iceland for purposes of discussion, to review in advance of the expected 1987 summit the full range of bilateral and multilateral issues of concern to each superpower, including such issues as the resolution of various regional conflicts, bilateral trade, and human rights. The Soviets, by contrast, were determined to utilize the sessions to score a substantive breakthrough in relations. Gorbachev and his advisers arrived in Reykjavik armed with a package of arms control proposals so sweeping in scope, they appeared to believe, that Reagan would be unable to resist its allure. Appropriately dazzled, the American president would seize on this unparalleled opportunity to make negotiating history and cut a deal. The particular deal the Soviets had in mind was an agreement to slash INF deployments and vastly reduce long-range offensive forces, all in exchange for a commitment on the part of the United States to confine to the laboratory all SDI-related research, development, and testing for a period of ten years.

In retrospect, it is remarkable how close the two leaders came to reaching agreement at Reykjavik, or at least on the terms of a framework accord to guide subsequent negotiations. Following a series of marathon negotiating sessions, at which small teams of U.S. and Soviet officials labored through the night of October 11–12 to arrive at agreed positions on INF and strategic offensive forces, the principals reconvened. Amidst considerable excitement (and more than a little confusion), Reagan and Gorbachev sought to close the deal, only to discover that despite determined efforts, they could not compose their differences over SDI. The negotiations ended abruptly late in the afternoon of October 12, with a stiff handshake and a minimum of ceremony. Each party departed Reykjavik convinced that the other had torpedoed potentially the most important arms control agreement since the start of the process almost eighteen years before.[13]

For the Soviets, in particular, the outcome at Reykjavik constituted a keen disappointment. To have come so close, only to have the negotiations founder over Reagan's refusal to guarantee U.S. compliance with the narrow interpretation of the ABM Treaty, was deeply frustrating. At the press conference convened in the immediate aftermath of the meetings (and for days and weeks afterward), Gorbachev emphasized that were it not for the American president's refusal to bargain on SDI, the path would now be clear for the conclusion of a series of bilateral arms control agreements more far-reaching than any previously under consideration.[14]

Among the achievements at Reykjavik, Gorbachev noted, were two prospective accords. The first, on intermediate-range nuclear forces, would have resulted in the elimination of all but 200 U.S. and Soviet INF warheads—100 for each side—and none within range of targets in Europe. The second, on central offensive systems, would have required Washington and Moscow to reduce their forces to 1,600 "strategic nuclear delivery vehicles" and 6,000 strategic warheads by 1991 (the extent of second-round reductions, to be carried out between 1991 and 1996, was a point of contention between the sides; see below). In connection with the latter, the two sides also had agreed on the desirability of warhead sublimits, to be applied against the systems that made up each leg of the strategic triad—ICBMs, SLBMs, and heavy bombers. The Soviets had even consented to some reduction (as yet unspecified) in the number of deployed "heavy" or large ICBMs, since the early 1980s a key U.S.

demand and one to which the Kremlin had consistently turned a deaf ear. Finally, the negotiators achieved visible progress in a number of other areas, including agreement on procedures to facilitate verification and to ensure effective compliance, a source of contention throughout the talks.[15]

Exactly what happened at Reykjavik—what had and had not been agreed to—was anything but clear in the immediate aftermath of the discussions. Each side did its best, however, to assign to the other primary responsibility for the failure to nail down an agreement, while simultaneously leaving the door open for a return to the bargaining table. Predictably, the Soviets blamed the Americans for the impasse, focusing, in particular, on Reagan's refusal to sanction a ten-year extension of the ABM Treaty and to commit the United States to abide by a narrow interpretation of that accord. As to what might be salvaged from Reykjavik, Gorbachev's initial judgment was equivocal; while acknowledging that the superpowers had reached a new level of understanding on several key issues in Iceland, the Soviet leader also warned that their work was in danger of being subverted by an American administration still determined to press ahead militarily and to manipulate the negotiating process to U.S. advantage.[16]

On October 14, Gorbachev, in a televised address to the Soviet people, expressed regret at the outcome of the meetings, which he attributed directly to Reagan's stubborn defense of SDI. He also cautioned the United States that the Soviet proposals at Reykjavik constituted a single, integrated "package."[17] Moscow was likely to resist, therefore, any U.S. attempt to pick apart the Kremlin's position and to claim Soviet concurrence on one or another point of special interest to the administration. In underscoring the holistic nature of the Soviet negotiating stance, Gorbachev threw into question Moscow's readiness to cut a deal over INF along the lines agreed to in Iceland. Additionally, he rendered conditional, and therefore subject to reconsideration, the various understandings reached in Reykjavik on strategic launcher and warhead limits. At the same time, the Soviet leader assured Washington of his strong interest in capitalizing on the momentum generated by the episode in Reykjavik in order to reach prompt agreement in the Nuclear and Space Talks.[18]

The Americans too sought to put a positive spin on Reykjavik, while holding Moscow responsible for the meeting's disappointing conclusion.[19] Given the latent inconsistency in the administration's position regarding SDI, however, the U.S. case was the more difficult one to make. As Moscow never tired of asking, what *was* the rationale for SDI, especially Reagan's vision of an impenetrable defensive "shield," once the two sides had eliminated all strategic offensive forces, as the Soviets claimed they apparently had agreed to do at Reykjavik? Even allowing for the possibility, as administration spokesmen later argued, that the president had assented to the abolition of long-range ballistic missiles over ten years—and not, as Moscow insisted, on the elimination of *all* strategic offensive arms— the U.S. position was a weak one. Adding to the administration's public relations problem was the content of the Soviet offer regarding SDI, which would have permitted research, development, and testing of strategic defensive systems, consistent with a strict reading of the ABM Treaty. For an administration long accustomed to being on the political offensive in arms control—advancing compelling, if deceptively simple proposals that conservative Soviet leaders had heretofore rejected out of hand—the experience of having to defend the American position must have come as something of a shock.

At Reykjavik, the U.S. administration learned firsthand just how far Gorbachev was prepared to go to revitalize the bilateral arms control process. They also began to perceive that for Gorbachev the successful conclusion of the NST negotiations, an important goal in and of itself, was significant for a second reason.

His larger purpose, it seemed, was to use a breakthrough in the negotiations to engineer a qualitative change for the better in U.S.–Soviet relations. Specifically what this change might entail— how relations might develop in the months and years to come—was, of course, impossible to know in late 1986. For Washington, the one certainty was that from this point forward, relations with Moscow were going to be different, perhaps radically so, from anything that had come before.

Endgame in INF

In the weeks following Reykjavik, neither side seemed quite certain what to do or how to proceed. Did they or didn't they have a new set of understandings to guide future discussions on INF- and START-related issues? Out of the febrile negotiations in Iceland, what—if anything—should U.S. and Soviet policymakers regard as binding? Meeting in Vienna in November 1986, Shultz and Shevardnadze agreed to emphasize the positive. While noting (in separate statements)that serious differences continued to divide the sides, each seemed to suggest that the negotiations should take up where they had left off.[20] In other words, such progress as Reagan and Gorbachev had attained in elaborating the terms of both an INF and a START agreement should constitute the new baseline for the NST negotiations. To a degree, however, the Shultz-Shevardnadze recommendation to press ahead left the most important question unanswered. Press ahead toward what, exactly? Toward a comprehensive accord, as discussed at Reykjavik, or toward discrete agreements on INF and START (including limitations on strategic defensive and space weapons)?

The Soviet answer to that question came in late February 1987, when Gorbachev announced his government's willingness to conclude a treaty to reduce intermediate-range nuclear forces along the lines discussed at Reykjavik, without waiting for a breakthrough in START. The United States responded enthusiastically, tabling within several days of Gorbachev's announcement a draft INF treaty for Moscow's consideration. Gorbachev's decision to decouple INF from START provided a powerful boost to the arms control process; for the first time since U.S. and Soviet negotiators had reconvened in March 1985, a substantive agreement between the superpowers appeared within reach.

Several major issues, and a number of more minor complications, stood in the way of final agreement. All were resolved with remarkable speed. The most important question was how to dispose of U.S. and Soviet shorter-range missile systems (those with ranges between 500 and 1,000 kilometers). The Soviet Union enjoyed a marked advantage in the number of deployed systems in this category, a fact that aroused considerable anxiety among Western decision-makers, particularly those attached to NATO. Unless the shorter-range missiles were eliminated or otherwise constrained, alliance officials warned, Moscow would be left with a virtual monopoly on such weapons. An intense (and arcane) debate quickly ensued among Western defense analysts about the wisdom of leaving Moscow's European-based shorter-range systems undisturbed in the wake of an INF accord.[21]

Gorbachev abruptly cut short the debate in April, when he proposed the simultaneous elimination of U.S. and Soviet systems with ranges of 500 to 1,000 kilometers. Those in the West who had expressed the gravest misgivings about Moscow's superiority in short-range missiles were, if anything, more distressed by Gorbachev's proposed solution than they were about the disparity in the number of weapons. To many in NATO, it seemed that the Kremlin's longstanding ambition to initiate a process leading to Europe's eventual "de-nuclearization" was about to be realized. To make matters worse, the Soviet Union seemed poised to attain this cherished objective not at the cost of deep reductions in Warsaw Pact conventional forces, long a staple of NATO's negotiating strategy, but as a result of U.S. eagerness to strike a deal—any deal. The controversy raged until mid-June, when the NATO foreign ministers, at the Reagan administration's strong urging, lent their endorsement to what had come to be known as the Double Zero.

A second issue that threatened to delay conclusion of an agreement was the disposition of 171 Soviet INF missiles (as well as an undisclosed number of shorter-range systems) deployed in Central Asia and the Far East. The understanding reached at Reykjavik would have allowed each country to retain 100 INF warheads and to station these weapons in areas beyond the reach of targets in Europe. The logic behind this residual force had never been very compelling to either side, however, and following NATO's endorsement of the global "double zero" in June, the Soviets indicated that they were prepared to go along. In August they agreed to a worldwide ban on the production and deployment of both long- and shorter-range INF. With Moscow's consent to the complete elimination of intermediate-range missile systems (including, in addition to the missiles themselves, launchers and support facilities), U.S. and Soviet negotiators began to put the final touches on the joint draft text of the agreement. Three times during the fall, in September, October, and finally late in November, Shultz and Shevardnadze met to clear away the remaining obstacles—none of them sufficiently weighty to threaten conclusion of the accord—and on

December 8, at the White House, Reagan and Gorbachev affixed their signatures to the Treaty Between the United States of America and the Union of Soviet Socialist Republics on The Elimination of Their Intermediate-range and Shorter-range Missiles.[22]

The treaty, which against the larger backdrop of U.S.–Soviet security relations may be judged a fairly minor achievement, was nonetheless a landmark agreement. Its significance derived from three factors. At a symbolic level it marked the end of one era—"the second Cold War"—and the start of another, one characterized by an unmistakable determination on the part of the two governments to ease bilateral political tensions and to reassert a measure of control over the nuclear arms competition. It demonstrated, in particular, the willingness of the two countries to set aside past (and continuing) political differences in order to arrive at consensus in a vital area of mutual concern. As recently as 1985, the give and take essential to the negotiating process had been nowhere in evidence; seldom, in other words, had so much changed in the relationship in just two years. With the successful conclusion of the negotiations, a new and more hopeful era had dawned in superpower relations.

The agreement was also important because of what it suggested about Moscow's new approach to negotiating security. In INF the Soviets agreed to dismantle and destroy some 1,836 intermediate-range missiles, as well as 850 missile launchers. The agreement required the United States to do away with fewer than half as many missiles (867) and only a third as many launchers (283).[23]

Such a disparity in the scope of reductions was new in the history of superpower arms control. For almost seven years, the Reagan administration had insisted on strict numerical equality in the number of deployed weapons as the logical end point of the negotiating process. "Unequal reductions to an equal outcome" became the administration's rallying cry. Since 1981, the Soviets had forcefully rejected the U.S. formula, alleging that the deployment of several hundred SS-20 missiles between 1977 and 1984 was a defensive measure, undertaken to ensure a stable balance of forces in Europe. (U.S. Pershing II deployments, by contrast, constituted a military "provocation," according to Moscow, because of their pinpoint accuracy and extremely short flight times to targets in the European USSR).

At Reykjavik, Gorbachev simply abandoned the line bequeathed to him by Brezhnev and Andropov and embraced a variant of the Zero Option. In so doing, the Soviet leader effected a key departure in Kremlin policy, established an important precedent, and, at least potentially, simplified the search for a new series of accords to regulate the U.S.–Soviet military balance. At the same time, he seemed to have set Soviet arms control diplomacy on something of a slippery slope: if "unequal reductions to an equal outcome" was acceptable in the INF context, then why not apply it to other dimensions of the military competition—conventional forces in Europe perhaps—where Moscow also enjoyed a decided quantitative advantage in most indices of power?[24] Once so affirmed, the logic of asymmetrical reductions would prove difficult to contest.

In the view of many analysts, Soviet and American, it was, however, the treaty's detailed provisions regarding verification that imparted to the agreement its real significance. Fully six of the treaty's seventeen articles, as well as two separate protocols ("Protocol on Procedures Governing the Elimination of Missile Systems" and "Protocol Regarding Inspection") dealt directly with this historically sensitive issue. In addition to the "national technical means" at their disposal, the United States and the Soviet Union agreed in INF to the establishment of an intrusive verification regime to guard against cheating. Among the agreed measures were the right to station personnel from one country at designated facilities of the other to monitor the cessation of missile production, the right to dispatch observers to confirm the destruction of missiles, launchers, and associated equipment, and the right to conduct short-notice "challenge" inspections of all major installations involved in the production, storage, and deployment of intermediate-range missile systems. The regime was to be in effect for thirteen years, with the destruction of the weapons in question to be completed within three years of the agreement's ratification.[25] No other U.S.–Soviet arms control treaty then in effect featured on-site inspection procedures remotely comparable to those incorporated in the INF accord.

With the signing of the INF Treaty, policymakers in Washington and Moscow turned their attention to several complex issues delaying completion of a START agreement. Work on the accord had slowed in the months following Gorbachev's February 1987 decision to break out and accelerate the negotiations on INF. When Reagan and Gorbachev met in Washington in December 1987, they instructed their START negotiators to redouble their efforts to reach agreement, with an eye toward producing a final, agreed text in time for the American president to sign before the expiration of his term in January 1989. Although the two sides failed in that attempt, they did succeed in coming to terms on a number of questions—agreeing, for example, to a limit of 4,900 for ballistic missile warheads, to 50 percent reductions in Soviet "heavy" missiles, and to a set of counting rules for air-launched cruise missiles—during fall 1987 that had posed problems earlier in the negotiations. The differences that remained were not inconsequential, however, and in the end, the treaty could not be readied in time for Reagan's signature.[26]

On balance, Gorbachev's early (1985–1989) arms control strategy—to induce the United States to negotiate seriously with Moscow by offering up a "cascade of concessions"[27]—must be considered a major success. As a result of Gorbachev's constant prodding, the two sides secured a treaty to eliminate over 2,500 intermediate-range missile systems. In addition, they achieved closure on most major issues in START. Gorbachev also shattered the Western stereotype of Soviet leaders as intransigent and short-sighted negotiators, constitutionally incapable of advancing innovative or creative proposals. In short, he injected new life into a process that many in the United States believed had breathed its last.

But the price of progress had been high, measured against past Soviet policies and preferences. By the terms of the INF Treaty the Soviets were forced to demobilize and destroy roughly three missiles for every single U.S. weapon so affected—hardly the type of precedent most governments welcome as they prepare to head into a fresh round of negotiations. In START, the Kremlin's advantage of approximately 3:1 in the number of deployed, high-accuracy, land-based ballistic missile warheads—acquired over time and at great effort and expense—was also scheduled to disappear, as the two sides headed toward a new agreement on the limitation of strategic offensive forces.

What made the concessions acceptable to Gorbachev (and apparently tolerable to others in the leadership) was the lure of a fundamentally new chapter in East-West relations, a chapter in which the competition between the superpowers to acquire and deploy weapon systems of dubious military value would be replaced by a carefully regulated balance of power at substantially reduced levels of armament. With the arms race thus contained, and relations between Washington and Moscow rendered less threatening, Soviet leaders could at last turn their full attention to what in their judgment constituted *the* central issue currently before them: how to overcome the trend toward entropy so evident in virtually all aspects of Soviet life, from economics to culture, as well as the terrible sense of inertia that seemed to have taken hold at all levels of society, from those the system had endowed with special privileges to those with none.

ARMS CONTROL IN EUROPE: FROM THE COLD WAR TO THE COLLAPSE OF SOVIET POWER, 1989–1990

The same set of problems that prompted Gorbachev and those around him to sweep aside decades of Soviet diplomatic practice in order to produce a rapid breakthrough in superpower relations also led the Soviets to embrace what can only be considered, especially in retrospect, a high-risk strategy toward Europe. The link between Gorbachev's opening to Washington and the extraordinary shift in the Kremlin's European policy between 1985 and 1989 operated on a second level, as well. Given the strong political, economic, and military ties that bind the United States and Western Europe, Soviet leaders could hardly have expected to restrict the implications of the "new political thinking" to the American side of the Atlantic. Once discarded, the principles that for some forty years had informed the conduct and content of Soviet foreign policy could not, it turned out, be resurrected selectively and reapplied to a single region. The restructuring of relations between the superpowers logically dictated, then, a fundamentally new Soviet approach toward Europe, both East and West. The transformation of Moscow's European policy began within months of Gorbachev's election as CPSU general secretary, and the pace of change rapidly accelerated as the decade progressed. The reconfiguration of relations continues to this day, albeit in ways and to a degree that could scarcely have been imagined at the outset of the process.

Soviet policy toward Europe during the second half of the 1980s is perhaps best understood as a well-conceived, if long-overdue effort on the part of the Kremlin to end four decades of self-imposed political and economic isolation from the West by adopting a strategy of controlled revolution, or "revolution from above." The strategy, which the leadership sought to invest with a thematic unity sufficiently broad and compelling to attract devotees from across the European political spectrum, was in practice directed at two distinct audiences: to policymakers in Western Europe (and the United States) without whose assistance Gorbachev's vision of a "common European house," stretching from the Atlantic to the Urals, could never be realized; and to reform-minded forces in Eastern Europe, whose support Gorbachev had come to regard as indispensable in the developing drive to dislodge the conservative, corrupt, and inept communist governments then in place throughout the region.

The first thrust, to enlist Western help in overcoming the division of the continent, turned out to be the easier of the two tasks. The second, which began as an attempt to reform and invigorate East European communism by encouraging the participation in the political process of "progressive" forces loyal to Marxism (and to Moscow) but hostile to the reactionary leaderships in East Germany, Czechoslovakia, Hungary, Romania, and Bulgaria, went terribly wrong from the Kremlin's perspective and ended up destroying, rather then affirming, the foundations of Soviet power in Eastern and Central Europe.

Soviet leaders looked to arms control to assist the realization of this two-part strategy to transform the continent's political landscape and to secure Moscow's place in the new Europe of the 1990s. In the Soviet vision, the military confrontation between NATO and the Warsaw Pact, both cause and symptom of Europe's division, would give way over time to a sustained and broadly based East-West détente. Negotiations would be required both to structure this process and to impart the requisite stability. Over time, Gorbachev appears to have believed, a single community of sovereign states, capitalist and socialist, would emerge in Europe, linked to one another through a complex and reinforcing series of bi- and multi-lateral political and economic ties. A democratized and economically revitalized Soviet Union would then be free to assume its rightful place as the largest and most powerful actor within this European collective.

The vision was flawed, however, in one critical respect. It assumed that political leaders, particularly in Moscow and Washington, would be in a position to control the pace and character of change. Central to the ability to control events during this transitional period would be the maintenance of the postwar continental system—that is, the continuation, throughout the interregnum, of Europe's de facto division into two separate blocs. Absent this essential feature, Moscow's ambitious strategy could easily go awry, generating pressures for change far beyond those contemplated by Gorbachev, to say nothing of political leaders elsewhere on the continent.

Regrettably, from Gorbachev's perspective, the institutions that sustained the communist systems in Eastern Europe turned out to be far more brittle than he had anticipated. Once challenged, they crumbled with breathtaking speed. The result was widespread political turmoil and the shattering of regime legitimacy in one country after another along the Kremlin's western border. The revolutions of 1989–1990 also eviscerated the system of relations that linked the individual states of the Warsaw Pact to one another and to the Soviet Union. In a matter of months, from the election of Tadeusz Mazowiecki as Poland's non-Communist premier in August 1989 to the execution of Romanian dictator Nicolae Ceauşescu the following December, the "socialist community" in Europe ceased to exist.

With its demise, the Soviet Union's carefully conceived design for Europe's orderly transition to a new age unraveled. An important casualty of the chaos was Moscow's European arms control policy, to which the leadership had looked both to undergird the larger process of political change and, equally important, to place limits around it.

Setting the Stage: The Development of Moscow's European Security Policy, 1985–1987

As with most of Gorbachev's early forays in foreign policy, his first initiatives in the areas of European security and arms control were notable mostly for their caution. In the foreign policy section of his February 1986 report to the twenty-seventh CPSU congress, for example, the Soviet leader dealt with the subject of the military confrontation in Europe only in passing and in the most general of terms. When he next addressed the topic, at an April 1986 meeting of East Germany's ruling Communist party, he did call upon the West to renew its commitment to secure an agreement in the long-running and stalemated Mutual and Balanced Force Reduction negotiations. However, his proposed solution to the impasse in MBFR—to extend the geographic reach of the negotiations to all of Europe "from the Atlantic to the Urals"—could hardly be considered a breakthrough, or even helpful, given the manifest inability of NATO and Warsaw Pact negotiators (despite thirteen years of effort) to achieve consensus on the terms of a modest accord to limit armed forces and armaments deployed in Europe's central region.[28]

The issuance in June 1986 of the so-called Budapest Appeal—the proposal by the seven Warsaw Pact countries to their sixteen NATO counterparts to undertake a "substantial" reduction in ground force personnel, conventional and nuclear weapons, and tactical aircraft—was more successful in capturing the attention of Western policymakers. Under terms of the proposal, the two alliances would agree to implement force reductions on the order of 100,000 to 150,000 within two years, to be followed by an "immediate" second wave of cuts. At the conclusion of this second phase, Warsaw Pact and NATO troop strength would stand at some 25 percent below 1986 levels; simultaneously, the two sides would undertake corresponding reductions in tactical aircraft, as well as in conventional armaments, nuclear weapons, and nuclear delivery systems.[29]

Apart from the proposed scale of the reductions, the most noteworthy features of the appeal were the explicit call for steps to lessen "the danger of a sudden attack" in Europe and expressions of support for confidence-building measures to guard against "sudden offensive operations." The signatories of the appeal also conveyed their support for "a reliable and effective" system to ensure compliance with any agreements that might emerge from this process, "including on-site inspections." That the potential to mount offensive military operations might constitute a source of instability in the military relationship between the two alliances was a novel admission by the Pact; the unequivocal endorsement of on-site inspection also came as something of a surprise to Western observers. Less appealing to the NATO states was the Pact's expression of interest in aircraft and nuclear weapons reductions, both of which the West had long regarded as vital compensation for the East's numerical advantages in deployed manpower, artillery holdings, and armor.[30]

Three months later, in September 1986, representatives of thirty-three European countries, the United States, and Canada, meeting in Stockholm, concluded the first phase of the Conference on Disarmament in Europe (CDE) with an agreement on confidence- and security-building measures, or CSBMs. The Stockholm Accord, under active negotiation since the first part of 1984, imposed significant restrictions on a wide range of military activities in Europe, mostly in the form of stringent requirements for the advance notification of troop movements and military maneuvers, ranging from a minimum of forty-two days (for operations involving 13,000 or more troops) to a maximum of two years (for those involving more than 75,000 forces). The agreement also provided for a limited number of on-site, "challenge" inspections (not to exceed three in any given year) on the territory of a signatory state and for the right of all CDE countries to dispatch military observers to exercises featuring upwards of 17,000 troops.[31]

Of limited practical significance, the Stockholm Agreement was nonetheless an important branch-point in the mostly unhappy history of postwar European arms control. It marked a clear shift on Moscow's part in the direction of greater openness and flexibility that Western governments were quick to note and eager to exploit. Contributing to the sense of optimism that attended the signing of the agreement was the Kremlin's high praise for the accord, as well as the suggestion, from Gorbachev among others, that the time had come to return to the issue of mutual force reductions with a renewed sense of vigor and purpose.

Seeking to capitalize on the momentum generated by the Stockholm Agreement, NATO foreign ministers, meeting in Brussels in December 1986, proposed to convene two separate negotiations: the first, involving the CDE 35, would develop and enact additional confidence- and security-building measures; the second, in which the twenty-three NATO and Warsaw Pact states would take part, would seek to stabilize the European military balance through joint reductions in armaments and the elimination of force disparities. Under the NATO plan, constraints on manpower and tactical aircraft would be set aside, at least temporarily, in favor of deep reductions in conventional weapons. High on the NATO list of priorities were large, asymmetrical cuts in Soviet tanks and armored troop carriers deployed in Eastern Europe and the western military districts of the USSR.

Given Moscow's traditional aversion to "balanced" (i.e., unequal) force reductions, the leadership's response to NATO's December initiative—either yea or nay—would be taken by the West as something of a litmus test regarding Soviet intentions. The Kremlin's answer was not long in coming. Within several weeks of the Brussels appeal, the Soviets endorsed both sets of initiatives, and in February 1987 East and West began the first of a series of informal discussions to develop a mandate for what would come to be the negotiations on conventional forces in Europe, or the CFE Talks.

Several factors appear to have motivated Moscow's affirmative response to the NATO initiative and the leadership's seemingly strong interest in moving the European arms control process forward as expeditiously as possible. At one level, Moscow's enthusiasm could be traced to the leadership's clear determination to accelerate the nascent East-West political dialogue and to affirm the trend toward greater cooperation (and away from confrontation). Just as superpower relations had improved dramatically in the months since the October 1985 Geneva Summit, so might relations between the Soviet Union and Washington's NATO allies, given the proper stimulus. An important start in that direction had been made with the conclusion of the Stockholm Agreement; better to seize on an existing opportunity than to delay, in the (probably vain) hope that future conditions might be even more favorable from the Soviet perspective. The Conventional Stability or Mandate Talks also would afford Soviet leaders a chance to gauge the West's understanding of and responsiveness to Gorbachev's "new political thinking."

At a second level, negotiations between NATO and the Warsaw Pact—whatever their outcome—tended to ease Western fears of the military threat said to emanate from Soviet soil. For all their faults, the MBFR talks had offered valuable reassurance to the people of Western Europe that the Soviet government was, or at least seemed, as interested in avoiding war as they were, despite the massive display of military power to their east. The Mandate Talks could do the same, even in the absence of substantial progress toward a new agreement. Less cynically, the discussions could produce a mandate to guide subsequent negotiations that might, in turn, eventuate in real reductions, thereby underscoring Gorbachev's contention that the overarching security problem in Europe was not so much the relatively remote prospect of war, but the seemingly endless preparations to wage one.

Finally, assuming success during this first phase, a new set of negotiations might enable the Soviet Union to scale back on its military presence in Eastern Europe, an increasingly urgent goal to a political leadership eager to find ways to cut military expenditures and to shift resources from the defense to the civilian sectors of the economy. The financial burden to Moscow of maintaining over 700,000 ground troops and air force personnel on the territory of its Warsaw Pact allies was not inconsequential; while the redeployment to the Soviet Union of some percentage of these forces might not save the Kremlin much money (costs might even increase), their demobilization could result in significant savings over the medium-to-long term. A force reduction agreement in Europe also might help to neutralize opposition on the part of senior military authorities to even a modest drawdown in the country's defense potential in the absence of at least some reductions in NATO's military capabilities.

Similar goals—particularly the desire to alleviate Western threat perceptions and to curtail military expenditures—had induced Moscow to take part in previous European arms control negotiations, and yet nothing of lasting substance had ever been achieved. In MBFR, for example, the Soviets repeatedly affirmed their interest in an accord. At the same time, they effectively stymied the negotiations by insisting throughout the process that a "rough" balance of forces already obtained in Central and Eastern Europe, in spite of the sizable Warsaw Pact lead in most indices of military power. The logic of the Soviet position required the Eastern negotiators to submit proposals calling for equal reductions in NATO and Pact manpower and military equipment. When they finally abandoned this tactic and admitted the existence of various asymmetries in personnel and weaponry, they also deflated their force estimates so as to minimize the imbalances (giving rise to what came to be known in MBFR as the "data-base" problem). The predictable outcome was a negotiating impasse.[32]

Faced with a choice, in other words, between securing an agreement in MBFR that would have cost them more in the currency of military power than they wanted to pay, and destroying the prospects for an accord but retaining their existing force posture in Europe, Soviet leaders consistently chose the latter. In 1987, under new management, the Kremlin confronted very much the same issue. How high a price was the leadership prepared to pay in order to obtain an agreement with the West to regulate the European military balance? If anything, the choice before Gorbachev was more painful than the one that had confronted his predecessors, as the NATO countries were now demanding even deeper cuts in Warsaw Pact conventional forces than they had at earlier junctures. It was, for the leadership, perhaps the most sensitive and potentially far-reaching foreign policy decision it had yet been called upon to make.

The CFE Negotiations and the Collapse of Soviet Power in Europe, 1987–1990

Three assumptions appear to have guided Soviet leaders as they considered whether to keep or to break faith with past Soviet arms control policies in Europe during the critically important two years that separated the start of the Mandate Talks in February 1987 and the first round of the CFE negotiations in March 1989. Their first assumption was that the danger of war in Europe between the countries of NATO and the Warsaw Pact had all but disappeared in recent years—however real that prospect might have been, or seemed, at an earlier time. Their second assumption, derived from the first, was that a military posture of "reasonable sufficiency," the precise character of which they had yet to determine, was more than enough to deter any Western military adventures against the countries of the Warsaw Pact. Both propositions, while controversial, seemed rooted in a combination of experience and common sense.

The leadership's third and boldest assumption was that socialism had struck sufficiently deep roots in Eastern Europe to withstand domestic political changes comparable in scope and magnitude to those beginning to work their way through the Soviet system, as well as some limited restructuring of relations between Moscow and its Warsaw Pact allies in the direction of greater autonomy and voluntarism. It was on this basis that the Kremlin believed it possible to undertake potentially deep reductions in Soviet armed forces and armaments deployed within the "northern tier" states of East Germany, Poland, and Czechoslovakia without either undermining the legitimacy of those regimes or endangering the foundations of Soviet hegemony in the region. As the Soviets were soon to discover, however, their confidence in this third judgment proved to be misplaced—disastrously so from their perspective. It was an error of profound proportions that would eventually cost them an empire—notwithstanding doubts they may have begun to harbor about the wisdom of maintaining their imperial prerogatives in a region of declining economic value and questionable political importance.

In 1987 the events that were to precipitate the transformation of the European political order still lay several years in the future. The Kremlin's more immediate problem was what position to stake out in connection with the Mandate Talks, which convened for the first time in Vienna on February 17. In a speech in May 1987, Polish president Wojciech Jaruzelski floated a proposal in which "offensive" weapons of the two alliances, including tactical nuclear weapons, strike and fighter aircraft, tanks, and artillery, would be singled out and targeted for reduction, so as to decrease the likelihood in Europe of a "sudden attack" and to assist the development of "defensive" military postures.[33] Formally, the Soviets neither associated themselves with nor distanced themselves from the Jaruzelski plan, although Moscow's influence was difficult to miss.

One month later, in June 1987, the Warsaw Pact states proposed that the thirty-five countries that had signed the Stockholm Agreement also take part in the upcoming negotiations and that reductions in European-based nuclear weapons constitute a key part of the negotiating mandate. Neither suggestion found its way into the Western plan, presented in July, which called for limiting the negotiations to the twenty-three NATO and Warsaw Pact states and for barring consideration of nuclear weapons entirely. The first real break in the discussions occurred in December, when the sides agreed that only the member states of the two alliances should take part in the negotiations to reduce military capabilities; a separate but parallel forum would develop additional confidence- and security-building measures for Europe as a whole.

Despite the apparent progress, a host of issues needed to be resolved before actual negotiations could begin. Between December 1987 and the initialing of the draft mandate thirteen months later, representatives of the twenty-three worked to achieve agreement on the types of weapons to be reduced, the disposition of military equipment to be withdrawn from the reduction zone, the exact geographic extent of the prospective negotiations, and procedures for monitoring compliance following the conclusion of an accord.

As vital as the resolution of these (and related) questions were to the ability of the two alliances to complete the draft mandate and thereby clear the way for the start of negotiations, they were in a sense secondary to a more basic question that only the Soviets could answer: how high a price were they willing to pay for an agreement? During much of 1988, the leadership seemed not to know, vacillating between a posture that suggested resistance to deep cuts, particularly on the basis on asymmetry, and a more flexible approach, including incorporation of the principle of "unequal reductions to an equal outcome."

In February 1988, for example, Soviet defense minister Dmitri Yazov, in an obvious attempt to undercut Western arguments in support of asymmetrical reductions, alleged that an approximately equal balance of forces could be said to exist between NATO and the Warsaw Pact.[34] Yazov's contention was highly reminiscent of the Soviet position during the MBFR talks, by reference to which the Kremlin had turned aside successive Western demands that the East absorb a disproportionately larger share of the proposed reductions in personnel and weaponry. Gorbachev, during President Reagan's visit to Moscow in May 1988, and Shevardnadze, before the United Nations the following June, contradicted Yazov by underscoring the Soviet Union's support for the elimination of force imbalances and the establishment of true military equality between the two alliances.

Eventually, the Gorbachev-Shevardnadze position prevailed— as later Soviet initiatives were to reveal—although not without, it appears, a spirited contest for control over the content of Soviet arms control policy between the country's leading civilian authorities, who seemed disposed to sanction relatively large cuts in Soviet weapons stocks in order to advance the prospects of a deal with the West, and several of the USSR's highest-ranking military officers, who looked upon the expressions of interest in asymmetrical reductions with a barely concealed sense of fear and loathing.[35]

The low point for the Soviet military may well have come in December 1988, when Gorbachev, speaking before the UN General Assembly, revealed plans to reduce unilaterally the country's armed forces by 500,000, including the withdrawal of some 50,000 Soviet troops from Eastern Europe. In all, according to Gorbachev, over the next two years the Soviet Union would remove from the western military districts of the USSR and the territory of its Warsaw Pact allies 10,000 tanks, 8,500 artillery systems, and 800 combat aircraft.[36]

One week later, *Krasnaya zvezda*, the organ of the Ministry of Defense, announced the resignation of Marshal Akhromeyev as chief of the General Staff, "in connection with his transfer to other work," and the appointment of General Mikhail Moiseyev as Akhromeyev's successor.[37] Almost immediately, Akhromeyev began a new assignment, as military adviser to Gorbachev. The unusual circumstances surrounding Akhromeyev's career change suggested that his sudden departure from the General Staff might have come at the behest of his fellow officers, at least some of whom were likely to have lost confidence in Akhromeyev and in his ability to defend the military's interests against the political leadership's increasingly determined forays into issue areas customarily left to the armed forces. Akhromeyev also might have decided to leave the General Staff fully at his own initiative. Having played a key role in the development of the unilateral initiative the previous summer, by the time of its unveiling in December 1988 the marshal might have had second thoughts about the wisdom of the plan and opted to disassociate himself from its implementation. With Akhromeyev's suicide in September 1991, the full story may never be known.

Gorbachev's dramatic UN initiative settled, for a time at least, the question of who in Moscow was in charge of the development of Soviet military policy. After December, Western skeptics also found it harder and harder to challenge the authenticity of Gorbachev's commitment to restructure Soviet military forces by reference to the twin dictates of "reasonable sufficiency" and "defensive defense." In addition, the initiative served to enhance Gorbachev's image as a statesman, as a political leader willing to run major risks in the pursuit of peace. In a more practical vein, Gorbachev's UN address had the effect of generating pressure on the West to respond in kind at the CFE negotiations, now just weeks away, by offering up reciprocal concessions.

If such were in fact the purposes of the December initiative, the Soviet leadership must have taken only limited comfort from the results of the opening round of the CFE talks, held between March and May 1989. The Warsaw Pact position, which Shevardnadze outlined on March 6, called for reductions in manpower and military equipment in three stages. During the first phase, the two alliances would agree to eliminate all force "imbalances and asymmetries" (including personnel), after which tactical aircraft, combat helicopters, tanks, armored fighting vehicles, armored personnel carriers, and artillery tubes would be capped at some 85 to 90 percent of existing NATO totals. Following completion of this initial step, NATO and Warsaw Pact manpower would be reduced by a further 25 percent over a two- to three-year period. During the third phase, "the armed forces [of the two alliances] would be given a strictly defensive character, and agreements would be reached on ceilings limiting all other categories of arms. . . . " In his remarks, Shevardnadze proposed a verification regime for a CFE agreement that would supplement the two sides' reliance on "national technical means" with far more intrusive measures, such as the right to conduct frequent challenge, as well as scheduled, on-site inspections.[38]

The NATO position, presented by British foreign minister Geoffrey Howe, was as specific as the Soviet proposal was vague. Howe, like his Soviet counterpart, called for parity in deployed weapon systems. Unlike Shevardnadze, he attached numbers to the Western reduction plan. Under terms of the NATO proposal, each alliance would be permitted to retain 20,000 main battle tanks, 16,500 artillery pieces, and 28,000 armored troop carriers. The Western proposal excluded limits on manpower, tactical aircraft, and short-range nuclear weapons. In addition to the aggregate limitations, Howe suggested two additional kinds of constraints. The first came to be known as the "sufficiency rule," whereby no single country could account for more than 30 percent of a given type of weapon system deployed within Europe "from the Atlantic to the Urals." The second set precise limits on the number of weapons that a particular country could station on the territory of its European allies. In practice, only the Soviet Union and the United States would be effected by this latter proposal, as only they maintained large numbers of stationed forces in Europe.[39]

All things considered, it was not a bad start. Both sides agreed on the need to negotiate a balance of forces in Europe; both recognized, at least implicitly, that the Warsaw Pact would be required to undertake substantial and asymmetrical reductions in certain weapons stocks to reach this desired end state; and both were prepared to live with an intrusive verification regime to ensure compliance. On the other hand, *what* and exactly *how much* to reduce remained very much at issue.

Militarily, the Soviets looked to CFE to impose meaningful limits on Western strike and ground-attack aircraft and to compel the relocation of NATO's forward-deployed tactical nuclear weapons to rear areas. In exchange, they were willing to absorb disproportionately large reductions in manpower, armor, and artillery. NATO priorities were to sidestep the former while securing the latter. As the Soviets must have sensed, however, in March 1989 their leverage in the CFE talks was less than impressive and could diminish further in the weeks and months to come. Economic pressures alone were making it increasingly difficult for the Soviets to maintain a military presence in Eastern Europe totaling well in excess of 700,000 troops (including air force personnel). Something had to be done—and quickly—to ease the mounting burden. To keep the West at the bargaining table, Moscow would very likely have to make new concessions.

Two items were of particular interest to the West at this early juncture in the negotiating process: an exchange of data on forces and military equipment and some concrete numbers to go along with the Warsaw Pact's proposed weapons ceilings. Gorbachev supplied the numbers in May 1989 when he conferred with Secretary of State James Baker in Moscow—20,000 main battle tanks, 24,000 artillery systems, and 28,000 armored troop carriers—figures clearly within striking distance of the Western proposal. On data, Moscow continued to resist, arguing that the exchange should be deferred to the concluding round of the negotiations, once the agreement was ready for signature.

The dispute over when to compile and then to review the relevant data troubled Western negotiators, although far less than it had during the MBFR negotiations, when much of the emphasis had been on *reductions*, rather than on *ceilings*, as in CFE. The Pact could always claim, of course, that a particular tank or artillery system was not subject to reduction, given its characteristics (what the West saw as a main battle tank, the East could contend was actually a "light" vehicle, and therefore not to be included in the new weapons ceiling). The Soviets had engaged in precisely such definitional haggling during the MBFR talks, when the two sides found themselves unable to come up with a mutually acceptable definition of "regular" armed forces. The gambit was less likely to succeed this time around, however, in light of Moscow's seemingly high interest in a CFE treaty, as well as agreement between the sides on the desirability of on-site inspections.

Notwithstanding differences over manpower, tactical aircraft, combat helicopters, and nuclear weapons, East and West were obviously serious about the CFE negotiations and eager to keep the process moving forward. Between March and October 1989, each side amended its negotiating position in important ways. Early in the second round, for example, the Warsaw Pact conceded on both the "sufficiency rule" (holding out, however, for a limitation of 35 to 40 percent for the weapons contribution of a single country, rather than the 30 percent favored by NATO) and the proposed regulations governing the equipping of stationed forces. At the NATO summit meeting in Brussels in May, President George Bush endorsed the idea of constraints on tactical aircraft and combat helicopters. On the same occasion, he suggested a limitation of 275,000 for U.S. forces in NATO and Soviet troops in Eastern Europe, effectively extending the Western CFE position to include reductions in manpower. In October, during the third round, the Pact responded to the Bush initiative by proposing a limit of 300,000 on stationed forces—down 50,000 from its previous offer. The two sides also began to focus on the imposition of weapons ceilings within certain regions of Europe (a further Warsaw Pact concession) and exchanged detailed proposals on verification. Conditions seemed right for the conclusion of an agreement as early as the first half of 1990.

The rapid pace of the negotiations had only partly to do with an apparent meeting of the minds between senior political figures in Moscow and Washington (and in the capitals of Eastern and Western Europe) on the urgency of a continent-wide military détente. At least as central to the process was the unmistakable erosion of Soviet authority in its dealings with allies during 1989, as insurgents in one East European country after another successfully challenged the region's communist parties for political control.

In April 1989 the Polish "Roundtable" talks adjourned with an agreement between the government and the heretofore outlawed Solidarity organization to permit partially contested parliamentary elections. Two months later, Solidarity and its political allies captured 99 of 100 seats in the reconstituted Polish Senate, as well as all open seats in the Sejm, or lower house.[40] In August, President Jaruzelski asked Solidarity's Mazowiecki to form a government—a request Mazowiecki accepted—thus bringing to power in Warsaw the first noncommunist ministry since World War II. Hard on the heels of these events, Hungary, the German Democratic Republic, Czechoslovakia, Romania, and Bulgaria all underwent revolutions of their own, similar in outcome (if not always in style and method) to the drama unfolding in Poland.

By the end of the year, three of Moscow's European allies—Poland, Hungary, and Czechoslovakia—were well launched on the path of substantial political and economic reform. Two others, Romania and Bulgaria, occupied an uncertain middle ground between reaction and revolution. Most unsettling from the Soviet perspective was the situation in East Germany, where the regime, cleansed of its most notorious hard-line elements, found itself unable to restore public order in the aftermath of the opening of the Berlin Wall on November 9. Home to almost 400,000 Soviet ground troops, a stable, pro-Soviet GDR was central to the maintenance of the Kremlin's political-military position on the continent. Collapse of the communist government in East Berlin—a near certainty by December—threatened to shatter the very foundation of Soviet power in Europe.

It is in this context that Moscow's conduct during the first year of the CFE negotiations must be apprised. As the revolutions of 1989 gathered force, Soviet objectives in Vienna began to change. Whatever leverage Soviet leaders once held in CFE was ebbing away. As a consequence, no longer could they look to the negotiations to induce the West to pay a steep price for the restructuring of their own forces in Europe; even less could they count on the talks to constrain the most threatening elements of the West's military posture. Time was running out. For Moscow, the Vienna negotiations were rapidly becoming a device to underpin legally whatever residual military presence they could convince their reluctant Eastern European allies to accept.

By the start of the new year, the overriding Soviet goal in CFE was no longer to utilize the talks to accelerate the pace of political and military change in Europe, as it had been during the deceptively calm months leading up to the start of the negotiations in March 1989. Rather, the new objective was to slow the process, or, failing that, to impart to it a measure of predictability. As the NATO and Warsaw Pact negotiators prepared to resume their deliberations in January 1990, it was impossible to predict which of these two broad tendencies—managed change or political disintegration—would ultimately prevail in Eastern and Central Europe. For the leadership in Moscow, nothing less than the Soviet Union's future as a great power, both within Europe and beyond, hung in the balance.

ARMS CONTROL IN ASIA: MAKING UP FOR LOST TIME

Events in Europe overshadowed all other international and foreign policy developments in 1989. Even U.S.–Soviet relations, long the centerpiece of world politics, receded into the background during the second half of the year as the revolution the Poles ignited in April spread uncontrollably from one Eastern European country to the next. In Asia, by comparison, the pace of change seemed almost glacial. Although is some ways no less profound, the shifts in relations between and among Asian countries between 1985 and 1990 were accompanied by little of the drama that typified events half a world away. Beneath the surface calm, however, developments had been set in motion throughout the region that had the potential to transform the contemporary international political landscape.

As in Europe, the primary catalyst for change was the reorientation of Soviet foreign policy. The turn from confrontation to accommodation that enabled the marked improvement in relations between the Soviet Union and the West during the late 1980s also led to a distinct warming of the political climate in Asia. Soviet relations with several of the continent's leading countries—cool to frigid at the decade's midpoint—were clearly on the mend. By 1990 ties between Moscow and Beijing, for example, were better than they had been in thirty years; even Soviet-Japanese relations, among Asia's worst, had begun to recover from their most recent low point, after the downing of Korean Airlines Flight 007 in September 1983. Everywhere in Asia, it seemed, the Soviets were eager to distance themselves from the discredited policies of the past and to demonstrate their commitment to the development of friendly, equitable, and mutually advantageous relations.

Although to a lesser degree than in Europe, where negotiations to limit NATO and Warsaw Pact armed forces and military equipment had come to dominate the East-West political discourse, Soviet security and arms control policies in Asia played an important part in easing regional tensions and in helping to restore relations between Moscow and several of the region's most powerful actors. Again, as in Europe, most of the concessions came from the Soviet side—a reflection of the deep suspicion with which many Asian leaders continued to view Moscow's intentions, despite the advent of Gorbachev and the "new political thinking." In contrast to Europe, however, where the negotiations were both highly structured and multilateral, the process in Asia was decidedly less formal and, to the Kremlin's chagrin, exclusively bilateral. Moreover, if, as in the CFE talks, European arms control had acquired a kind of autonomous momentum, in Asia the act of limiting the military capabilities of the Soviet Union and neighboring countries remained very much a product of developments at the political level between Moscow, on the one hand, and its negotiating partners, on the other.

The Vladivostok and Krasnoyarsk Initiatives, 1986–1988

Perhaps in no other part of the world had the Soviet Union's political fortunes fallen so low as they had in Asia during the final years of the "era of stagnation." By 1985, the Soviets could count on the friendship and support of but a handful of Asian countries, principally India, Vietnam, and North Korea. Soviet leaders had nurtured ties with India carefully over several decades, both as a counterweight to (and later as compensation for the "loss" of) China and to serve as an example of how relations between Moscow and Third World countries, with proper tending, could operate to the advantage of both parties. From the Kremlin's perspective, the link to New Delhi was the one solid, enduring achievement of the Soviet Union's postwar Asian diplomacy—Moscow's "jewel in the crown." Relations with Vietnam and North Korea, part of the USSR's burden of empire, were more constraining to the leadership than liberating, given Hanoi's image as an aggressive, regional actor with hegemonic pretensions, and Pyongyang's status as an international pariah.

Moscow's biggest problem in Asia, of course, was China. For more than thirty years, Soviet and Chinese leaders had eyed one another suspiciously across the world's longest unbroken border, trading insults and occasionally coming to blows. As relations deteriorated, the Soviets increased the number of troops deployed opposite China by a factor of five—from roughly ten divisions in the early 1960s to more than fifty by the mid-1970s. Hundreds of tactical nuclear weapons and theater-range surface-to-surface missiles also found their way to Soviet Asia, in addition to whatever fraction of their long-range nuclear forces Kremlin military planners earmarked for possible use against the People's Republic. Chinese leaders reciprocated by augmenting their own forces, particularly those deployed in and around Manchuria, and by procuring a modest arsenal of nuclear weapons, which they paired with a small holding of ballistic-missile launchers of sufficient range to strike most Soviet cities, including Moscow.

The death of Mao Zedong in 1976, whom the Soviets held personally responsible for the dangerous state of relations between the two communist giants, failed to end the standoff. The situation went from bad to worse, in fact, as China and the United States, after a number of false starts, moved to establish full diplomatic relations in fall 1978, and as Chinese leaders, confident in their new relationship with Washington, undertook a determined campaign to create what they themselves labeled a global, anti-Soviet "united front." Before relations could improve, the Chinese cautioned, the Kremlin would have to satisfy three conditions: a reduction in Soviet troop strength along the Sino-Soviet frontier; the evacuation of Soviet forces from Afghanistan; and the withdrawal by Vietnam— Moscow's Southeast Asian ally—of its military contingent in Cambodia.[41] The Soviets dismissed the Chinese demands out of hand.

Soviet-Japanese relations were in a similar state. Never warm to begin with, ties between Moscow and Tokyo had been frozen since the mid-1970s, when the Kremlin's unwillingness even to acknowledge the existence of a territorial dispute[42] between the two countries provided Japanese policymakers a convenient excuse to defer consideration of bilateral issues to the indefinite future. High-level political contacts were infrequent and unproductive; trade and commercial relations suffered accordingly. Leaders in both countries seemed either unwilling or unable to break free of the accumulated suspicion and distrust that had build up over the forty years since the conclusion of the war in the Pacific in 1945. Absent some flexibility on the part of either country concerning, in particular, the Northern Territories issue, the prospects for a Soviet-Japanese détente appeared slim.

Several diplomatic initiatives, undertaken by the Brezhnev leadership during the 1970s to burnish Moscow's image as an Asian power, had fallen flat. If anything, the proposals to establish an Asian collective security system worked against the Kremlin's efforts to normalize relations within the region. Whatever Moscow's true intent, many in Asia saw the proposals as a transparent attempt to disrupt U.S. alliance relationships (with Japan, South Korea, and the Philippines, for example) and to isolate and contain China (which was, in the Soviet estimate, the overarching threat to regional peace and security). While a number of Asian leaders shared Moscow's antipathy toward Mao and his successors, few were willing to align themselves openly with the Soviet Union in order to balance China's power and influence.

In Asia, then, the task confronting Gorbachev was indeed formidable. In a July 1986 speech, delivered in the Far Eastern port city of Vladivostok, the Soviet leader did his best to distinguish his policies from those of the Brezhnev era and to signal the start of a fundamentally new chapter in Soviet-Asian relations. At Vladivostok, Gorbachev took positive note of the "great Chinese revolution," praised the PRC's commitment to far-reaching economic reform, and spoke warmly of the tradition of friendship between "the two biggest socialist states" of Asia. He characterized Japan as "a power of paramount importance" that had been elevated to greatness during the postwar years by virtue of the "single-mindedness, self-discipline, and energy" of the Japanese people. In accordance with the program of the twenty-seventh CPSU congress, Gorbachev declared, the Soviet Union stood ready to cultivate good relations with all countries in Asia (most of which he proceeded to list), "without exception."[43]

Gorbachev also advanced at Vladivostok a five-point plan to relieve regional tensions that combined elements of the "old" and the "new political thinking." Three of the proposals—for the establishment of a South Pacific nuclear-free zone and a nuclear-free Korean Peninsula, for restrictions on U.S. and Soviet naval activities, and for the consideration of confidence-building measures and the nonuse of force—had found their way into previous Soviet initiatives. None had stirred much interest in Asia at the time, and none seemed likely to do so in 1986. The fourth, on the settlement of regional conflicts, was long on rhetoric and goodwill but short on substance. The fifth proposal—a call for "radical" reductions in

Soviet and Chinese conventional armed forces "to the limits of reasonable sufficiency"—*was* new, although just how important the departure in policy might turn out to be was difficult to judge without knowing what the Soviet leader had in mind by way of numbers.[44]

Gorbachev's announcement in February 1988 that Soviet combat forces would withdraw from Afghanistan within twelve months was a key development in this context. As one of Beijing's "three conditions," Moscow's exit from that war-torn country could only enhance the prospects for improved Sino-Soviet relations by demonstrating to Chinese leaders the seriousness of Gorbachev's desire to break with the policies of his predecessors. When Vietnam, later that year and at Moscow's urging, revealed plans to reduce its military presence in Cambodia by 50,000 troops, relations between China and the Soviet Union took another modest turn for the better.

Notwithstanding the apparent progress in relations with China, the Vladivostok initiative failed to win any converts to the Soviet cause in Asia. The United States, professing not to see the need, consistently turned aside Moscow's expressions of interest in negotiations to limit naval activities in the Pacific.[45] The Japanese government proved no more cooperative, insisting that a sustained improvement in relations between Tokyo and Moscow was simply impossible without a prior resolution of the dispute over the Northern Territories. Member states of the Association of Southeast Asian Nations (ASEAN) welcomed the increasing number of Soviet goodwill visits, but declined to move much beyond symbolic return gestures in the absence of a settlement of the conflict in Indochina. Indicative of the generally low level of interest in the Vladivostok appeal was the lack of response to Gorbachev's proposal to convene a regional conference on confidence- and security-building measures, patterned after the Helsinki process in Europe. Clearly, something more was needed to spark interest in the Soviet program to promote "peace and cooperation" in the Asia-Pacific region.

Gorbachev gave a second speech on regional security in September 1988, in Krasnoyarsk. Billed as a major new statement on Soviet policy toward Asia, the speech amounted to little more than a recapitulation and refinement of the themes first articulated in Vladivostok two years before. As in his earlier address, Gorbachev called for the convocation of a Helsinki-like meeting and for negotiations to restrict naval activities. He also urged the start of talks to limit regional military capabilities, particularly among the countries of Northeast Asia—the Soviet Union, China, Japan, and the two Koreas. The most interesting part of the speech was the section devoted to Sino-Soviet relations, in which Gorbachev declared himself in favor of full normalization, and proposed "preparations without delay" for a summit meeting between Soviet and Chinese leaders.[46]

Taken on its own terms, the Krasnoyarsk speech could hardly be considered a breakthrough; in all major respects, it corresponded closely to the line that had emerged at Vladivostok. What had changed was the larger political context, both within the region and beyond. In July 1986, Soviet troops had yet to begin their withdrawal from Afghanistan, while in Cambodia Vietnamese troops persisted in their defense of the Hanoi-backed regime in Phnom Penh. Relations between Moscow and Washington remained cool, despite the Geneva Summit and the preparations, then at an early state, for a second meeting between Reagan and Gorbachev sometime in the fall. In Europe, work on the Stockholm Accord continued but an agreement was still several months away.

By September 1988, political conditions were very different. The majority of Soviet forces had already left Afghanistan and Vietnam was floating proposals for the complete withdrawal of its army from Cambodia (the Vietnamese made it official in January 1989). The superpowers had signed and ratified the INF Treaty. In Europe the CFE negotiations were about to commence, following the all-but-certain completion of the Mandate Talks. All that was required, it seemed, was a final, powerful stimulus from Moscow to precipitate the kind of movement—or "dynamism" to use the word preferred by Gorbachev—then beginning to characterize Soviet relations with the United States and the countries of Western Europe.

Pressing Ahead: Soviet Security Policy in Asia, 1989–1990

The impetus came in the form of unilateral Soviet force reductions, first outlined by Gorbachev in his December 1988 address to the UN General Assembly. Over the next several months, he and other high-ranking Soviet officials provided important details about the reduction plan, including the fact that of the 500,000 forces to be demobilized by the end of 1990, fully 40 percent—some 200,000 troops—were to come from military districts east of the Ural Mountains and west and north of China. Of these, Shevardnadze revealed in February 1989, 120,000 would come from units deployed in the Soviet Far East, opposite Manchuria. The foreign minister also confirmed that 50,000 Soviet troops would soon depart Mongolia, in accordance with an agreement worked out between Moscow and Ulan Bator during the final months of 1988.[47] During his trip to Beijing in May 1989, Gorbachev further delighted his Chinese hosts by announcing the deactivation of eleven air force regiments located in Soviet Asia, as well as sixteen warships attached to the Pacific Fleet.[48]

A number of factors determined the timing of Gorbachev's troop-reduction plan. Doubtless one factor was the Soviet leader's desire to accelerate the political dialogue with his Chinese counterparts, then at a delicate stage. Shortly after Gorbachev's December 1988 UN speech, Chinese foreign minister Qian Qichen journeyed to Moscow—the first such visit in thirty years—for consultations with senior Soviet leaders. Two months later, Shevardnadze flew to Beijing for an additional round of discussions. In May Gorbachev traveled to the PRC for three days of intense meetings with ranking Chinese officials, including Deng Xiaoping.

Although Gorbachev's reception in Beijing was less than he might have hoped for—the Chinese were correct, though reserved, in their dealings with the Soviet reformer—the mission was a major success from Moscow's perspective. In addition to the full restoration of relations, a vital Soviet objective, the two sides agreed to expand trade and commercial relations and to intensify their economic and technical cooperation. They even discussed reestablishing party-to-party relations, severed twenty-five years before during the darkest days of the Sino-Soviet conflict. More to the point, while it is possible that the summit might have come about in the absence of the Soviet decision to trim the number of its forces deployed near the Chinese frontier, it is just as likely that China's leaders would have held back, waiting for Moscow to concede on the third of their "three conditions." Gorbachev, who by the spring of 1989 had invested considerable time and energy in the normalization of relations with Beijing, chose not to run that risk.[49]

Détente with China freed the Soviets to devote greater attention to several other pressing issues in Asia, including relations with Japan. Before the Beijing Summit, in December 1988, Moscow and Tokyo had agreed to establish a permanent bilateral working group, to be co-chaired by Soviet and Japanese deputy foreign ministers, to explore the conclusion of a peace treaty. Press reports accompanying the first meeting of the working group, held in Tokyo in March 1989, suggested that the territorial question—the status of the four southernmost Kurile Islands—would occupy a central place in the deliberations. Soviet deputy foreign minister Igor Rogachev took the opportunity to affirm once more the legitimacy of Moscow's claims to the disputed islands, while at the same time insisting that the controversy should not be allowed to stand in the way of normalized relations. His Japanese counterpart, Kakakazu Kuriyama, faithfully reiterated the now familiar Japanese position: good relations with Moscow must await resolution of the territorial question.[50] A similar dynamic characterized the colloquy between Gorbachev and Foreign Minister Sosuke Uno when the latter journeyed to Moscow in April 1989 for the second high-level review of Soviet-Japanese relations in six months.[51]

Notwithstanding the ostensible rigidity of the Soviet position, a subtle change in the Kremlin's line had begun to emerge. During Uno's Moscow visit, for example, Shevardnadze raised the possibility of some kind of accommodation, as yet undefined, regarding the two islands closest to the island of Hokkaido.[52] In November 1989 Aleksandr Yakovlev, one of Gorbachev's principal foreign policy advisers, traveled to Tokyo for a round of discussions with senior Japanese leaders. In a startling departure, Yakovlev spoke of a "third way" in reference to the dispute over the Northern Territories, and argued that the problem could and should be resolved in concert with other issues on the bilateral agenda. Yakovlev also described Gorbachev's upcoming visit to Japan, scheduled for sometime in 1991, as an event of potentially far-reaching significance. How significant, Yakovlev implied, would likely turn on the success of the two sides in surmounting at least some of their differences in the period separating his visit and that of the Soviet president.[53]

Despite these indications of flexibility, in the end the Soviets refused to countenance the one outcome regarding disposition of the Northern Territories—their outright return to Japan—that might have made possible the full normalization of relations with Tokyo. One possible formula, which circulated in Moscow during the second half of 1990, called for the immediate restoration of Japanese sovereignty over the islands, in exchange for which Tokyo would agree to the maintenance of Soviet military installations on the two northernmost islands—Etorofu and Kunashiri—for a fixed number of years. Gorbachev could have proposed such a deal either in advance of or during his 1991 visit. He did neither.

Elsewhere in Asia, Soviet efforts to advance relations with powerful regional actors met with somewhat greater success. As a direct result of its role in promoting Vietnam's withdrawal from Cambodia, for example, Moscow's standing among ASEAN states had improved dramatically since the mid-1980s. The leadership's decision to press ahead with the establishment of full diplomatic relations with South Korea, despite the Soviet Union's close ties with the North Korean regime, was yet another illustration, second in importance only to the normalization of relations with Beijing. As in its dealings with Japan, Moscow's primary incentive for reaching out to Seoul was economic. Unlike the Japanese, however, the South Koreans had no territorial dispute with the Kremlin and were at least as eager as the Soviets to formalize their burgeoning political and commercial contacts.

That its new relationship with Seoul had a manifestly negative impact on its relations with Pyongyang seemed not to concern the Soviet leadership unduly. The North Koreans had few other friends to whom they could turn for support, in any event. China, Pyongyang's other Asian ally, itself moved to expand relations with South Korea during this period, and evinced no more interest than the Soviet Union in pressing North Korean claims against the South. On the contrary, both Beijing and Moscow were quietly supportive of efforts to reduce political and military tensions on the peninsula through such mechanisms as the on-again, off-again ministerial talks between the North and the South.

Despite the obvious achievements of Gorbachev's Asian policy between 1985 and 1990—the rapprochement with China, limited movement in relations with Japan, the establishment of diplomatic and economic ties with South Korea—the Soviet leader's larger vision for the region remained substantially unrealized. In contrast to Europe, where the shifts in Soviet foreign policy resulted in the remaking of the continent's political map, in Asia relations between and among the region's primary actors retained much of their traditional character. For the most part, the changes that did occur were accommodated within the existing structure of relations, frustrating Gorbachev's plans to move beyond the regional political system that had been in place in Asia for the better part of twenty years.

The fundamental reason for the durability of the regional system in East Asia was the lack of interest of most countries in changing it. The anti-Soviet thrust, so evident in the diplomacy of China and Japan, persisted because leaders in both countries believed that it served their interests. The rush in Western Europe to respond in material ways to Moscow's bid for integration and inclusion found no echo in the policies of Beijing and Tokyo, for example. Compounding Gorbachev's dilemma was his lack of negotiating leverage. In relations with China, it was the Soviets who offered most of the concessions (including a sizable unilateral reduction in their Asian-deployed armed forces and an unconditional withdrawal from Afghanistan). For them to have made real progress in relations with Japan, comparable concessions would have been required. They were never forthcoming.

The major Asian countries were content, on balance, to let their Soviet problem resolve itself. Gorbachev's promise to further curtail Soviet military capabilities in the region if Moscow's Asian neighbors would only consent to formalize and multilateralize the search for security was hardly compelling, as most Asian leaders seemed persuaded that the Soviets would be forced to slash deployments on their own in order to shrink the country's bloated defense budget. It was for this reason, above all others, that Gorbachev's efforts to transform the basis of Soviet power in Asia by, among other gestures, underscoring the modesty of the Kremlin's regional ambitions, failed to generate the desired results.

FLYING BLIND: GORBACHEV AND SOVIET ARMS CONTROL POLICY, 1990–1991

Within months of his election as CPSU general secretary, Gorbachev moved to seize the initiative in arms control by advancing a number of bold proposals, much as he had done and would do again in other policy arenas, foreign and domestic. He acted to correct what he and others in the leadership had come to regard as grievous errors committed by those who had preceded them in office and to establish control over a process he was eager to set in motion with the Soviet Union's most powerful rivals. In so doing, he seems to have believed, developments could be made to conform to his agenda, rather than to the agendas of others.

Maintaining control over events—having the ability to determine the rate and character of change—was a vital component of Gorbachev's arms control strategy. Only by retaining the initiative could he hope to engineer a series of outcomes that would simultaneously allow for major cuts in Soviet defense spending, deep reductions in force deployments, stabilization of the East-West military competition, and the perpetuation of Moscow's status as a great power.

By 1990, the forces that Gorbachev had unleashed *within* Soviet society had all but deprived him of the ability to control events *beyond* the country's borders. The rapid deterioration of conditions within the Soviet Union—the deepening economic crisis, the breakdown of civil authority, the rapid decline in Communist party prestige and influence, the sharp intensification of ethnic, religious, and national tensions—all combined to limit Gorbachev's capacity to maneuver internationally. And, as existing problems intensified, new ones appeared, further undermining the Soviet leader's domestic base of support and eroding popular confidence in his policies.

For better than four decades an important foundation of the regime's authority, both at home and abroad, was the widespread conviction that Soviet leaders would take whatever actions might be required, up to and including the use of force, to safeguard "the postwar gains of socialism," particularly in Europe. When that turned out not to be the case—when the leadership itself, in responding to the systemic crisis within the Soviet Union, became a primary catalyst for change—events moved rapidly out of control. In Eastern Europe what began as gradual reform turned virtually overnight to out-and-out revolution, forcing Moscow, on short notice, to choose between two equally unappealing courses of action: direct military intervention, in an attempt to restore order and maintain the empire; or inaction, to substantiate its support for and adherence to the principles of the "new political thinking." Soviet leaders determined that the costs, material and otherwise, associated with the first option were prohibitive. In deciding as they did, however, they effectively shattered the foundations of Soviet power in Europe and eviscerated their own negotiating position in the CFE talks.

When NATO and Warsaw Pact negotiators finally reached agreement in CFE, the treaty itself was an anticlimax. While the signing ceremony in Paris in November 1990 was an elaborately staged affair, attended by heads of state and foreign ministers from twenty-two European countries, it was an event oddly bereft of drama. Since the onset of the negotiations in March 1989, the European political and military landscape had changed profoundly, to say the least. Most significantly, the German Democratic Republic had simply disappeared, having been absorbed by its powerful neighbor to the west the month before.

The military situation in Europe had also changed. At the time of unification, more than 300,000 Soviet troops remained on the territory of the former GDR, where they were scheduled to stay for at least four more years, while the government of German chancellor Helmut Kohl helped fund sufficient new housing in the USSR to accommodate the returning soldiers and their families. Their military value to Moscow had essentially evaporated, however, with the disappearance of the host government in East Berlin. Also underway in November 1990 was the redeployment of some 150,000 Soviet forces stationed in Czechoslovakia and Hungary that Moscow had already pledged to withdraw in their entirety by mid-1991 (a timetable the Soviets met).

The scope of the reductions in the CFE Treaty was indeed breathtaking—well over 20,000 pieces of military equipment were to be destroyed under the terms of the agreement—but, again, less spectacular than the political revolutions in Eastern Europe that had made the cuts possible in the first place. In the topsy-turvy world that was beginning to emerge by early 1992, inducing the several successor states of the USSR to commit themselves to the terms of the CFE Treaty completely overshadowed the terms of the actual agreement and momentarily, at least, undercut the sense of relief and celebration that Western governments had felt at the time of the agreement's signing. If the West's primary interest in the accord in 1989–90 had been to legislate military equality between NATO and the Warsaw Pact, thereby reducing the likelihood of an East-West conflict in Europe, less than two years later one of NATO's major goals in affirming the agreement was to make it harder for the newly independent countries of the former Soviet Union to wage war against one another.

The conclusion of the long-awaited START Treaty, in July 1991 in Moscow, was similarly low-key, and for many of the same reasons. The agreement, which required Washington and Moscow to reduce strategic nuclear forces to a common ceiling of 1,600 launchers and to effect warhead reductions on the order of 15 percent for the United States and 33 percent for the Soviet Union, came at the end of a prolonged process of negotiation during which the character of superpower relations had changed in fundamental ways. What made the agreement possible, above all, was Moscow's determination to normalize ties with the United States as soon as possible and at virtually any price, to signal the final, irrevocable end of the Cold War, and to enshrine cooperation as the central organizing principle of a new era in bilateral relations.

As with the CFE Agreement, the fate of the START Treaty was immediately thrown into doubt when the Soviet Union ceased to exist as a legal entity less than five months after the treaty's signing. Gorbachev's promise in October 1991 to match President Bush's unilateral pledge of the month before to eliminate all U.S. land- and sea-based tactical nuclear weapons was also rendered problematic by the USSR's collapse.

Much of the diplomacy involving the United States and the four republics of the former USSR with nuclear weapons on their soil that followed in the immediate aftermath of the Soviet demise focused on the issue of compliance with the terms of the START

Treaty and on securing the adherence of Ukraine, Belarus, and Kazakhstan as non-nuclear weapons states to the 1968 Nuclear Nonproliferation Treaty. As of this writing, the status of the START treaty remains unresolved, despite its ratification by the U.S. Senate and the Russian parliament in October 1992. Although Belarus and Kazakhstan formally accepted the agreement's terms in the months following U.S. and Russian legislative action, as of February 1993 Ukraine has yet to lend its official sanction. (To date Kiev also has declined to join the nonproliferation treaty as a non-nuclear weapons state, notwithstanding its May 1992 pledge to do so at its earliest convenience.)

Ratification of START by all four successor states is, of course, essential to ensure implementation of the treaty's many and complex provisions; it is also important, however, because without such joint action, the Bush-Yeltsin agreement of June 1992, which moves considerably beyond the reductions in strategic forces mandated in START, cannot be finalized and made ready for executive and legislative action in either the United States or Russia.

Detailed consideration of these and related questions lies well beyond the scope of this study, which extends only to the point in December 1991 when Gorbachev resigned as Soviet president. It is perhaps sufficient to note that the problems the United States now confronts as its seeks to structure strategic relations with the Russian Republic (and with Ukraine, Belarus, and Kazakhstan) are dramatically different from those that characterized superpower relations in the past. That they are so different is a direct outgrowth of the revolution that Gorbachev initiated in Soviet security policy beginning in 1985 and over which he subsequently lost control. How and why events moved beyond Gorbachev's reach, and what remains of the Soviet leader's legacy, particularly in arms control, is the subject of the final chapter.

Chapter 4

Perestroika and the Soviet Military

SOME OF THE MOST DRAMATIC TELEVISION FOOTAGE OF THE FAILED coup d'état in Moscow in August 1991 featured units of the Soviet military rolling toward the heart of the country's capital in an apparent effort to assist the Committee for the State of Emergency in the USSR in its illegal attempt to seize power. The more powerful visual, and, as it turned out, the more consequential act, was of Boris Yeltsin, president of the Russian Federation, climbing atop one of the tanks sent to dislodge him from his headquarters at the Russian White House to denounce the actions of the conspirators and to rally his supporters.

The attempted coup forced the Soviet military, battered and dispirited after six years of experimentation with radical reform, to choose sides between the country's constitutionally sanctioned, if unpopular, head of state, Mikhail Gorbachev, who had been forced into an uneasy alliance with the charismatic Yeltsin, and those determined to oust the embattled Soviet president in order to arrest what they saw as the country's precipitous slide toward political, economic, and social chaos. In the end, most of the military leadership, by staying in their barracks and refusing to take up arms in support of the old guard, sided, in effect, with Gorbachev and Yeltsin. While those who sought to oust Gorbachev might well have failed in their poorly planned and clumsily executed bid for power even without the military's de facto desertion, the decision by many in the leadership of the armed forces to remain on the sidelines doomed the conspiracy to failure within hours of its initiation.

Why did the military leadership of the Soviet Union, next to the party *nomenklatura* the most privileged of the institutions associated with communist rule, fail to take up arms in defense of the system? Why would senior commanders, who in 1991 could only expect additional cutbacks in spending, deeper reductions in forces, and a further diminution in status, elect to do nothing rather than to throw their considerable weight behind those promising to restore their position in society?

The question has no simple answer. The sources of the military's conduct during the August crisis are numerous, and as difficult to pinpoint as the factors that determine the actions (or inactions) of any large, complex, and hierarchical organization attempting to function during a period of radical change. The perceived political legitimacy of Gorbachev (and Yeltsin), especially as compared to that of the group seeking to overthrow them, clearly played a role. Poor planning on the part of the conspirators, most notably the failure to consult widely with at least the most important military officials and to secure their support *in advance* of the declaration of the state of emergency, also contributed to the armed forces' relatively low profile. Another explanation, it seems, was the longstanding tradition of the Soviet military of steering clear of politics in any direct sense, which Western analysts attribute, both then and now, to a combination of vigilance on the part of Communist party authorities (especially during the early years of the country's history), conscious political design (the creation of a "loosely coupled" system of civil-military relations), and military professionalism.[1]

The argument advanced in the pages that follow, however, is that the military as a disciplined force could not have acted in defense of the ancien régime, even had it harbored such ambitions. Like every other major Soviet institution of the time, by 1991 members of the armed forces, officer and enlisted men alike, were thoroughly caught up in the larger struggle over the country's future, resulting in a degree of politicization, resentment, fear, and confusion within the military that was without precedent in the Soviet experience. An army riven by such dissent is an unreliable instrument, unable to act collectively and decisively in the interests of the state, or on behalf of those presuming to act in its name.

In this sense, the failure of the Soviet military to take sides during the attempted coup—to champion forcefully the cause of one faction or the other—was part of the larger failure of Soviet society either to embrace with conviction or to reject the radical reform program unleashed by Gorbachev and his supporters. The paralysis so evident in virtually every Soviet institution by the late summer of 1991, in other words, had come to afflict the armed forces in equal measure, depriving it of the ability to act coherently and in a manner likely to influence, if not determine, the outcome of events.

For this reason, the disintegration of the armed forces as an institution cannot—and should not—be separated from the larger saga of the Soviet Union's decline. One of the largest and arguably the most lavishly supported of the country's myriad institutions, the military was wholly dependent on the largesse dispensed by the civilian leadership, whatever its particular cast, thereby linking its fate in the closest possible way to that of the Soviet system more generally. To a greater degree than with any other Soviet organization except the Communist party, the unraveling of the military proceeded in tandem with the unraveling and subsequent collapse of the Soviet state. How this came about is the subject of this chapter.

The chapter begins with a review of the state of civil-military relations in the Soviet Union at the time of Gorbachev's accession to power in March 1985. The second section is devoted to an analysis of Gorbachev's early attempts (1985–1989) to reform the armed forces as an institution, in keeping with the principles of perestroika and the logic of "the new political thinking." The third section examines the impact on the military of the centrifugal forces at work in Soviet society, particularly during the last several years of Gorbachev's tenure, and the efforts of the uniformed military to respond to these unwelcome developments. The final section assesses the conduct of the armed forces both during the attempted coup in August 1991 and in its immediate aftermath.

THE PATTERN OF SOVIET CIVIL-MILITARY RELATIONS

From his immediate predecessors Gorbachev inherited one of the world's most stable and predictable systems of civil-military relations. Particularly in the period following the ouster of Nikita Khrushchev in October 1964, relations between civilian decision-makers and ranking military officials had become for the most part harmonious and routine, a function both of the willingness of the political leadership to leave operational military matters to those with the competence to manage them and the uniformed military's respect for and deference to civilian control of the armed forces. The decision by the Brezhnev leadership to increase the defense budget 4 to 5 percent each year between 1965 and 1977 doubtless helped preserve its good working relations with the military establishment.

The dismal performance of the Soviet economy from the mid-1970s on introduced elements of discord. As discussed in chapter 1, the controversy that attended the doctrinal pronouncements of then chief of the General Staff, Marshal Nikolai Ogarkov, which culminated in his dismissal in September 1984, had as much to do with the allocation of resources both to and among Soviet armed forces as it did with the marshal's impolitic way of framing the issues. At a time of budgetary retrenchment, Ogarkov was demanding (among other things) more money for military investment, especially for the development and acquisition of high-technology "smart" weaponry, only a portion of which could be obtained by redirecting resources from the military's existing accounts, such as those devoted to the modernization and expansion of the Strategic Rocket Forces. The balance, Ogarkov seemed to imply, would have to come from elsewhere in the system, by raiding Soviet social programs, for example. To delay in this vital task, Ogarkov warned, was to place the Soviet Union at risk, given the revolutionary advances in conventional weaponry and in advanced, military-related technologies being developed in the West.

In another sign of discord, two weeks before his death Brezhnev addressed an unusual gathering of senior Soviet military officials in Moscow in which he seemed to chide the armed forces for their wasteful ways and urged them to make more effective use of the resources placed at their disposal. "The Party Central Committee," Brezhnev reminded his audience, "takes measures to meet all your needs. The Armed Forces should always be worthy of this concern." Somewhat elliptically the aging leader went on to note:

> The times are now such that the level of combat readiness of the Army and the Navy should be even higher. We must deal with the improvement of combat readiness constantly and in the most responsible fashion, on the basis of growing requirements. Then no eventuality will catch us unawares.
>
> We must be able to operate with consideration for the latest achievements of military science and the art of war. It's important to persistently strive for positive results in combat training. At the same time, special attention should be given to troop command and control.
>
> It's extremely important to wield weapons skillfully, to be able to fully use their combat potential.
>
> The Soviet Army must be up to the mark in all respects: equipment, structure, training methods. It should meet today's tasks. *And you, comrades, bear the responsibility for this* (emphasis added).[2]

To whom precisely Brezhnev was directing his remarks—and with what exact purposes in mind—remains something of a mystery, even ten years later. His death on November 10 only added to the confusion, as Yuri Andropov, his successor as party general secretary, chose at least initially not to follow up on Brezhnev's critique. Instead, in an effort both to ensure their support and to calm their fears, Andropov lavished praise on the armed forces and promised to attend to their considerable material needs.

Although by late in 1983 Andropov, or those speaking on his behalf, had begun to hedge a bit on his support for the military,[3] Konstantin Chernenko, who took over from Andropov upon the latter's death in February 1984, retreated to orthodox formulas when discussing the Soviet military and its role in "safeguarding the gains of socialism" during his brief thirteen-month stint as general secretary. In none of Chernenko's pronouncements was there any direct criticism of the military's performance or of its management of resources, although he did lobby obliquely for a continuation of the investment mix for Soviet society—increasing appropriations for social programs, consumer industries, and agriculture, with a freeze on military spending—favored by Brezhnev during the second half of his stewardship.[4] Gorbachev, elevated to the pinnacle of power in the Soviet system with the assistance of at least some of the party's ranking conservatives, such as Andrei Gromyko, adopted an equally cautious, even celebratory tone during his first year in office.

At a May 1985 Kremlin meeting to commemorate the fortieth anniversary of the defeat of Nazi Germany, for example, Gorbachev pointedly denounced U.S. "imperialism" and West German "revanchism" and drew special attention to the role of the Soviet military in restraining the dangerous intrigues of the West. "Realizing the scope of the military threat and cognizant of our responsibility for the fate of peace," the Soviet leader declared, "we will not allow the military-strategic equilibrium between the USSR and the U.S. and between the Warsaw Treaty Organization and NATO to be upset. We will continue to adhere to this policy because we have learned well, once and for all, what the past has taught us."[5]

Less than a year later, however, as Gorbachev sought to escape from the self-limiting implications of the Brezhnev legacy in foreign and defense policy, the new general secretary began to sound the themes in military policy that in three short years were to transform the character and conduct of world politics. In place of the traditional Soviet argument that in times of great East-West tension the most reliable guarantee of Soviet security was to maintain and, if possible, further augment the armed forces of the state, Gorbachev suggested just the opposite. In his address to the twenty-seventh CPSU Congress in February 1986, he observed that "the world today has become too small and fragile for wars and a policy of force. It cannot be saved and preserved unless there is a break—a decisive and irrevocable break—with the way of thinking and acting that for centuries has been built on the acceptability, the permissibility, of wars and armed conflict."[6]

Gorbachev's introduction in 1986 of what amounted to a fundamental departure in at least the expression of Soviet security policy had less of an impact on his audience—both at home and abroad—than the impatient Soviet leader might have expected. In Washington, the Reagan administration, deeply skeptical about the sincerity of the new Soviet leader, dismissed the general secretary's call for a new beginning in East-West relations as bombast. Closer to home, Gorbachev's own military, including Defense Minister

Sergei Sokolov (appointed by Chernenko in December 1984 to succeed Dmitri Ustinov) seemed to believe it was business as usual. In his address to the party congress, for example, Sokolov relied almost exclusively on the vocabulary developed during the first ten years of the Brezhnev regime in depicting the heroic contributions of the Soviet military to the cause of peace and socialism.[7]

Other senior military, most especially Sergei Akhromeyev, Ogarkov's successor as chief of the General Staff, proved more willing to break with the failed policies of past, although even among those so inclined the definitions they offered of Soviet doctrine, as well as their pronouncements on force postures, weapons procurements, and arms control tended to lag behind the latest encyclicals issued by Gorbachev and those in the political leadership most closely associated with him.

The real mystery, given the stakes, is why Gorbachev moved so cautiously in his military personnel policy. Not until two years into his tenure as general secretary did he sack the aging and conservative Sokolov, and when he finally acted it was in apparent response to the unauthorized surprise landing on Red Square in May 1987 of a small, single-engine private plane, piloted by a disturbed West German teenager. While other heads rolled at the same time, including that of General Aleksandr Koldunov, chief of air defense forces and first deputy minister of defense, the reshuffling within the Defense Ministry fell short of the kind of purge that had accompanied the installation of previous Soviet leaders, most notably that of Khrushchev in the 1950s.

From his election as general secretary in March 1985 to the attempted coup d'état in August 1991, Gorbachev had but two ministers of defense—and only one of his own choosing—and two chiefs of the General Staff, a relatively low rate of turnover for a man seeking to remake his country's institutions. And while those he appointed to senior positions within the armed forces pursued a relatively aggressive personnel policy, liberally restaffing positions billeted at the third and fourth echelons of the Soviet military establishment with individuals of their own choosing, such officers were seldom promoted, demoted, or reassigned, it appears, because of their perceived support for or opposition to Gorbachev's new line on security policy.

In what he would come to characterize in succeeding years as a determined effort to effect a revolution in Soviet military affairs, Gorbachev was apparently content, curiously, to allow those with the most to lose as a result of his proposed changes to oversee and implement the reform agenda. It was a pattern that he was to repeat over and over again in other dimensions of Soviet life and with very much the same results: the promulgation of a collection of well-intentioned and seemingly far-reaching directives that were either sabotaged by unsympathetic officials or, at best, partially discharged and inconsistently applied. That Gorbachev, at once a product of the old system and its most determined critic, would countenance such behavior was a reflection of his own deep ambivalence about transformative change; it also highlights the particular dilemma that bedevils any *reform*-minded political leader who confronts the need for *revolutionary* solutions.

Gorbachev's respect for the "rules of the game" during the first few years of his administration worked at cross purposes with his plans for the reform of the Soviet military system. Perhaps, as his detractors alleged in the wake of the failed coup attempt, he placed a higher value on loyalty than he did on competence; perhaps he believed that the military, cognizant of the imperative for reform, would embrace (or at least not reject out of hand) new approaches to the resolution of existing and prospective problems, much as he was to do. Perhaps he felt that his power to intervene in something as important to the military establishment as personnel policy was and should remain limited and, if exercised too readily, could breed resentment and additional resistance (leading, perhaps, to an attempt to remove him from power).

Whatever the explanation, in his relations with the leadership of the armed forces Gorbachev was a traditionalist almost to the very end and respectful of the division between civil and military authority that had grown up in the wake of Khrushchev's forced retirement twenty years before. The irony is that had he struck at the military early on, when at least arguably his power was at its greatest, he might have been able to assemble a team willing to enact his subsequent reforms more or less in their entirety. As it was, he proceeded cautiously at the beginning so as to preserve good relations with the military, only to see his own power to effect change gradually slip away, thereby reducing the political risks to the defense bureaucracy as it set about the task of frustrating important elements of his reform program.

THE POLITICS OF MILITARY REFORM, 1985–1989

Virtually all of the problems that greeted Gorbachev upon his election as CPSU general secretary could be traced to the lackluster performance of the Soviet economy over the course of the preceding ten years. Beyond the most direct consequence of stagnation, namely the consignment of the vast majority of the population to a kind of perpetual quasi poverty, the failure of the economy to post even modest gains after 1980 eroded popular support for and confidence in the Soviet system more generally; over time the tendency toward cynicism and alienation on the part of the people, already well-developed features of Soviet life, became pervasive, as did the retreat into private culture, which came, predictably, at the expense of state-supported civil society. By the mid-1980s no major strata of Soviet society, including the party, seemed to have much faith in the renewability of socialism.

Gorbachev on the Offensive

To combat these enormously destructive tendencies, Gorbachev in 1985 embraced two key elements of the Andropov reform program: the drive to "accelerate" the country's economic performance, mostly by convincing the population to work harder and smarter (and to drink less); and the anticorruption campaign, or the attempt to bring to justice those believed to have profited unfairly and at the expense of ordinary people during the Brezhnev era. The military leadership, deeply concerned about the manifest decline in civic discipline, was broadly supportive of the attempt both to jump-start the economy and to root out corruption.

Neither initiative produced much by way of results, however, and by his second year Gorbachev had begun his search for more radical prescriptions. If during the early stages of his stewardship Gorbachev had been content to leave undisturbed the formula for the allocation of resources to the military that had been developed late in the Brezhnev years and respected ever since, by the time of the

CPSU congress in 1986 the Soviet leader was having second thoughts. Gradually, it seems, the political leadership was coming to understand that reform on the scale necessary to reignite the country's stalled economy would take money—lots of it—and that the only possible source of new funds over the near-term were the budgets of the military services.

For the military, this was the real significance of Gorbachev's pronouncements on the nonwinnability of nuclear war and the sudden interest in the concepts of "reasonable sufficiency" and "defensive defense." If implemented, such ideas would likely result, first, in smaller appropriations to the armed forces and, later, in actual reductions, both in the size of the services and in their capabilities. In an effort to convince the general secretary to look elsewhere for additional resources—and to buttress the case of those within the political leadership disturbed by the implications of Gorbachev's statements on doctrine and strategy—the military relied on two time-tested techniques for the defeat of policy initiatives that it believed threatened Soviet national security.

The first technique was to point to the intensification rather than the diminution of the military threat confronting the USSR and its allies. Such assessments were nothing new, of course, having become a staple of Soviet military analyses during the final two years of the Carter administration, and continuing through the Reagan defense buildup of the early to mid-1980s.

General A. T. Altunin, deputy minister of defense and head of the Soviet civil defense effort, warned in February 1986, for example, that "reactionary imperialist circles in the West, especially the United States" were continuing to step up their military preparations. "Under such conditions," Altunin declared, "the Soviet people are forced to display great political vigilance and not to relax their efforts to strengthen the country's defense capability."[8]

Defense Minister Sokolov, in his address to the party faithful the following month, used very similar language in portraying the grave threat to socialism posed by the war-prone imperialists.[9] As late as February 1988—some twenty months *after* release of the June 1986 declaration of the Warsaw Pact in which the signatories had pronounced the emergence of political conditions in Europe suitable for a new and far-reaching détente—very senior representatives of the Soviet military, including chief of the General Staff Akhromeyev in a *Trud* article, were still issuing stark warnings about "imperialism" and "the danger of war in present-day conditions."[10]

The second technique was to cite without specifying the date or the audience or to quote out of context passages from Gorbachev's speeches that seemed to affirm the positions of the defense establishment on such issues as the likelihood of war, resource allocation, and doctrine and strategy. For example, in an article published in February 1986 in *Rude Pravo*, the organ of the Czechoslovak Communist party, Colonel General V. F. Yermakov, commander of the Central Group of Soviet Forces, highlighted a statement by Gorbachev that the political leadership would provide the armed forces of the Soviet Union "everything" necessary to defend the country and its allies, without, however, indicating where or when the words had been uttered.[11] Akhromeyev, in the February 1988 *Trud* article referred to above, relied on the identical technique—quoting Gorbachev approvingly so as demonstrate the political correctness of the marshal's analysis, but failing to inform his readers of the occasion for the general secretary's remarks or to whom they had been directed.[12]

Undaunted, Gorbachev persisted in his campaign to justify reductions in defense spending by reference to the declining threat of war and to reorient Soviet military doctrine in the direction of greater defensiveness. The Soviet leader took particular exception to the tendency on the part of certain ranking military officials to draw direct (and frightening) parallels between the prewar environment of the 1930s and the military-political situation of the 1980s—a device he and others dismissed as profoundly mistaken and ill-informed.

Much to the annoyance of the General Staff, Gorbachev enlisted the support of several of his well-placed civilian allies, including Foreign Minister Eduard Shevardnadze and Politburo member Aleksandr Yakovlev, neither of whom cared much about the sensitivities of the military leadership concerning the formulation of doctrine, budget share, or the role of the armed forces in society. He also encouraged wider discussion of military and doctrinal issues among analysts known to be critical of existing Soviet policies, particularly those attached to several of the social science institutes of the Academy of Sciences, including the Institute for USA and Canada Studies and the Institute of World Economics and International Relations.[13]

Next to Gorbachev himself the most important and forceful exponent of the "new political thinking" was Shevardnadze. In remarks delivered to a Foreign Ministry–sponsored conference in June 1987, he was explicit in his condemnation of certain actions undertaken in ostensible support of the Soviet Union's global interests, including the lavishing of funds on the military, and on the need for an entirely new basis for the conduct of foreign and security policy. "The main thing," Shevardnadze lectured his audience,

> is that the country not incur additional expenses in connection with the need to maintain defensive capability and protect its lawful foreign policy interests. This means that we must find ways to limit and reduce military rivalry, eliminate confrontational features in relations with other states, and suppress conflict and crisis situations.[14]

In a repeat performance a year later, Shevardnadze was, if anything, even more explicit in his criticism of those responsible for the development of Soviet military policy during the Brezhnev years. "The idea, which gained a firm hold in the minds and deeds of certain strategists, that the Soviet Union could be as strong as any possible coalition of states opposing it," the foreign minister lectured, "is absolutely groundless. To follow it means to act clearly against the national interest." In what the military could only have read as a direct challenge to its competence and professionalism, Shevardnadze concluded that section of his report by declaring that "we cannot . . . permit ourselves the luxury of 'imitating' the United States, NATO, and Japan in all their military-technical novelties."[15]

The forced resignation of Defense Minister Sokolov in May 1987, and the appointment of army general Dmitri Yazov to succeed him, resulted in a decline in the military's guerrilla campaign against Gorbachev's security and foreign policies. Yazov, whom Gorbachev had plucked out of relative obscurity to head the Defense Ministry, proved more willing than his predecessor to reproduce the views of the general secretary and those allied with him on most issues. He also was prepared, particularly during the early years, to impose these perspectives on the military press, which prior to his appointment had demonstrated a notable lack of enthusiasm for the "new political thinking." Under Yazov's direction, then, and at least for a while, most of those in uniform charged with writing on military affairs were careful to frame the issues in such a way as not to run afoul of the defense minister and his superiors.

The Military Fights Back

Notwithstanding the advent within the military of a more consistently sympathetic line in support of the Gorbachev reform agenda, important differences persisted, both between civilian and military leaders and within the military establishment itself. Between 1985 and the first part of 1989, some of the most intense debate centered on the operational implications for the armed forces of the proposed shifts in doctrine. The military's discomfort with the concept of "reasonable sufficiency" as a guide to the sizing of both nuclear and conventional armed forces, as well as its profound skepticism regarding the utility of "defensive" operations in the event of war, have already been discussed at length in chapter 2.

Suffice it to say in this context that the determination of Yazov and Akhromeyev, in particular, to adopt a proactive stance with regard to the debate over doctrine—as evidenced by the spate of detailed analyses prepared under their guidance that appeared in the Soviet press during the second half of 1987 and throughout 1988[16]—sprang at least as much from the perceived need to retain control over the "military-technical" dimension of doctrine, long the prerogative of the professional military in Soviet society, as it did from a sense of growing apprehension about the direction of change. While the debate over doctrine had a strong substantive component, in other words, it also had an important political dimension: given that the "new political thinking," together with the failure of the reform program to spark even a modest economic recovery, required the downsizing of the country's armed forces and the adoption of a less offensively oriented military strategy, who better to restructure the armed forces than the military professionals associated with the Ministry of Defense and the General Staff?

This turf war intensified during 1988 and 1989 as senior members of the political leadership, joined by a small group of civilian analysts, pressed the case for reform and, in a new development, leveled attacks against the military as an institution. Echoing charges made by Shevardnadze in his remarks to Foreign Ministry personnel in July 1988 that excessive secrecy in the conduct of Soviet foreign policy had led to multiple disasters, Georgi Arbatov, director of the Institute for USA and Canada Studies, argued in a piece that appeared in *Pravda* in October that the military, too, was in immediate need of a dose of glasnost. Characterizing the meeting among the Foreign Ministry *aktiv* as "an unprecedented event" in the development of Soviet foreign policy, Arbatov went on to declare that "[o]ne would like to hope that a similar event will take place at the Defense Ministry."[17]

Even Yazov and Akhromeyev, while eager to shield the military as much as possible from the rising chorus of criticism emanating from civilian quarters, took the defense bureaucracy to task for its halfhearted response to perestroika and its failure to implement reform-oriented directives in their entirety. In a series of articles published during the summer of 1988, and again toward the end of the year, both the defense minister and the chief of the General Staff were scathing in their assessments of the responsiveness of the ministry to the new developments in doctrine and strategy.[18]

According to Akhromeyev, many directorates of the General Staff were elaborating decisions slowly and timidly. "Certain commanders and staffs," the Marshal declared, "have not fully grasped the demands of the defensive strategy and operational art."[19] The plans and timetables developed by the General Staff had consumed many hours, Akhromeyev argued,

> but this quantity on paper has not been translated into quality. The USSR defense minister has issued instructions for a serious restructuring of combat training in light of the demands of the new military doctrine. This restructuring has been partially begun during the summer period. It must be vigorously continued.[20]

Yazov was no kinder. The military's persistent reliance on "formal, bureaucratic" methods, the defense minister alleged, was the primary force holding back the development of military science, "not only by dint of people's own inability to produce anything new, valuable, or useful, but also because mediocrity can exist comfortably only by pulling everyone and everything down to its own level and reducing . . . really creative natures and talents to its own common denominator."[21]

Predictably, tensions also surfaced over the defense budget and various initiatives to curb military spending. On this issue, and in contrast to the discussions over doctrinal change and organizational responsiveness, the uniformed military did its best to maintain a united front. Prior to 1988 the need to rein in military expenditures, while perhaps assumed within the Gorbachev leadership, had yet to be made explicit, at least in such a way as to provoke overt opposition on the part of the armed forces. Not until January 1989, in fact, did Gorbachev and Nikolai Ryzkhov, chairman of the government's Council of Ministers, offer specific targets for the reduction of military spending—14.2 percent from 1989 to 1991—and for cuts in the procurement of weapons.[22] And it was not until May 1989, in a speech to the Congress of People's Deputies, that Gorbachev provided a figure for total military outlays—77.3 billion rubles—by reference to which one might assess the significance of the proposed reductions.[23]

Gorbachev's revelation, which he insisted on characterizing as the "real figure," sparked considerable controversy. Critics, both of Gorbachev and of the military, alleged that the figure significantly understated actual spending on the armed forces by excluding the costs of some kinds of forces (such as border troops) and by ignoring research and development costs for weapons. Others alleged that the figure, constituting an estimated 9 percent of Soviet GNP, could be off by a factor of two or three, given the artificiality of prices in the Soviet system; the prices charged to the military for the goods and services it consumed, in other words, bore little, if any, relation to the actual costs of production, owing to the military's status as a privileged demander of resources, as well as the absence of market forces by which the real value of commodities might be determined.

The leadership of the armed forces, even as it lent rhetorical support to the idea of reducing defense expenditures in response to the country's worsening economic situation, sought to limit the extent of the projected reductions in three ways: by minimizing the existing defense burden on Soviet society; by advocating at most modest cuts in defense appropriations; and by suggesting to the country's political leaders that they spread out the anticipated reductions over a period of years.

The first line of defense—that the Soviet Union spent no more, and probably less, than the United States on the maintenance of its military—failed to win the military many new supporters, judging by the response in the Soviet press to an analysis to that effect offered by Yazov, which appeared in the U.S. newsweekly, *U.S. News and World Report*, in March 1989.[24]

At least initially, the second and third arguments proved more popular with the political leadership, which for reasons of its own was less than eager to sanction drastic, near-term reductions in military spending. The specter of widespread unemployment certain to result from the sudden discharge of thousands of Soviet military personnel, officers and enlisted men alike, induced a degree of caution on the part of political leaders who, in the absence of such concerns, might have been more inclined to impose truly draconian cuts. The prospect of a loss of negotiating leverage with the West also might have served to restrain Gorbachev, at least for a time, particularly given the approach of the conventional force reduction negotiations between NATO and Warsaw Pact countries, scheduled to begin during the first half of 1989.

The attempt to have it both ways—reductions in budget and force deployments large enough to generate measurable savings and to convince Western policymakers of the seriousness of the proposed military reforms, while at the same time sufficiently modest to preserve the country's essential force structure and to prevent widespread social unrest—reached a crescendo of sorts with Gorbachev's dramatic announcement to the UN General Assembly in December 1988 that the Soviet Union would reduce its armed forces unilaterally by some 500,000 over the ensuing two years, including the withdrawal of 50,000 troops from Eastern Europe.

In the context of ongoing developments in Soviet civil-military relations, the most interesting aspect of the December 1988 initiative was the military's seemingly strong support of the measure. After the fact, leading spokesmen for the armed forces, including two chiefs of the General Staff, emphasized the military's direct and sustained involvement in both the design and implementation of the proposed package of reductions.[25] They also underscored their determination to prevent a repetition of the 1960s experience with conventional force reductions, in which the army, at Khrushchev's behest, had been forced to absorb deep reductions quickly and without due regard for the human costs, let alone the practical military consequences, including the ability of the armed forces to defend the country against aggression. Finally, the military characterized the reductions, which were to proceed in an orderly fashion over a two-year period, as a perfectly reasonable response to the shift toward greater "defensiveness" in Soviet doctrine; a posture of "reasonable" or "defense sufficiency," they argued, would require a smaller number of deployed forces than earlier, more offensively oriented strategies.

The armed forces were less supportive of the December 1988 initiative than they appeared at first blush, however. Akhromeyev's explicit criticisms of the military's way of doing business during the summer of 1988 have already been noted and might have had something to do with the latter's lukewarm support for, or perhaps resistance to, unilateral force reductions, plans for which would have been under active consideration and debate at the time. A second sign of discontent was the publication of letters in the military press, in the wake of the December 1988 announcement, expressing open skepticism about the wisdom of the reduction scheme, none of which were likely to have appeared without high-level sponsorship.[26] Most pointed to the likely economic hardships that could befall those cashiered, took exception to the poor timing of the reductions in light of the upcoming negotiations with NATO, or counseled against the reductions because of the continuing threat to Soviet security posed by Western military forces.[27]

Notwithstanding these and other hints of opposition, the December 1988 initiative for the unilateral reduction of Soviet forces might well have served as a model for cooperation between civil and military authorities during a period of great stress and transformative change had the country held together long enough for the reform agenda to be implemented. Despite the expressions of concern after the fact, the Gorbachev UN initiative appears to have been developed in close consultation with the appropriate military authorities and shaped in such a way as to alleviate their worst fears. Especially important in this regard was the provision of ample time to adjust to the reductions, thereby avoiding at least some of the mistakes of the 1960s reduction edict and enabling a relatively smooth transition to a new force structure. With two years to implement the proposed changes, the military leadership appears to have believed that it could accommodate both lower levels of forces and armaments and a smaller share of the national budget.[28]

As it was, the General Staff's carefully laid plans for the development of a new military doctrine and the downsizing of the armed forces came to naught as the 1989 anticommunist revolutions in eastern Europe shattered the foundations of the Soviet Union's postwar position on the continent and as powerful centrifugal forces at home eroded the Communist party's—and ultimately Gorbachev's—capacity to direct the affairs of state.

THE MILITARY AND THE DISINTEGRATION OF THE UNION, 1989–1991

Between the first part of 1989 and August 1991, the attention of the military shifted from the orderly consideration of such issues as doctrinal reform, budget share, and manpower levels, to far more fundamental and contentious questions concerning, for example, the relative advantages and disadvantages of a conscript versus a professional (or militia-based) army, the use of regular armed forces to suppress large-scale outbreaks of domestic violence, and the preferred relationship between a democratizing civil society and its instruments of coercion. Ultimately, circumstances also forced the military to confront the problem of determining where, precisely, its loyalties lay—to the Soviet system and the Communist party, as the country's constitution suggested, or to the people and their elected representatives, whatever the latter's political orientation. It was for the armed forces, having been insulated from such sensitive and potentially dangerous issues for seventy years by a Communist party confident in its capacity to govern and determined to maintain the military's subordinate position, both an unprecedented and an unwelcome choice.

The final three years of Gorbachev's tenure began, however, with little of the drama that was later to engulf the Soviet leader and his country. In military affairs, implementation of the December

1988 unilateral initiative continued to preoccupy the leadership of the armed forces, as did preparation of a comprehensive draft program of military reform for presentation to the government, sometime in 1990, and consideration later by the Supreme Soviet, the standing legislature of the newly formed Congress of People's Deputies.

The military, particularly its planning arm, the General Staff, had begun consideration of a comprehensive program of reform during the summer of 1988, well in advance of Gorbachev's address to the United Nations in December. The tempo of the work accelerated, however, during the first half of 1989, as the pace of the country's political life quickened, primarily in response to the decision to hold contested, multicandidate elections in March for some two-thirds of the seats in the Congress of People's Deputies. Eager to restrict direct civilian involvement in defense planning as much as possible, senior military leaders moved quickly to shape the anticipated debate by sketching out their preferred program for the reform and restructuring of the armed forces.

Initially they sought to limit the debate to the three issues about which they felt most strongly and over which they believed they could exercise the most influence: defense spending; reductions in manpower; and modifications to the existing structure of forces. As noted, on spending, the military proposed, and Gorbachev later endorsed, a 14.2 percent reduction that was to be implemented over a two-year period, with a vague hint of additional cuts to follow in succeeding years. On reducing the size of the armed forces, during the first half of 1989 the military was disinclined to consider any downward adjustments in excess of those already announced— namely the 500,000 troops scheduled for demobilization under Gorbachev's December 1988 reduction edict—arguing that a military establishment numbering 3.7 million (down from the 4.2 million on active duty in January 1989) was the minimum required to safeguard the security of the Soviet state.[29]

A similarly conservative assessment informed the General Staff's recommendation regarding the future structure of the armed forces. In the plans previewed in the military press both before and after the convening of the Congress of People's Deputies in May 1989, the organization of the military, including the highly centralized arrangements for the command and control of forces, the division of the armed forces into five services, and the existing system of military districts—would all be preserved, more or less in their entirety.[30] Encouraged by many outside the professional military to consider a truly radical reconfiguration of forces, the leadership of the armed forces resisted, proposing instead a combination of predominantly cosmetic (or marginal) changes, the practical effect of which would be to leave intact the system that had been in place since the post-Khrushchev reforms of the mid-1960s.

Conflicts over Conscription, Extraterritoriality, and Depoliticization

The attempt by the military leadership to retain control over the debate concerning the future character of the armed forces failed miserably. While some newly elected members of the Supreme Soviet seemed content to quibble with the Defense Ministry's pronouncements on defense spending, force levels, and various organizational matters, other deputies launched a more wideranging assault against the military from which the latter was never to recover.

These so-called "radical" deputies, who included several relatively junior members of the armed forces, struck at three features of the existing system that constituted the very bedrock of modern Soviet military organization. The first was *conscription*.

Since resolution of the debate over a conscript versus a professional army in the 1920s, no representative of the Soviet state had seriously questioned either the necessity for or the desirability of a military draft. Beyond its presumed operational utility—for example, in enabling the country to maintain sufficient forces in being to mount large-scale offensive operations—in the judgment of the political leadership, universal military service constituted the regime's most effective weapon in the struggle to combat parochialism and "narrow-minded nationalism" on the part of those inducted and to foster an appropriately "Soviet," or supranational, set of values. For most male citizens of the USSR, service in the military was their one sustained exposure to and participation in a genuinely multinational institution; as such, the regime was loath to sanction its replacement with a system of voluntary enlistment.

Conscription also afforded the military an uninterrupted supply of manpower at bargain basement prices and, given the three-year terms of service, adequate time to train the draftees to perform the wide range of tasks associated with the operation of a complex military organization. Few features of the modern Soviet military mattered as much to its architects, in other words, as did retention of the draft.

Those who advocated abolishing conscription dismissed as wishful thinking the contention that universal military service promoted patriotism and loyalty to the Soviet state, pointing instead to the persistence of ethnically and religiously inspired violence among service personnel, as well as an increase in the incidence of *dedovshchina*, the violent hazing of young recruits, all of which in their opinion underscored the social costs, rather than the social rewards, of involuntary military service. They also alleged that a professional military could be maintained for approximately the same amount of money as a conscript army, particularly since the need to maintain the large force structure assembled during the Brezhnev era had all but disappeared with the rapid winding-down of the Cold War—a proposition to which the military leadership took exception.[31]

Repeatedly during 1989 and 1990, very senior representatives of the military denounced as unworkable, too expensive, and even dangerous various proposals to replace the conscript system with an army based on voluntary enlistments. In March 1989, at a Defense Ministry conference convened for the benefit of the military press, Yazov criticized as "bearing the stamp of incompetence and haste" a number of proposals calling for the radical reform of the armed forces. He was especially critical of plans to do away with conscription. "When people talk about manning the Army on the basis of voluntary hired recruitment for military service," the defense minister observed, "they usually cite the high professionalism of this kind of army." "Yes," he admitted, "its quality in this respect is indeed high. But this approach overlooks the economic aspect of the question. The point is that a hired army is at least several times more expensive for society than an army manned on the basis of universal military service."[32]

As for what Yazov termed "the purely military aspect of the question,"

> . . . this was demonstrated with the utmost clarity by V. I. Lenin, who noted at the beginning of this century that "the times when wars were fought by hired men have receded beyond recall into oblivion . . . ." Because of the limited nature of the reserves that get trained under such a manning system, a hired army is incapable of conducting protracted military operations, particularly in defense of extensive territories. In other words, from a military viewpoint, too, it is ultimately not capable of ensuring the guaranteed resolution of the tasks of repulsing aggression and defending our motherland's borders. And, finally, a substantial flaw in a hired army is the direct dependence of its morale on material incentives. History testifies to the unreliability of depending solely on incentives of this kind, . . . when the high moral content of military service is replaced by material advantage and becomes devalued.[33]

In his appearance before the Supreme Soviet in July 1989, called to confirm his appointment as defense minister, Yazov was considerably more succinct. "Let me say straight away," he declared to the country's legislators, "we cannot afford a professional army."[34]

Akhromeyev, in his capacity as Gorbachev's principal adviser on military affairs, also condemned the fascination with a volunteer army as militarily unsound, citing the need to maintain large forces because of what he termed the Soviet Union's unique "geo-strategic situation"—by which, it seems, he meant the country's large number of potential enemies—and the requirement for rapid mobilization in the event of war.[35] As did a number of his colleagues, the former chief of the General Staff extolled the virtues of a "people's army," especially its capacity and willingness to act reliably in defense of communism, the socialist system, and the Soviet constitution.[36]

These and other efforts to demonstrate the unworkability of voluntary military service in the USSR notwithstanding, the campaign among the most radical of the people's deputies to abolish conscription continued unabated; the issue, like so many others broached publicly for the first time during the country's final three years, was still unresolved when the union expired in December 1991.

The second and related aspect of the existing system against which a number of radical deputies took aim was the principle of *extraterritoriality*, or, in the Soviet context, the power of the central government to deploy military personnel, including draftees, to wherever in the country it saw fit. For the most part, those who argued against the right of the regime to dispatch forces to any part of the Soviet Union declined to frame this extraordinarily sensitive issue in such explosive terms. Rather, they proposed that the military forces of the USSR be reconfigured, either in whole or in part, as a collection of "territorial militias," or military groupings made up of draft-age males from a particular region, which, during peacetime, would fall under the jurisdiction of regional (probably republic-level) political authorities. If proposals to end the draft aroused profound misgivings on the part of senior military officials, schemes to divide the armed forces among the Soviet Union's fifteen republics struck them as suicidal.

Consideration of this issue was further complicated by the fact that some advocates of reform, particularly those with military backgrounds, meant something quite different when expressing their interest in a territorially based system than did other supporters, especially those representing the interests of the various republics. Moreover, the differences in perspective widened over time.

The first group tended to support the concept only in the context of the adoption of a so-called mixed system for Soviet armed forces—a system in which a large core of enlisted personnel, recruited on a voluntary basis, would be supplemented in times of need (e.g., national emergencies and war) with territorially based militia units. In this sense, the militias would act in the Soviet context much the same way that National Guard and reserve units function in the United States. Such a system had in fact been in place in the Soviet Union during the 1920s and early 1930s. More to the point, in this variant the principle of extraterritoriality would be preserved. By contrast, the second group, for whom the question of military organization was above all a political one, were inclined to favor the territorial option as a way to undermine the authority and coercive capacity of the central government and to buttress the claims regarding sovereignty emanating from a number of the USSR's increasingly restive republics. For this group, acceptance of the territorial principle by the larger polity could be a vital step on the road to statehood and full independence from Moscow.

Predictably, the military leadership was both forceful and un-ambiguous in its opposition to the establishment of territorial militias in whatever guise, characterizing such discussions as "far removed from present-day realities and the actual requirements of the country's defense."[37] To organize the armed forces in such a manner, according to deputy minister of defense Vitali Shabanov, was "simply impossible," given that "the concentration of Army and Navy Forces is planned and effected on the basis of ensuring the defense capacity of the country as whole and not of individual republics."[38] At different times during 1989 and 1990, both the defense minister and the chief of the General Staff echoed Shabanov's warning.[39]

These and other military leaders also pointed to the negative impact of territorially based militias on combat effectiveness and the quality of recruit training, asserting, for example, that such a system would preclude "both the mastery of modern weapons at short-duration periodical camps and, especially, the achievement of the necessary combat harmony among personnel and the requisite level of organization, discipline, and combat readiness . . . ."[40] According to Yazov,

> Militia units are stationed not where the situation requires but where they are manned and camps are held, and as a result they cannot gain control of a theater of operations and in fact are incapable of resolving the task of repulsing aggression and reliably ensuring the country's security.[41]

Unfortunately from the perspective of Yazov and his colleagues in the defense ministry, the increasingly rapid pace of change at the political level in the Soviet Union rendered less and less relevant the many militarily sound arguments they advanced in favor of maintaining the existing structure of forces. In April 1989, for example, the Gorbachev government ordered the dispatch of Soviet troops to Tbilisi, Georgia to quell antigovernment protests, resulting in the deaths of some twenty protesters. This action, which proved highly unpopular throughout the country and further undermined the prestige of the armed forces, provoked renewed calls in the troubled Caucasian republic and beyond for the immediate and complete withdrawal of Soviet forces and the creation of an all-Georgian militia to maintain the peace. Even more alarming to the Soviet high command were the Baltic declarations of independence from the Soviet Union in spring 1990, one effect of which, if implemented, would have been to exempt the citizens of Lithuania, Estonia, and Latvia from their obligatory service in the Soviet military.

As events unfolded throughout 1989 and 1990, the military found itself less and less able to control or to limit the terms of the debate regarding military reform because, at its core, the debate was about the future of the Soviet system as a whole—and not about the reorganization of the armed forces. At the same time, political leaders in the republics had fewer and fewer incentives to heed the military's dire warnings about the likely consequences of radical reform for the country's security and material well-being; many, in fact, embraced the reform process openly—the more radical, the better—apparently seeing in the potential dissolution of a unified military a sure way to accelerate the collapse of the union itself.

Attempts to *depoliticize* the armed forces, or to sever the link between the military and the Communist Party of the Soviet Union, constituted the third element of the radical reformers' campaign to restructure the existing system. Under the terms of the 1977 constitution (the so-called Brezhnev Constitution), the Soviet military was pledged to defend the USSR against external aggression and to safeguard the country's "socialist gains."[42] As part of that commitment, the armed forces were legally obligated to help preserve the Communist party's monopoly on political power, which was itself guaranteed in Article Six of the constitution. The party's conception of the military as an extension of the regime—as an instrument to enforce the "right" of the CPSU to govern—had operated as a given in Soviet politics for several generations, and prior to 1990 no one in a position of authority had seriously questioned this durable arrangement.

The situation began to change in the first half of 1990, when the CPSU Central Committee, at Gorbachev's urging, suggested to the Congress of People's Deputies that it "consider" eliminating the Communist party's constitutional guarantee of political power. The Congress, meeting in March, was only too happy to oblige, voting 1,771 to 24 (with 74 abstentions) to repeal Article Six of the constitution. In so doing, the national legislature made it possible for opponents of the existing system of civil-military relations to challenge openly the legal basis of the military's obligation to place the interests of the Communist party on an equal footing with the interests of the country.

The leadership of the armed forces was slow to adjust to this revolutionary development. In April 1990, for example, in an interview carried in the weekly *Argumenty i fakty*, General Boris Gromov, commander of the Kiev military district and former commander of Soviet forces in Afghanistan, argued that since the time of Peter the Great "we have had . . . special organs to promote the policy of the forces governing the state." The army, in Gromov's judgment, could not "lie outside of politics." In response to a question about whose policies the military should promote under current conditions, the general responded without hesitation, "those of the ruling party," or the CPSU.[43]

When Akhromeyev addressed the issue one week after Gromov's pronouncement, the marshal was equally direct, if rather more subtle in his interpretation of the military's obligation to support the system. Where Gromov had explicitly linked the interests of the armed forces to those of the Communist party, Akhromeyev, by contrast, drew a connection between the military and "socialism." In the marshal's words, "A political struggle is under way in the country between those people who favor and those who oppose socialism. The opponents of socialism know that the main forces in their way are the Communist Party and the Armed Forces. That is why they are attacking them so virulently."[44] Leaving no doubt as to where he stood on the issue, Akhromeyev concluded, "There is an oath in the Armed Forces whereby every serviceman swears to defend the Soviet socialist motherland and the Constitution. The socialist system will be preserved as long as the Army and Navy are monolithic, trained, and instructed."[45]

Here, it seems, was precisely the point the reformers were trying to make. Even with the elimination of Article Six, as of mid-1990 the military was apparently unwilling to distinguish between its obligation to protect the country against external aggression and its role as defender of the "socialist" system, which included, it appeared, de facto preservation of the ruling party's political status as *primus inter pares*. A leading voice of reform, People's Deputy and army major Vladimir Lopatin, put the matter directly in the course of a June 1990 interview in *Nedelya* when he asserted that "all of the military managers, beginning with the commander of a division and above, are approved by the Central Committee. For an officer to advance in the service requires not so much professionalism as membership in the party and personal loyalty to the CPSU leadership." Lopatin continued, "It seems to me that it is necessary to eliminate the party structures in the Army. The Armed Forces must serve the people, not parties."[46]

Lopatin returned to the issue the following month in the course of a panel discussion on military reform organized by *Krasnaya zvezda*. Again, the reform-minded major was explicit regarding the need to remove the military from politics and to place the armed forces under the control of the country's duly elected officials. "Through constitutional procedures," Lopatin argued,

> the CPSU has given up its monopoly on power in favor of the state organs. The Army should be subordinated to these organs. However, in our opinion these organs still remain an instrument of the party. Certain political circles are holding on to this instrument, this force, in every way possible; they may try to use it in the struggle for power in the environment of the emerging multiparty system.[47]

Lopatin's proposed solution was straightforward: "We see a way out in discontinuing the operation of political parties within the framework of the structures which ensure the stability of our society and state security, such as the Army, the KGB, the militia, the procuracy, and so on."[48]

The logic of Lopatin's case was unassailable, much to the annoyance of the Defense Ministry. By comparison, the military's counterattacks, which continued through the summer and fall, seemed feeble and atavistic, particularly those ascribed to spokesmen for the Main Political Administration, the department within the ministry charged with maintaining the ideological purity and political correctness of the armed forces. The critiques of Lopatin-style depoliticization offered by Yazov and Moiseyev fared no better.[49]

In an effort to put the matter behind him and the country, Gorbachev, who had broken ranks with the military on the issue as early as August 1990, issued a decree in January 1991 instructing the armed forces to establish vaguely defined "military-political bodies" to carry out state-oriented educational tasks;[50] these "bodies," according to the explanations offered subsequent to the president's announcement, were to operate in parallel with Communist party military organizations already in place.[51]

Not surprisingly, Gorbachev's attempt at compromise pleased almost no one: neither the political and military traditionalists, for whom anything less than a reaffirmation of the undivided loyalty of the military to the Communist party bordered on treason; nor the reformers, for whom any kind of formalized political activity within the armed forces, regardless of its source, was to be avoided. Only anticommunists determined to repoliticize the military in favor of their particular political orientation had reason to celebrate Gorbachev's solution.

Into the Abyss

At one level 1991 was to be a banner year for the advocates of radical reform of the Soviet military. Under the pressure of events, the political leadership, with a reluctant Defense Ministry in tow, was to consider, and in some cases sanction, a number of the measures—including a possible phasing out of conscription, the establishment of territorial militias, and depoliticization—favored by those seeking to remake the military establishment (and Soviet society in general). In the end, of course, it mattered very little, given the demise of the country. On a second level, however, it mattered a great deal, at least to those waging the struggle, because until very nearly the end the fate of the union remained a live issue—if just barely—and worth fighting about.

Once again, however, as the new year began, the military's senior leadership seemed woefully unprepared for the cascade of crises about to descend upon it. In August 1990 the Defense Ministry completed its long-awaited draft program of military reform, sending it to Gorbachev and the Defense Council for comment and review.[52] Several months later, it submitted the plan to the Supreme Soviet for legislative action. This detailed and carefully drawn document, to which the General Staff in particular had devoted hundreds of hours, for the most part sat unread on the desks of the country's civilian leaders and was still awaiting implementation in August 1991 when the failure of the attempted coup placed all such union-level plans on political hold.

As it turned out, the more salient and pressing issues for the military were whether it would be called upon to intervene in a series of rapidly escalating, ethnically based regional disputes in an effort to restore order (and if so, how it should respond); and whether force would be used to defeat the Lithuanian, Estonian, and Latvian bids for political independence, then seen to constitute the most acute threat to the integrity of the union. The sudden increase in the incidence of draft evasion during the second half of 1990 and into 1991 also preoccupied military authorities, who found themselves for the first time in the country's history short of recruits.[53]

On the first of these issues—intervention in regional conflicts fired by ethnic and religious antagonisms—the military was reluctant to act, in part because of the bloodshed that had resulted from its actions in Tbilisi in April 1989, and in Baku nine months later, when regular army units were dispatched to protect the city's thousands of Armenian nationals from violence at the hands of the Azerbaijani majority. In each instance, acting on instructions from central political authorities, the army had both inflicted and sustained casualties numbering in the scores. To make matters worse, the interventions served to intensify rather than reduce the level of violence in the effected areas. Of probably equal concern to the military command in Moscow, the use of force against the Georgians and Azerbaijanis had provoked outrage among some segments of the Soviet population located far from the fighting, who condemned the military's action on the grounds that as a "people's army," Soviet armed forces should never be turned against the citizens of the state.

In an attempt to defuse the violence, in July 1990 Gorbachev issued a decree ordering ethnic militants to surrender their weapons within fifteen days or face action by troops of the Interior Ministry. Evidence of the failure of the edict to accomplish its desired objective came barely two weeks later, when the Soviet president extended the deadline for compliance to October. He could have saved himself the effort.

By early 1991 the situation had, if anything, deteriorated further. In the disputed enclave of Nagorno-Karabakh, the district of Azerbaijan inhabited largely by ethnic Armenians, fighting between the two populations intensified, despite repeated efforts to negotiate a cease-fire. Soviet forces assigned to separate the combatants and to keep the peace were singularly unsuccessful, as hundreds of local inhabitants, Armenians and Azeris, civilians and combatants, continued to die in perhaps the most intense ethnically based conflict in Soviet history. Other outbreaks of violence elsewhere in the country, in Tadjikistan and Uzbekistan, for example, kept Soviet forces on the move during much of 1991.

In the latter two instances, in a conscious political decision to shield the army from popular criticism and to prevent any further erosion of its fighting élan, the authorities in Moscow dispatched forces assigned to the Interior Ministry, rather than troops under the command of the Ministry of Defense, to subdue the fighting. In an ironic twist, Defense Minister Yazov, along with Marshal Akhromeyev a staunch defender of the proposition that the military and society could not and should not be separated, had either initiated or acquiesced in the decision to relieve the army of any direct responsibility for the maintenance of domestic order, at least in those instances where the root causes of violence could be traced to ethnic or religious discord.

A separate, if related, challenge confronted the military leadership in the crisis surrounding the attempted secession of the three Baltic republics. Would the military, if so ordered, intervene to preserve the Union? Here, it seems, the problem could not be finessed by assigning the task to the other instruments of coercion at the disposal of the regime. Given both the scale of the crisis and the clear constitutional mandate to protect and serve the "Soviet socialist fatherland"—a directive that included, presumably, preservation of the country's existing borders—how could the regular armed forces refuse to act?

In possible preparation for military action against the Lithuanians, in particular, Yazov announced in November 1990 that the government had authorized the use of force to defend Soviet military installations and service personnel at risk in any and all of the country's fifteen republics.[54] Two months later, in January 1991, elite units of the Interior Ministry (so-called Black Berets) seized selected installations in Latvia and Lithuania, and the Defense Ministry revealed plans to dispatch army paratroopers to various of the republics, including the Baltic states, to round up would-be conscripts who had failed to report for duty and to enforce the law on universal military service. Lithuanian president Vytautas Landsbergis denounced the latter move as a provocation and warned his population to expect bloodshed.[55]

When the military did in fact act on January 13—employing thousands of troops in an attempt to seize key Lithuanian government buildings and to dislodge the country's elected leaders—Gorbachev, responding to pressure from the West, quickly distanced himself from the move and blamed the local military commander who had acted, according to the Soviet president, on his own initiative and not at the behest of the government in Moscow.[56] Within hours of Gorbachev's statement, the Soviet troops that had been involved in the operation were ordered to return to their barracks. During their brief deployment, some fifteen Lithuanians had perished.

Whatever the truth, the decision not to the remove the Landsbergis government by force signaled Moscow's de facto recognition of Lithuania's independence, and, by extension, that of Latvia and Estonia, as well. More than two years later it remains unclear whether the Soviet military, had it received orders from Gorbachev to persist in its efforts to topple the independence-minded government in Vilnius, would have complied. The fact that elements of the army, at someone's direction, forcibly took up positions from which they could have launched large-scale operations suggests that at least some units of the regular army were prepared to act in conformance with such orders.

If this was in fact the case, those so inclined might have reasoned that it was better to act against the Lithuanians in January than to wait, when conditions inside the Soviet Union and the breakaway republic might have been even less favorable. They also might have believed that one massive, well-executed, and successful show of force, while expensive in human terms, might have been sufficient to convince other rebellious republics, such as the Ukraine, Moldova, and Georgia, to rethink their campaigns for political independence and to stop short of defying outright Moscow's orders to cease and desist in their "illegal" activities.

Gorbachev's decision neither to confirm nor support the actions of the Soviet commander in Lithuania renders all such speculation moot; the possible consequences of a thorough and violent crackdown in that Baltic republic will never be known. It is interesting, nonetheless, to speculate about how events might have turned out had the Soviet leader settled upon a different course of action. For the military leadership in Moscow, the outcome of the Lithuanian crisis cut both ways: on the one hand, the failure to act decisively probably saved hundreds, if not thousands, of lives, military and civilian; on the other hand, never again, senior commanders might have reasoned, would there be so clear an opportunity to demonstrate the resolve of the armed forces to defend, by violent means if necessary, the Soviet Union's existing frontiers.

In countermanding the orders of the local commander in Lithuania, Gorbachev signaled that he was unlikely to turn to the army at a later juncture to hold together the rapidly disintegrating Union by force of arms, or even, in all probability, to preserve his own position or that of his government. He might well have believed by this point that as an instrument to preserve the Soviet Union the military itself was unreliable, subject as it was to the very same stresses and strains then tearing at the fabric of Soviet society. To call upon it to act might only serve to expose its inability to do so, at least as a disciplined, centralized organization able to receive and give orders. In other words, by early 1991 Gorbachev might not have trusted the armed forces to carry out his directives or to act collectively in defense of anything. If this was Gorbachev's assessment, it turned out to be close to the mark.

THE MILITARY AND THE AUGUST 1991 COUP D'ÉTAT

The ad hoc committee that attempted on the morning of August 19, 1991, to impose a state of emergency on the people of the Soviet Union and to relieve Gorbachev of his duties as president was overwhelmingly civilian in composition.[57] Among its members, however, was the senior-ranking military official, Minister of Defense Yazov. Thus, while it may be incorrect to label the attempted seizure of power a "military coup" as has one analyst,[58] Yazov's decision to take part in the conspiracy (and to do so in his capacity as head of the Defense Ministry) involved the Soviet military in an evident and important way.

Precisely *what* role the armed forces played both in the initiation of the coup and in its defeat remains something of a mystery even now, long after the fact. At a minimum, a number of very senior military officials, including many in Yazov's immediate retinue, most of those detailed to the General Staff, the heads of three of the five services, and the majority of the military district commanders, either supported or acquiesced in the attempt by the so-called Emergency Committee to assume control. Other high-level officers, we know, opposed this "unconstitutional" act and disregarded orders to comply with the directives of the plotters or actually came out in support of Russian Federation president Boris Yeltsin, the most visible and prominent political figure to defy the orders of the Emergency Committee.

The military's ambiguous conduct during those August days, coupled with the coup's ignominious failure, left the armed forces exposed and politically vulnerable in the immediate aftermath of the attempt to unseat Gorbachev. Some political figures who had defied the conspirators took note of the military's "restraint" during the crisis and heaped praise on those commanders who had sided with Yeltsin; other, generally less senior officials were less charitable, however, detecting in the failure of the armed forces to act collectively and with determination to defend the country's elected officials a dangerous precedent and confirmation of their worst suspicions.

In retrospect, however, what is truly remarkable about the behavior of the armed forces during those difficult days—from the declaration of the state of emergency on August 19 to its cancellation upon Gorbachev's return to Moscow on August 22—is not what they did, but what they did *not* do. They did not place the country under martial law. They did not engage in massive displays of force to intimidate the population. They did not occupy all key government centers, including communications facilities. And, most importantly, they did not shoot unarmed civilians. They did not, in other words, do what other militaries have routinely done when so instructed by civilian authorities allegedly acting on behalf of the state.

They did not act collectively in support of the August 1991 coup, it seems, because they could not. Six years of political and economic reform, some of it radical, had taken its toll on the capacity of the military to behave in a disciplined fashion; deep divisions within the military apparently operated at all levels of command and within all five services. When called upon to lend their support to the conspirators, therefore, leading members of the armed forces found themselves caught between conflicting loyalties and incapable of concerted action. Torn between orders to take up arms in support of "Acting President" Gennadi Yanaev and repeated pleas to join forces with the democrats, for the most part they did nothing at all. In so doing they contributed to the rapid unraveling of the conspiracy, but also, and in a way they could not have anticipated, to the collapse of the country they were pledged to defend.

Rumors of a military coup against the Gorbachev government circulated freely in the Soviet capital more than a year before the actual attempt to seize power. In March 1990, for example, two correspondents from the independent newspaper *Argumenty i fakty* quizzed General Gromov, the Kiev military district commander, about the possible formation of a military junta to displace the civilian leadership. In the opinion of the interviewers, Gromov, one of the Soviet Union's most popular officers, was a likely candidate to head such a group. Gromov dismissed the speculation as an "absolutely groundless stupidity," promoted by "certain circles for whom the armed forces under conditions of perestroika stick in their craw."[59] In an interview the following month with a Western journalist, former Warsaw Pact commander Marshal Viktor Kulikov pronounced predictions of a military-led coup "sheer fabrication."[60]

Such disclaimers notwithstanding, the rumors persisted. They gained fresh credibility in June 1990 when General A. M. Makashov, commander of the Volga-Ural military district and a candidate for the presidency of the Russian Federation, delivered a blistering attack against the policies of the existing government in an address to a conference of Russian Communist party officials in Moscow. Although he stopped short of proposing Gorbachev's ouster, the general condemned the inactivity of the Central Committee and the Politburo in defending the interests of the armed forces and affirmed that "we [the military] have no intention of giving in ideologically."[61] More ominously, Makashov concluded his remarks with an explicit warning to those he considered traitors to the Soviet cause:

> We understand that things are difficult for everyone. But, believe me, the Armed Forces are not to blame for the fact they are in such a difficult situation today. And in spite of everything we army communists cannot conceive the Union without Russia or Russia without the Union. And for this we will fight.[62]

In the wake of Makashov's extraordinary statement, which elicited a sharply negative response from the country's increasingly liberal and outspoken press, fears of a military putsch increased markedly. When no such attempt materialized, they subsided once more, only to reappear with renewed vigor in the fall.

In early September a number of newspapers reported the sudden deployment to Moscow of a combat-ready paratroop regiment ordinarily based in Ryazan, some three hours by train from the capital. Other units were also reported to be on the move, most of these in the direction of Moscow. When confronted with the reports, the Defense Ministry offered two explanations, neither of which proved especially persuasive to a media (and a population) that had come to expect some form of military intervention before the onset of winter. The first reason offered for the surprise deployments was that the troops were needed to help with the local potato harvest; the second, and equally incredible, explanation was that the units were scheduled to take part in the annual parade on Red Square commemorating the Bolshevik victory on November 7 and had simply arrived a little early.[63]

A parliamentary commission later claimed that the most probable explanation for the deployment of the Ryazan regiment, in particular, was to ensure order in the event of possible disturbances during a scheduled rally of prodemocracy forces in Moscow on September 16 and to engage in a show of force of sufficient scale to intimidate the demonstrators.[64] In the event, the Defense Ministry ordered the regiment to stand down and on September 18, two days after the rally, the unit returned to Ryazan without ever having made an appearance in the city center.

The commission also found that the deployments were not part of a conspiracy to mount a military coup; neither, however, were they undertaken to assist in the picking of potatoes or to prepare for the November parade. Predictably, Yazov remained faithful to the Defense Ministry's initial justifications and in the wake of the mini-crisis journalists close to the military took to the pages of *Krasnaya zvezda*, *Izvestiya*, and *Sovetskaya Rossiya* to argue his and the ministry's case.[65] It is probably safe to say that almost no one accepted the defense minister's explanation at face value.

From October to April, concerns over the military's possible participation in politics shifted from the fear that it might seek to dislodge Gorbachev and his supporters by force of arms to suspicions that the embattled Soviet president might make common cause with the military to disband the government and establish an extraconstitutional committee for "national salvation." In January 1991 disgruntled Communists loyal to Moscow had attempted to establish themselves as de facto governments in each of the Baltic republics by declaring the existence of such commissions and his critics suspected that Gorbachev, whose politics had veered to the right in recent months, might be tempted to do the same in Moscow.

When the Soviet leader tacked to the left again during April and May, such talk abated. It did not, however, cease entirely; it re-emerged in a curious fashion three months later in the immediate aftermath of the actual coup attempt, when some observers speculated that Gorbachev might have had a hand in the plot that resulted, contrary to expectation, in his confinement rather than in his selection as supreme leader of a reconstituted government. Others argued that, at a minimum, Gorbachev had allowed the conspiracy to unfold in order to entrap his enemies and to provide an appropriate pretext to move decisively against them. No evidence has yet appeared to substantiate either claim, however.

Given the several false alarms over the preceding fifteen months, when the conspirators in fact moved, declaring a state of emergency in the early morning hours of August 19, it is, perhaps, surprising that the coup attempt appeared to catch some of the Soviet leadership off guard, including Gorbachev, who was vacationing with his family at the Black Sea. That Yazov, in particular, had cast his lot with Yanaev and company—notwithstanding the former's repeated affirmations of support for the government, the constitution, and perestroika—must have come as a bitter disappointment to the Soviet president, who had appointed Yazov defense minister in 1987 over the heads of literally hundreds of officers with greater seniority and experience.

Almost immediately, however, it became apparent that whatever the defense minister's intentions, Soviet armed forces were not rushing to implement the instructions of the Emergency Committee to ensure compliance with its directives. The passivity of the military might have been at least in part a consequence of poor planning; the attempted coup bore all the marks of a conspiracy cobbled together in haste and without adequate preparation.[66] Important elements of the armed forces, as well as units of the Interior Ministry and the KGB, appear not to have been apprised of the exact timing of events, and had, therefore, little or no time to receive and process their orders and to take up their positions. Inexplicably, the Emergency Committee did not, for example, direct loyal units to arrest Boris Yeltsin and other prominent non- and anticommunists, nor did it order them to seize and occupy the legislative and executive headquarters of the Russian Federation, located less than a mile from the Kremlin.

More bad news was on the way. When Yeltsin, now installed in the so-called Russian White House, defied the Emergency Committee and declared its actions unconstitutional, he did so perched atop a tank—one of several such vehicles that had heeded the call of the Russian president (and of his chief military adviser, Colonel General Konstantin Kobets, former deputy chief of the General Staff) to ignore the orders of their superior officers and to embrace the cause of democracy.[67] As it turned out, units from three elite army divisions that the Defense Ministry had dispatched to Moscow to police the streets—the Taman Motorized Rifle Division, the 106th Airborne Division, and the Kantemirov Tank Division—had also defected and, according to press accounts, were on their way to the Russian White House to take up positions inside the barricades that had been hastily erected by Yeltsin's supporters.[68]

Of greater consequence, three senior officers broke ranks and refused to implement the orders of the Emergency Committee. Lieutenant General Viktor Samsonov, commander of the Leningrad

Military District, met with Mayor Anatoli Sobchak and agreed that his forces would neither take up positions inside the city limits nor use force against the civilian population.[69] Colonel General Yevgeni Shaposhnikov, commander-in-chief of the Soviet air force, also abandoned the conspirators, assuring the Russian parliament on August 19 that none of his forces would engage in any military action against those loyal to Yeltsin. General Pavel Grachev, commander of the country's airborne forces, had promised Shaposhnikov earlier that day that he, too, would issue no orders in support of the junta.[70]

The defections of Generals Samsonov, Shaposhnikov, and Grachev—together with chief of the General Staff Moiseyev's convenient absence from Moscow during the first two days of the coup attempt[71]—revealed the military's deep ambivalence about the actions of the Emergency Committee and further diminished the prospects for its success. While the splits within the military did not cause the coup attempt to collapse, they did contribute to its unraveling and provided Yeltsin and those who stood with him a much-needed political boost.

During his first day back in the capital, Gorbachev appointed Moiseyev acting defense minister to replace Yazov, who was placed under arrest (along with the six other surviving members of the Emergency Committee) on August 22 by the Russian prosecutor's office.[72] To replace Moiseyev at the General Staff, Gorbachev named General V. N. Lobov, head of the Frunze Military Academy; during the attempted coup Lobov, who had earlier served as chief of staff of the Warsaw Pact, had adopted a position of "nonrecognition" of the Emergency Committee.

The real purge of the armed forces began the following day, however, when the restored Soviet president, under pressure from Yeltsin, fired Moiseyev and appointed General Shaposhnikov as head of the Defense Ministry. Shaposhnikov, whose defection had contributed to the collapse of the conspiracy, began a thorough sweep of the military leadership that resulted in the arrest of several Defense Ministry officials and the cashiering of many more.[73] By mid-September, for example, Shaposhnikov had ordered the removal of nine of the fifteen members of the Defense Ministry Collegium, including most of the first deputy and deputy ministers of defense, and the forced retirement of several military district commanders. On December 7, again at the insistence of Yeltsin and his advisers, Gorbachev relieved Lobov of his duties as chief of the General Staff, installing in his stead Leningrad district commander Colonel General Samsonov. More personnel changes followed.

The following day, December 8, Yeltsin, Ukrainian president Leonid Kravchuk, and Belorussian Supreme Soviet chairman Stanislau Shushkevich announced the end of the USSR "as a subject of international law and a geopolitical reality" and declared the formation of the "Commonwealth of Independent States," or the CIS. Both Shaposhnikov and Samsonov remained in place, becoming, after Gorbachev's resignation as president of the Soviet Union, commander-in-chief of CIS military forces and chief of the General Staff of CIS Armed Forces, respectively.

With the lowering of the Soviet flag over the Kremlin on December 25, and its replacement with the standard of the Russian Federation, the USSR ceased to exist. At the same moment, as an object of contemporary inquiry, the study of *Soviet* civil-military relations also came to an end. At a second level, however, the story continues under radically different circumstances. As of this writing, relations between the military of the former Soviet Union and the government of the Russian Federation, which inherited much of the equipment and most of the personnel of the USSR's armed forces, seem more "consensual" than "conflictual" in nature, but the relationship is a young one and has yet to be tested. In this context it is perhaps useful to note that in the Russia of the 1990s, the only real certainty is change.

Chapter 5

Gorbachev, Security Policy, and the Soviet Collapse

COMING TO A BALANCED AND FAIR-MINDED ASSESSMENT OF THE role of Mikhail Gorbachev in the transformation of Soviet security policy between 1985 and 1991 is no simple matter. Whatever the perceived significance *at the time* of the Soviet leader's achievements in the areas of military policy and arms control, in particular, their consequence inevitably pales in importance when cast against the larger backdrop of radical social and political change set in motion by the Soviet Union's first—and last—great reformer. Compared to the collapse of the system he struggled so hard to preserve, what Gorbachev managed to achieve in engineering the most profound shift in Soviet military and arms control policies in the country's seventy-year history may seem, if not irrelevant, then of decidedly secondary importance.

Just as it would be a mistake, however, to ignore the fact that Gorbachev failed, ultimately, to attain many of the goals that he and others elaborated for the reform of Soviet security policy—most notably the failure to complete the revisions to military doctrine and the restructuring of the armed forces—so too would it be a mistake to dismiss as inconsequential the several very real products of those policies, which, despite the disappearance of the country in whose name the initiatives were undertaken, continue to exercise a vital influence on the development of regional and international security relations in the post–Cold War era.

THE GORBACHEV LEGACY

Most concretely, what remains of the Gorbachev legacy in security policy are three arms control agreements that the Soviet government concluded with the United States and NATO Europe between 1987 and 1991:

- *The INF Treaty* (December 1987). Under its terms, the United States and the Soviet Union agreed to dismantle and destroy 1,600 intermediate-range ballistic and cruise missiles, including some 900 deployed in NATO Europe and the USSR. The treaty contained what was at the time the most far-reaching provisions for monitoring compliance ever negotiated between the superpowers. Also eliminated were approximately 1,100 shorter-range missile systems (500–1,000 kilometers), deployed on the territory of the Federal Republic of Germany, East Germany, Poland, and Czechoslovakia, and in storage.

- *The CFE Treaty* (November 1990). Signed by sixteen NATO states and six members of the Warsaw Pact, the Treaty on Conventional Armed Forces in Europe places binding and complex restrictions on the number of tanks, armored personnel carriers, artillery pieces, and tactical aircraft each country can maintain within the agreed reduction zone. Arguably the most important consequence of the treaty was to deprive the Soviet Union (and its allies) of the ability to mount a credible surprise attack against NATO countries in Europe. The treaty remains in force, despite the dissolution of both the Warsaw Pact and the USSR in 1991, its obligations having been assumed on the Soviet side by seven of the "successor states"—the Russian Federation, Belarus, Ukraine, Moldova, Armenia, Georgia, and Azerbaijan.

- *The START Treaty* (July 1991). The Strategic Arms Reduction Treaty limits each side to a total of 1,600 long-range land- and sea-based ballistic missiles and heavy bombers; it also requires a 50 percent reduction in the number of so-called heavy, or large, Soviet ICBMs and mandates meaningful reductions—on the order of 15 percent for the United States and 25 percent for the Soviet Union—in the number of ballistic missile warheads, air-launched cruise missiles, and bombs permitted each side. Provisions for monitoring compliance are extensive and intrusive. The collapse of the Soviet Union in December 1991 rendered the fate of START uncertain; in May 1992, the four republics of the former USSR with nuclear weapons on their soil—Russia, Belarus, Ukraine, and Kazakhstan—formally conveyed their willingness to abide by the agreement's terms. In October 1992 the U.S. Senate and the Russian parliament approved the treaty; Belarus and Kazakhstan followed suit early in 1993. As of this writing, the Ukrainian *Rada* is still considering the accord and while ratification of START seems more likely than not, the outcome of the debate cannot be taken for granted.

The agreements negotiated during Gorbachev's tenure revolutionized superpower security relations in at least three ways: by eliminating hundreds of missiles and thousands of warheads on both sides; by opening the door to future agreements by which U.S. and Russian strategic arsenals might be further reduced on the order of 50 to 60 percent; and by legitimizing the most intrusive of inspection regimes in order to assure compliance and build mutual confidence. Of the U.S.–Soviet arms control accords of the 1970s, only the 1972 ABM Treaty, with its outright ban on the deployment of nationwide anti-ballistic missile systems, compares favorably with the three treaties concluded between 1987 and 1991. Were this the sum total of Gorbachev's contributions to security policy, his record would stand alone—far surpassing that of Leonid Brezhnev, before Gorbachev the Kremlin's most ardent deal-maker.

Of greater significance than the arms control agreements, however, are the several tectonic shifts in geopolitics that occurred between 1989 and 1991 that upended regional and international relations, ended the Cold War, and, if less directly attributable to the Soviet president than the INF, CFE, and START treaties, probably did more to secure his place in history.

The first of these developments—*the de-Sovietization and de-communization of Eastern Europe*—began in August 1989 as Polish voters elected Warsaw's first noncommunist government of the postwar era. Four months later communist governments in four other Eastern European countries—Hungary, East Germany, Czechoslovakia, and Bulgaria—had been swept aside by large, loosely organized popular movements emboldened by the example of Poland's peaceful revolution. In December even the highly repressive regime of Nicolae Ceauşescu was overthrown, and Ceauşescu and his wife murdered, in a violent coup d'état that brought to power an unstable coalition of anticommunists, "reformed" communists, political opportunists, and members of the dreaded Securitate, Ceauşescu's internal security apparatus. With the election in 1992 of a noncommunist government in Albania, the most remote and isolated of the continent's communist countries, the revolutionary process within Europe's "socialist community" was essentially complete.

Gorbachev's role in the liberation of Eastern Europe remains a matter of some controversy. While it is doubtless true that the Soviet leader, in calling for the "renewal of socialism" in Eastern Europe, never anticipated that the reform process he championed would soon give way to revolution, it is also true that at no point—before, during, or after the Polish political crisis of the spring and summer of 1989—did he threaten Soviet military intervention to preserve the hegemony of the Eastern Europe's communist parties or to secure Moscow's hegemony within the region.

This stands, of course, in sharp contrast to the actions of Khrushchev and Brezhnev, who, when faced with similar challenges in the 1956 Hungarian Revolution and the 1968 "Prague Spring" in Czechoslovakia, dispatched Soviet (and in the latter case Soviet and Warsaw Pact) forces to squelch dissent, "restore order," and preserve communist orthodoxy.

At a minimum, then, Gorbachev's posture toward the liberation of Eastern Europe should be construed as permissive in character; unable to conceive of a real alternative—save, perhaps, direct and massive military intervention—to the reformist course he himself had articulated, he chose to make a virtue out of necessity. A more compelling interpretation is that by fall 1989, with the outcome of the Polish case as precedent, Gorbachev and his closest foreign policy advisers, Foreign Minister Shevardnadze and Politburo member Aleksandr Yakovlev, understood only too well that other challenges to communist rule in Eastern Europe were likely to materialize in the near future. And that having failed to halt the emergence of a democratic opposition in Poland, they could hardly, at this late juncture, reverse course and seek to apply a different standard to political developments elsewhere throughout the bloc. Rather than oppose Eastern Europe's democratic revival, then, Soviet leaders tried to steer an untested middle course, at once encouraging (or at least not resisting) reform, while also seeking to preserve with their erstwhile allies something of the special, or "fraternal," character of their earlier relations.

The decision not to oppose the decommunization of the region was also consistent with the logic of the "new political thinking" and Gorbachev's European policy after 1988, both of which held as integral and fundamental to the Soviet Union's new foreign policy a commitment to respect the right of all states to determine the character of their respective political and economic systems and not to interfere in their internal affairs. Having elaborated in some detail what Foreign Ministry spokesman Gennadi Gerasimov termed in October 1989 "the Sinatra Doctrine,"[1] only with the greatest difficulty could Gorbachev revisit the decision to set Eastern Europe free—and only then at the risk of subverting the entire architecture of his foreign and security policies, a price he was unwilling to pay.

The second development that revolutionized world politics was *the unification of Germany* in 1990. And here it is difficult to regard Gorbachev's role in events as anything other than central. While the collapse of the East German state, like the overthrow of communism in other parts of Eastern Europe, caught Soviet leaders flat-footed and proceeded much more rapidly, once underway, than they had anticipated or would have preferred, the relative orderliness with which the process of unification unfolded had much to do with Gorbachev's conduct during this tumultuous period. Of particular significance was his decision in February 1990 to endorse the "2 Plus 4" formula for the negotiations that produced the final settlement on Germany,[2] to acquiesce in the Federal Republic's virtual absorption of its eastern neighbor (largely on terms set out by Bonn), and to accede to Western demands that a united Germany become a full-fledged member of the NATO alliance.

While the case can be made that Gorbachev had precious few cards to play once the East German political scene failed to stabilize in the aftermath of the collapse of the government of Erich Honecker and Willi Stoph in October-November 1989, it is also true that the Soviet Union was not without leverage. Nearly 400,000 Soviet troops remained on East German soil throughout 1990 and although unable to impose a settlement altogether to their liking, at the very least the Soviets could have significantly prolonged the 2 Plus 4 negotiations by rejecting this or that Western proposal or by escalating or suddenly changing their demands, much as they had done at other negotiating forums throughout the Cold War.

They did neither. That they did not is largely attributable to Gorbachev and, to a lesser extent, Shevardnadze, both of whom, it seems, had decided that there was more to be gained by demonstrating to the West, and particularly to the United States, their readiness to cooperate in the resolution of this extraordinarily central and historically sensitive security issue than there was by trying to obstruct progress in defense of a set of foreign policy goals they had already rejected and were then in the process of abandoning.

Expressed differently, for Gorbachev and those closest to him, the "game" in world politics had changed profoundly in the four years that separated his election as CPSU general secretary and the collapse of Soviet power in Europe; if prior to 1985 the overarching objective of Soviet foreign policy had been to strengthen the "positions of socialism" at the expense of the West, by 1989 a new goal— to secure Soviet admission to the elaborate collection of institutions that constituted the Western economic and political system—had arisen to take its place.[3] It followed, therefore, that working cooperatively with the United States and its allies on an issue as vital to the West as German unification could redound to Moscow's advantage in material ways.

The third critical development for which Gorbachev could claim considerable credit was *the radical upturn in U.S.–Soviet relations*.[4] While the détente between Washington and Moscow owed much to and proceeded in tandem with the collapse of communism in Eastern Europe and the unification of Germany, by the time of the Bush-Gorbachev summit in December 1989 at Malta the trend toward better and more cooperative superpower relations was already apparent and acquiring a momentum of its own. Relations continued to improve throughout the remainder of Gorbachev's term in office, as the two sides made slow but steady progress in START and found themselves in substantial agreement on a host of other, previously divisive issues, such as the desirability of a negotiated peace in Nicaragua and El Salvador and a reduction in the level of Soviet military and economic assistance to the Castro regime in Cuba. The Soviet leader also repeatedly affirmed for the benefit of the U.S. officials his thoroughgoing commitment to radical, but peaceful, reform and his determination to stay the course, whatever the need for the occasional feint to the right or the left to appease his domestic political opponents.

Increasingly, it seems, the administration came to believe that between hope and chaos in the USSR stood the embattled figure of Gorbachev and a handful of his supporters—a notion that the politically astute Soviet president did little to discourage. Dealing with Gorbachev was also easier and far more predictable for Washington than trying to negotiate with the collection of political actors eager to displace the Soviet president. So successful did Gorbachev prove to be in linking his own fate to that of U.S.–Soviet relations more generally that when, in December 1991, the leaders of the three Slavic republics of the USSR—Boris Yeltsin of Russia, Leonid Kravchuk of Ukraine, and Stanislau Shushkevich of Byelorussia— announced the creation of the Commonwealth of Independent States (and the effective end of the Soviet Union), the Bush administration seemed momentarily caught off guard and reluctant to embrace the new reality.

More than a year after his involuntary retirement, Gorbachev remains, in the United States at least, an immensely popular figure and an influential, if unofficial, ambassador of good will for the new Russia; this stands in sharp contrast to his stature within the former USSR, where his political views are neither sought nor, when they are offered, accorded much of a hearing.

THE WHY AND HOW OF GORBACHEV'S POLICIES

At least as interesting as the *what* of Gorbachev's policies are the *why* and the *how*. Given that the Soviet leader had an enormous, if controversial, impact on the content of the Kremlin's arms control and military policies between 1985 and 1991, what factor, or factors, could have impelled him to undertake what from the beginning constituted such a high-risk strategy of reform? And how did he propose to implement this radical agenda, in light of the many and predictable obstacles that he was certain to encounter both at home and abroad as he undertook to engineer shifts in policy of this magnitude?

The Economic Crisis

As this study has sought to demonstrate, if there was one central impetus to the reform of the Soviet system, including the need to rethink in fundamental ways the array of instruments by which the leadership sought to provide for the country's physical security, it was the dismal and declining performance of the economy. Among those who have sought to understand the causes of the "second Russian revolution," most are in agreement that the profound weakness of the Soviet economic system played a major part in sensitizing the leadership to the need for a broadly based program of reform; students of Soviet politics disagree, however, over what importance to attach to the economic crisis, relative to other factors.

For example, in seeking to establish a link between cause and effect, conservative observers tend to underscore the importance to the reform process of the Reagan administration's political and military challenge—the decision to "get tough with the Russians" in the early 1980s—as expressed in the form of the U.S. defense buildup between 1981 and 1986 and Washington's determination to negotiate with Moscow from a "position of strength." Liberal analysts, by contrast, often point to the declining appeal of communism generally and to the cumulative effects of what an earlier generation of Soviet authorities characterized as a conscious Western policy to subvert the socialist community ideologically through the importation of such "radical" values as consumerism and respect for individual human rights. Widespread corruption, lack of interest in or hostility to the existing political order on part of the population, and the reemergence of ethnic, national, and religious tensions are also cited as contributing factors to the decision by Soviet leaders to sanction far-reaching reforms.

Careful consideration of each of these factors is, of course, essential to a full and informed understanding of the causes of the Soviet turn toward radical reform. The argument that has been developed in the course of this study, however, is different. It is that none of these factors, taken either individually or in combination, is sufficiently powerful to account for the observed phenomenon. Moreover, each was either *derivative of* or *compounded by* the larger and preexisting problem of the continual decline in Soviet economic performance.[5] In other words, of the several explanations that have been offered for Gorbachev's willingness to embrace progressively more revolutionary solutions to the problems he confronted, only the country's deepening economic crisis meets the two criteria—that the explanation advanced constitutes both a necessary and a sufficient condition—central to establishing a convincing link between cause and effect.

Economic Reform as a Catalyst for Revolution

Since the mid-1960s, successive Soviet leaders—from Aleksei Kosygin to Yuri Andropov—had sought, without notable success, to restore the health and vigor of the Soviet Union's flagging economy, principally by improving labor productivity and making more efficient use of the country's vast resources. In the language of the economists, having largely exhausted the potential for additional extensive growth, which typified the development of the Soviet industrial base from the 1920s to the 1950s, Kremlin planners spent much of the 1960s and 1970s seeking to substitute growth parameters characteristic of countries experiencing intensive economic development, such as the United States, West Germany, and Japan.

These efforts produced extremely modest results. Whereas in the 1950s Soviet growth rates had equaled and in some cases exceeded those of the advanced industrial economies of the West, by the mid-1970s Moscow was falling further and further behind. In the early 1980s the Soviet economy was basically stagnant. By the time of Gorbachev's election as CPSU general secretary in 1985 the prognosis of the country's economists was that without substantial reform of the system the USSR could well experience "negative" growth.

The new leadership was advised to "streamline" the operation of the economy, although the economists differed sharply among themselves over whether the goals of improving efficiency and productivity would best be served by further centralizing the immense apparatus of the economy or by breaking it up into smaller, more manageable units. Some advisers urged a reform of the pricing system; the bolder among them even suggested the introduction of limited market-like mechanisms in some sectors in order to spur competition. In the mid-1980s, however, few were prepared to counsel the kind of economic "shock therapy" that was to be experienced by Poland in the early 1990s and, somewhat later, by Russia under Boris Yeltsin.

The failure of the Soviet economy to respond to any of these palliatives meant that the vast majority of the country's population, already living in a seemingly perpetual state of semipoverty, could anticipate no near- to medium-term improvement in their living standards. Deprived of the belief that whatever their current hardships, life was certain to improve tomorrow or the day after—a venerable article of faith among earlier generations of Soviets—the people of the USSR grew progressively more alienated from the system; increasingly they withdrew into the world of private culture, deriving what personal rewards and satisfaction they could from family and close friends and doing their best to minimize contact and association with the largely lifeless structures of the communist-dominated public apparatus.

The cumulative effect on the system of interlocking institutions that had sustained Communist party rule since 1917 was devastating, depriving the party and its many instruments of social, political, and economic control of the best and brightest of the country's population. It was this explosive combination of economic privation and the profound social alienation that this poverty induced that compelled Gorbachev to consider a much more far-reaching program of reform than even he had thought necessary when his Politburo comrades selected him to head the Soviet Communist party in March 1985. In short, something had to be done—and fast.

But what, precisely? For Gorbachev, especially during the first four years of his leadership, the answer was to renew socialism by "unleashing" its latent "potential" through a mix of material incentives, moral suasion, and appeals to duty, patriotism, and self-sacrifice. Thus, in 1985 he and others in the party's senior leadership unveiled plans to "accelerate" the country's economic performance by restoring labor discipline, rewarding hard work, eliminating waste, and reducing bureaucratic interference.

There followed in rapid succession the policies of perestroika and glasnost. Each was intended to attack a different aspect of the problem confronting the Soviet Union; each was also designed to reinforce the other and thereby advance or accelerate the process of reform.

Narrowly conceived, the purposes of perestroika were first to articulate and then to put in place an ambitious but realizable program for the transformation of the command economy, largely by freeing Soviet industry from the stultifying effects of centralization and bureaucratization. The key to the success of that effort, Gorbachev and his advisers believed, lay in making Soviet enterprises more accountable and therefore more efficient. Those enterprises that succeeded both in cutting costs and in retaining or expanding their market share would survive and profit; those that did neither would be allowed to fail.

Applied selectively and never rigorously enforced, perestroika did little more than introduce an additional layer of confusion into the process of central planning, complicate relations between enterprise managers and their superiors in Moscow (which were already poor), and exacerbate existing inefficiencies. By 1989 the prospects for recovery were, if anything, even more dismal than they had been in 1987 when Gorbachev first unveiled his eagerly awaited plan to reenergize the country's staggering economy.

To make matters worse, Gorbachev's decision in 1987 to ease press censorship and permit (limited) public debate of the ills besetting the Soviet system turned out to be an enormously consequential act, stimulating in short order a broad range of attacks on the policies of the Soviet government and on the perceived excesses of the Communist party. Once uncorked, moreover, this particular genie proved impossible to control. As the years passed, the press grew progressively bolder and more independent, criticizing by name, for example, political leaders—both alive and dead—for their part in policy decisions to which the editors of a given newspaper or journal took exception (viz., the Soviet invasion of Afghanistan in 1979). Even *Pravda*, long the party's faithful mouthpiece, joined the chorus of criticism, partly out of conviction and partly to keep pace with far more liberal newspapers and journals—such as *Literaturnaya gazeta* and *Moscow News*—which were leading the charge for an open and honest Soviet press.

Such license was unprecedented in the Soviet experience. And while it may have served to convince the population that dramatic social and political change was indeed afoot in the USSR, from the perspective of the leadership the results were altogether disastrous, undermining the Communist party's already fragile claims to legitimacy by further sullying its reputation as the tireless and principled defender of the interests of the working class. Far from restoring faith in the reformability of the system, in other words, the primary impact of glasnost was to reveal just the opposite: that the party, together with the entire system that it had spawned, was not only corrupt, but beyond redemption.

Now in a race against time, Gorbachev embraced more and more radical solutions in a determined effort to stay abreast of the demands for radical change. During the first half of 1990, for example, he sanctioned the elimination of Article Six of the Soviet constitution that guaranteed the Communist party's hold on political power, convinced the Congress of People's Deputies first to create and then to elect him to the post of executive president, and effectively deprived the Politburo of any real power by reassigning most of its duties to government ministers loyal to him in his capacity as head of state. In June 1990, with Gorbachev's assent, the Congress of People's Deputies passed legislation to assure freedom of the press; the following month, Gorbachev ordered an end to the censorship of Soviet radio and television. In the economic sphere, the Soviet leader manifested comparable impatience, at least initially, urging enactment of the so-called 500-Day Plan for the prompt marketization and privatization of the Soviet economy, before losing his nerve and rejecting the plan later in the year.

The Link between Economics and
the Reform of Soviet Security Policy

The visible unraveling of the Soviet political and economic system between 1987 and 1990 made all the more urgent Gorbachev's public, if equivocal, commitment to the reform of Soviet military doctrine and the restructuring of the country's armed forces. Only by freeing up and reallocating significant additional resources, such as those devoted to the maintenance of the military, might the leadership be able to arrest the dramatic deterioration in economic conditions and thus begin to stabilize the political environment. While the option of downsizing the Soviet military in order to improve the prospects for economic reform had been available to Gorbachev since 1985, by the Soviet leader's third year in power the merely attractive had become imperative. The issue, as always, was how to reduce military spending on a major scale, while also safeguarding the country's security.

As elaborated at length in the body of the text, Gorbachev came to rely on a strategy composed of three elements to implement safely his agenda for the reform and reduction of the Soviet military:

Adopt a New Calculus Regarding International Relations. Previous Soviet conceptions of international politics relied heavily on the notion of two unalterably opposed "world systems" locked in a state of perpetual, if mostly nonviolent, conflict. At the head of each community stood one of the two superpowers: the United States, protector and guarantor of the interests of world capitalism; and the Soviet Union, reliable ally of the international working class. In this contest for global hegemony, the security of one camp necessarily came at the expense of the other. The competition, in other words, could only be "zero sum." Accretions to the military, political, and economic power of the Soviet Union served the cause of peace and security by reducing the capacity of the imperialist community of states to impose its will on others and to foment international mischief and counterrevolution.

Gorbachev discarded this class-based architecture as a relic of the past, rendered inappropriate by the development and the subsequent widespread deployment of nuclear weapons. The nuclear danger, he insisted, transcended class and threatened civilization as a whole. Human values, the Soviet leader argued, must replace appeals to solidarity based on economic circumstance. In the nuclear age, Gorbachev repeatedly proclaimed, security could only be mutual.

With this fundamental revision of Soviet dogma, Gorbachev was able to distance himself from the foreign and military policies of his predecessors and to offer far-reaching proposals for ending the military competition between the superpowers (and between NATO and the Warsaw Pact). Since nuclear weapons threatened all countries with physical extinction, reducing the danger of nuclear war advanced the interests of all countries, capitalist and socialist alike.

Early in his leadership, between 1986 and 1988, Gorbachev conditioned his offers to facilitate the transition from confrontation to cooperation in international politics on the willingness of the West to recognize the legitimacy of Soviet foreign policy interests and to negotiate with Moscow on the basis of equality and mutual respect. Later in his tenure, as the domestic crisis intensified, Gorbachev lost leverage in negotiations with the West, forcing him to acquiesce in a series of outcomes not altogether to his liking, such as the INF Treaty, the decommunization of Eastern Europe, and the unification of Germany on essentially Western terms.

Prior to the fall of the Berlin Wall in November 1989, however, Gorbachev could, and did, insist to his domestic critics that agreements concluded with the West that some might consider a defeat for Soviet diplomacy actually constituted important victories. Among other advantages, they opened the way for more consequential accords with Moscow's former adversaries—such as the CFE and START agreements—which, when concluded, would bring to an end the ruinous military competition and thus liberate resources for the rebuilding of Soviet society.

Eliminate Both the Image and the Reality of the "Soviet Threat." A second element of Gorbachev's strategy was the determination to deprive the West, and particularly the United States, of the ability to portray the Soviet Union as a dangerous and growing threat to international peace and security. His foreign policy pronouncements, coupled with progress in arms control and the success of his several bilateral meetings with Presidents Reagan and Bush between 1985 and 1989, were of critical importance in this regard. By delivering on the promise to revolutionize both the tone and the substance of Soviet diplomacy, he undercut the political rationale developed by Western governments for sustaining their high rates of defense spending. With a decline in Western expenditures, Gorbachev would be in a much stronger political position at home to lobby for cuts in Soviet military spending and to argue in favor of actual reductions in the country's armed forces—both of which he did.

Gorbachev's decision to reduce Soviet armed forces unilaterally by some 500,000 troops, announced in December 1988 before the United Nations, was designed both to affirm the seriousness of the Soviet commitment to downsize its armed forces (in keeping with the logic of the "new political thinking") and to stimulate reciprocal concessions on the part of the United States and its NATO allies. And while it failed in the latter purpose, at least over the short term, it did serve to further the perception that the Soviet military threat to Europe (and, therefore, to the United States) was not what it had been.

By moving to eliminate Western fears that the Soviet Union stood poised to undertake offensive military operations against the NATO countries, the risk of war was itself diminished, making it easier politically for Gorbachev to argue to his own military that the Soviet Union could, without great risk, curb defense spending and persist in the effort to reorganize the armed forces along more defensive and less threatening lines.

Much of what Gorbachev sought to attain in his foreign and security policies between 1986 and 1991 was keyed, therefore, to what he was trying to achieve domestically—above all, a prompt reallocation of resources from the defense sector to such nonmilitary activities as investment and consumption of sufficient scope so as to reinvigorate an economy now perilously close to collapsing altogether.

Substitute "Need-driven" for "Threat-driven" Parameters for the Sizing of the Armed Forces, the Procurement of Weapons, and the Development of Doctrine. Reducing the perceived likelihood of war involving the Soviet Union enabled Gorbachev to press aggressively for the adoption by the military of the twin precepts of "reasonable sufficiency" and "defensive defense."

In essence, the Soviet leader argued that the very high rate at which the Defense Ministry acquired military equipment of all kinds—from nuclear delivery systems to armored personnel carriers—was unnecessary by any reasonable standard of sufficiency, given the remote possibility of *any* attack against the Soviet Union by the United States and its allies. Moreover, because procurement exceeded the requirements of defense, it also served to provoke the West and to spur it on to greater effort, thus perpetuating a military competition that neither side could win but that neither could afford to lose. At a minimum, the enormous production runs of the Soviet armaments industry amounted to a colossal waste of resources; at the extreme, they actually endangered the security of the state by providing a pretext for the more advanced military industries of the West to develop, test, and deploy new and ever more capable weapons systems that degraded the military utility of the Soviet conventional and nuclear arsenals. The United States' SDI effort was perhaps the prime example of this phenomenon, from Gorbachev's perspective.

To bring the situation under control, Gorbachev directed the General Staff of the armed forces to discard the previous standard of conventional (i.e., non-nuclear) military effectiveness—the capacity to defeat in relatively short order any possible combination of adversaries through large-scale offensive military action—and to prepare plans that would enable the Soviet Union to maintain only as many armed forces and only as much equipment as the military leadership believed necessary to mount effective *defensive* operations. The General Staff dutifully prepared such plans, submitting them to the Soviet president and to the country's parliament during fall 1990.

The reluctance of the military fully to implement Gorbachev's directives in this area—best symbolized by its spirited defense of the need to maintain the ability to mount "counteroffensive" operations within a generalized commitment to "defensive defense"—should not obscure the larger point that had Gorbachev continued in office (and had his country endured) most of the military reforms that he sponsored would have been implemented, the passive resistance of the General Staff notwithstanding.

THE FAILURE OF THE REFORM PROGRAM

Of course, Gorbachev did not continue in office and the Soviet Union did not endure. Roughly a year after the General Staff's submission of its program for the comprehensive reform of the Soviet military, the USSR ceased to exist as legal entity, replaced by a loose association of sovereign republics struggling to overcome the catastrophic consequences of seventy-five years of communist misrule.

In seeking to account for an event as dramatic and significant as the disappearance of one of the world's two great military powers, it is important to distinguish between factors that should be considered central to the collapse and those that surely contributed to or accelerated the country's undoing but did not cause it.

If, as this analysis asserts, the most important impetus to the reform of the Soviet system was the manifest need to revitalize and restructure the economy, then the most convincing explanation for the expiration of the USSR must be the failure of the Gorbachev reforms to generate anything approaching measurable and sustainable economic growth. Just as the decline in Soviet economic performance, both real and anticipated, had given rise to modest and, subsequently, to revolutionary demands for social and political change, so too did Gorbachev's inability to deliver on his promises embolden those who had lost faith in the renewability of socialism to seek its overthrow rather than its repair. Had the system begun to respond to Gorbachev's directives—in other words, had the Soviet leader succeeded at least in stemming the country's slide toward economic ruin—the story might well have ended differently.

In this sense, then, the marked upsurge in nationalist sentiment and in religiously and ethnically based violence, the collapse of morale within the Soviet armed forces, the rise of Boris Yeltsin and the democratic movement in Russia, even the creation of the Commonwealth of Independent States, may properly be attributed, at least in part, to the dismal record of perestroika and to the release, as a direct consequence of the regime's liberalization, of long-suppressed and extremely powerful social forces previously held in check by a government both able and willing to suppress dissent at the point of a gun.

It is well beyond the scope of this study to examine in detail why the reform program advanced by Gorbachev in fits and starts between 1985 and 1991 failed ultimately to save the USSR. It is perhaps sufficient in this context to take note of the powerful combination of factors—most having to do with the nature of the Soviet economic and political system that Gorbachev inherited—that conspired to frustrate his plans.

Most immediately, of course, it was the inability of Gorbachev's perestroika to spark the Soviet Union's economic recovery that sealed the fate of the old union. Their confidence in the existing system now thoroughly exhausted, the people of the USSR proved largely indifferent to the fate of the country and did nothing to prolong its existence. At a more aggregated level of analysis, it was the perceived nonreformability of the system as a whole—the conviction that the only sure road to recovery was to dismantle the myriad institutions of Soviet rule in their entirety—that led to the regime's collapse and to the unraveling of the Union.

Why this should have been the case is difficult to pinpoint. It may, however, have had something to do both with the reality of the situation—that is, the system *was* difficult to reform—and with the problem of relative deprivation: having learned a great deal since 1985 about the world beyond their borders, especially the marked difference in living standards between the USSR and the developed West, the people of the Soviet Union simply lost patience with the glacial pace of change and by 1991 were prepared to embrace the most radical of reform agendas, including the dismantling of the state itself.

The reluctance of the Communist party to reform itself—in particular, to relinquish its perquisites of power—and to commit itself wholeheartedly to the task of social and economic renewal could not have helped matters. Revelations of the CPSU's sordid past proved enormously costly in this regard, fatally undermining the party's claims that, whatever its shortcomings over seventy-plus years as the country's ruling party, it had consistently acted in defense of the interests of the Soviet working class and that it alone possessed the requisite dedication, skill, and experience to lead the people to a brighter and more prosperous future.

Whatever the precise interplay of events and personalities—the definitive story of the Soviet Union's collapse has yet to be written—by the time of Gorbachev's return to Moscow on the night of August 22, 1991, following the collapse of the conspiracy to remove him from power, the days of the old Union were clearly numbered. Even before the attempted coup, Gorbachev was convinced that the Soviet Union, as it was then constituted, could not endure and that a new entity would have to be created to take its place. What the

Soviet leader appears not to have anticipated was that this alternative political form—the Commonwealth of Independent States—would be erected without his participation and, in fact, over his strident objections. Gorbachev's time had run out.

THE COLLAPSE OF THE SOVIET UNION AND THE PROBLEM OF CHANGE IN INTERNATIONAL RELATIONS

The outright collapse of the Soviet Union as a sovereign state poses a number of important, if perplexing, questions for students of world politics. What, for example, does this unusual event tell us about the way we understand both the structure and the operation of the international political system? War, Robert Gilpin reminds us, is the traditional mechanism for transformative political change, including such consequential developments as the disappearance of major countries through conquest, absorption by others, and domestic revolution.[6] How, then, do we account for change of this magnitude, given that it occurred without recourse to force on the part of the Soviet Union's principal adversaries and, to date, without a nationwide civil war?

A second task is to explore, at a more theoretical level, what Gorbachev was trying to achieve in sponsoring the thoroughgoing reform of the Soviet system, especially during his last several years in office. And what was the connection, if any, between Gorbachev's domestic agenda, particularly between 1989 and 1991, and the nature of the international political and military order of which the Soviet Union was so much a part?

These are complex questions, the study of which is certain to preoccupy analysts of international relations and comparative politics for years to come. Coming, however, at the end of a book devoted to an examination of Soviet foreign and military policies under Gorbachev, they can, at best, be framed in the space that remains. The purpose of this final section, then, is less to answer this cluster of questions than it is to offer some admittedly preliminary observations, based on the book's findings, about the larger processes at work in the Soviet Union's collapse and the possible implications of that graceless fall for the way we think about the issue of change in world politics.

On the connection between change and organized inter- and intrastate violence, what the Soviet example suggests is that we have limited ourselves analytically by constructing an excessively narrow or parsimonious definition of war. Particularly in retrospect, it is difficult to regard the forty-plus years of U.S.–Soviet relations between the unveiling of the Truman Doctrine in 1947 and the fall of the Berlin Wall in 1989 as anything other than a period of prolonged systemic warfare, fought for the most part with an elaborate assortment of economic and political weapons. When the conflict between Washington and Moscow did turn violent, as it did in Korea in the 1950s and Vietnam in the 1960s and 1970s, U.S. and Soviet allies bore the brunt of the human, if not the material, costs. The term we assigned to this novel kind of rivalry—the Cold War—turns out to have been prescient.

What kept the Cold War from turning *really* hot across these four decades, it seems, was the paralytic effect of nuclear weapons, which imposed on the two superpowers new and altogether unprecedented constraints on the use of force.[7] Certainly by the mid-1950s, with the acquisition by Washington and Moscow of deliverable thermonuclear weapons, the option for either country to initiate hostilities in the expectation of emerging victorious had simply disappeared, occasional rhetoric to the contrary notwithstanding. One principal effect of the nuclear revolution was to limit each side to a strategy for the defeat of its rival that effectively ruled out the direct application of military power.

Whether the United States and the Soviet Union would have come to blows—absent this constraint—can never be determined. The more important point, in any event, is that after the deployment of megaton-range weapons they could not resort to war without almost certainly destroying themselves in the process.

Deprived of this reliable and familiar vehicle for the safeguarding of national security, both countries developed other ways to protect and advance their interests. Moscow, for example, in the 1960s and 1970s lent substantial financial and ideological support to so-called wars of national liberation and, later, to terrorist groups of various political stripes whose preferred targets were the West's public figures, economic interests, and military installations. For its part, the United States funneled enormous amounts of aid and money to scores of anticommunist groups over the forty years of bipolar competition and, through its intelligence services, often took a more direct hand in seeking to influence events in politically volatile regions. Each superpower also concluded a number of bilateral and multilateral alliances with friendly states, all ostensibly defensive in character, to secure its interests, communicate commitment, and ward off would-be opponents.

It was, however, Washington's success in denying the Soviet Union entry into the array of U.S.–led international economic institutions—the World Bank, the International Monetary Fund (IMF), the General Agreement on Tariffs and Trade (GATT), and the Organization for Economic Cooperation and Development (OECD)—that extracted the greatest cumulative toll on Moscow and on the community of socialist states it sought to nourish. The negative impact of the West's economic boycott on the Soviet Union and its allies, made all the more effective by the trade restrictions developed by and monitored through the Coordinating Committee for Multilateral Export Controls (CoCom), is difficult to overestimate.

Together, these steps deprived the socialist community of access to the larger system of international finance, trade, and commerce that the United States created in the aftermath of World War II and contributed in absolutely vital ways to that community's slow but ineluctable economic decline. Foreign Minister Shevardnadze admitted as much when he confessed late in his tenure that whatever else previous Soviet leaders, from Stalin to Andropov, thought they were doing, they were not creating an international economic and political system to rival that of the United States and its allies. The truth, Shevardnadze admitted, was that there was but one global system and that Moscow and its clients had been frozen out.

War, waged by other means, is still war. The struggle waged by the two superpowers was a conflict fought in slow motion, with quarter given, but on a global scale. It consumed enormous resources and cost thousands of lives. It defined the essential character of international relations for the better part of two generations. It also produced a victor—albeit one economically drained and without a clear organizing principle for the conduct of foreign policy in this new, post–Cold War world.

If, as Shevardnadze himself has suggested, the purpose of Gorbachev's foreign and domestic policies sometime after the midpoint of his career as president was to restore the Soviet Union's economic and political vitality, but not to revive the fading fortunes of communism on a global scale, how are we to understand the Soviet leader's experiment with reform? What was the distinction in Gorbachev's mind between socialism at home and socialism abroad? How could he and other Soviet leaders separate the two?

In an elegant essay published in 1990, C. John Ikenberry and Charles A. Kupchan advance an intriguing explanation of the process by which extremely powerful countries, such as the United States became after 1945, deploy their power.[8] They term the process "socialization." By altering the substantive beliefs of leaders in secondary nations, they argue, hegemonic states significantly enhance (and prolong) their influence within the international system. "Hegemonic control," they write,

> emerges when foreign elites buy into the hegemon's vision of the international order and accept it as their own—that is, when they internalize the norms and value orientations espoused by the hegemon and accept its normative claims about the nature of the international system. These norms and value orientations occupy the analytic dimension that lie between deep philosophical beliefs about human nature and more narrow beliefs about what set of policies will maximize short-term interests, and they therefore serve to guide state behavior and shape the agenda from which elites choose specific policies. Power is thus exercised through a process of socialization in which the norms and value orientations of leaders in secondary states change and more closely reflect those of the dominant state.[9]

And when do "the norms and value orientations of leaders in secondary states" change? Ikenberry and Kupchan argue that socialization occurs most often after wars and political crises, "periods marked by international turmoil and restructuring as well as the fragmentation of ruling coalitions and legitimacy crises at the domestic level." Such crises create environments "in which elites seek alternatives to existing norms that have been discredited by events and in which new norms offer opportunities for political gains and coalitional realignment."[10]

If, as this analysis asserts, the postwar rivalry between the United States and the USSR was indeed a contest for hegemony, and if by the late 1980s the Soviet leadership understood on some profound level that Washington had bested Moscow in that competition, then a potentially useful way to think about the larger purposes of Gorbachev's policies—especially in the period after the liberation of Eastern Europe—is by reference to the concept of hegemonic socialization.

As the endgame between the United States and the Soviet Union came into sharp relief, Gorbachev, having abandoned the fiction of an alternative international system made up of a collection of like-minded communist states, sought in essence to negotiate the entry of the Soviet Union into the Western-led community. To facilitate that process, he discarded many of the most hallowed precepts of existing Soviet foreign policy, including a belief in the zero-sum nature of world politics and an interpretation of international relations grounded in the concept of class (rather than interest and power). At the same time, he endorsed several features of the U.S.–dominated community of states—such as the democratization of political life, respect for the rule of law, and the superiority of market-oriented over centrally planned economies—that an earlier generation of Soviet leaders had either dismissed as bourgeois affectations or denounced as subversive.

The conditions that Ikenberry and Kupchan cite as conducive to elite socialization were all present in the Soviet case. The period between 1989 and 1991, in particular, was one of "international turmoil and restructuring"; within the USSR "the ruling coalition"—the CPSU—had become fragmented and Gorbachev was confronted with a legitimacy crisis of the first order. In seeking access to and membership in the most important of the West's institutions, the Soviet leader was pursuing a fundamentally high-risk strategy, one through which he hoped both to reconstitute his domestic political base by enlisting the support of reformed Communists and "democrats" ("coalitional realignment") and to secure sufficient material compensation (or "rewards") to justify this revolutionary shift in course.

In the late 1980s and early 1990s a number of Western students of political psychology and Soviet affairs cooperated in an attempt to generate new insights into the role of "learning" in the formation and conduct of postwar U.S. and Soviet foreign policies. They discovered that at least some learning had taken place on both sides, largely as a consequence of the constraining effects of nuclear weapons, the waning power of ideology, and, most of all, repeated interaction in a variety of negotiating forums.[11]

It now appears that learning of an entirely different sort was underway in the Soviet Union as a direct result of the failure of the USSR to "catch up and overtake" the West economically and to make good on Khrushchev's prediction of the early 1960s that within a generation the socialist countries would attain the highest standard of living in the world. What Gorbachev and his generation of Soviet leaders appear to have learned—ultimately—was that the system they inherited could not be fixed without a reform program so sweeping in scope as to invalidate the logic of the Great October Revolution and turn the meaning of socialism on its head.

As it has been elaborated on these pages, the Ikenberry and Kupchan argument about the susceptibility of "secondary nations" to the "socialization" efforts of hegemonic states is but one, preliminary explanation of the larger processes at work in the transformation of the Soviet polity between 1985 and 1991. Doubtless, there will be other attempts to account for this remarkable development. In presenting the argument here, the purpose is to stimulate discussion and, above all, to sensitize us to the need to reach beyond existing explanations in our attempts to understand the workings of the international political system and how transformative change comes about.

Few within the Western scholarly community predicted the retreat of Soviet power in Europe, or that a general secretary of the CPSU would abolish press censorship, sanction contested elections, and oversee the dismantling of the Soviet Communist party apparatus. Few of us foresaw that within four months of his return to Moscow in August 1991 to reclaim the mantle of political leadership, Mikhail Gorbachev would be out of a job as the country he had promised to save ceased to exist. The lessons, it seems, are obvious.

Notes

INTRODUCTION

1. This is not to suggest that "international-level" variables played no part in the Soviet Union's long-delayed turn toward reform. As discussed in the conclusion to this study, the systemic crisis that overtook the Soviet Union in the late 1980s and early 1990s was both intensified and accelerated by Western success in denying the USSR membership in the capitalist-dominated international economic and political order created by the United States and its closest allies in the aftermath of World War II. The effect of this policy was to force the Soviet Union (and its allies) to "go it alone" economically, which served both to exacerbate the structural weaknesses of the Soviet economy and to complicate the process of economic reform and systemic renewal.
2. Garthoff made this observation in March 1990 at the second of the Council on Foreign Relations working group sessions convened in support of this project.
3. Timothy J. Colton, *The Dilemma of Reform in the Soviet Union*, rev. ed. (New York: Council on Foreign Relations, 1986), pp. 4–5.

CHAPTER 1

1. N. V. Ogarkov, "Victory and the Present Day," *Izvestiya*, May 9, 1983, pp. 1–2.
2. N. V. Ogarkov, "Strategiia Voennaia," *Sovetskaya Voennaia Ensiklopediia* (Moscow: Voennoe izdatel'stvo, 1979), p. 564, from Dale R. Herspring, *The Soviet High Command, 1967–1989: Personalities and Politics* (Princeton: Princeton University Press, 1990), p. 131.
3. See, for example, "Speech by Comrade A. A. Gromyko, USSR Minister of Foreign Affairs," *Pravda*, April 4, 1971, pp. 8–9.

4. See, for example, Sh. Sanokoyev, "Foreign Policy and the Ideological Struggle Today," *International Affairs*, no. 5 (May 1974), pp. 70–78; Sanokoyev, "The World Today: Problem of the Correlation of Forces," *International Affairs*, no. 11 (November 1974), pp. 40-50; V. Zhurkin, "Détente and International Conflicts," *International Affairs*, no. 7 (July 1974), pp. 89–97; and A. Chembarov, "Socialist Countries and European Security," *International Affairs*, no. 1 (January 1974), pp. 8–14.

5. See David Holloway, "War, Militarism, and the Soviet State," *Alternatives* 6 (March 1980), pp. 59–92; and Franklyn Griffiths, "The Sources of American Conduct: Soviet Perspectives and Policy Implications," *International Security* 9 (Fall 1974), pp. 3–50.

6. See William Odom, "The Party Connection," *Problems of Communism* 22 (September–October 1973), pp. 12-26; and John J. Dziak, *Soviet Perceptions of Military Power: The Interaction of Theory and Practice* (New York: Crane, Russak, 1981).

7. See, in particular, Nathan Leites, *The Operational Code of the Politburo* (New York: McGraw-Hill, 1951); and Alexander L. George, "The 'Operational Code': A Neglected Dimension to the Study of Political Decision-Making," *International Studies Quarterly* 13 (June 1969), pp. 197–222. See also Coit D. Blacker, "Learning in the Nuclear Age: Soviet Strategic Arms Control Policy, 1969–89," in George W. Breslauer and Philip E. Tetlock, eds., *Learning in U.S. and Soviet Foreign Policy* (Boulder, Col.: Westview Press, 1991), pp. 429–68.

8. "The Program of the Communist Party of the Soviet Union," *Pravda*, November 2, 1961, pp. 1–9, as reprinted in *Current Digest of the Soviet Press* 13:45 (December 6, 1961), especially pp. 7–10.

9. See, for example, T. Timofeyev, "O nekotorikh tendentsiyakh rabochego dvizheniya na sovremennon etape obshchego krizisa kapitalizma," *Rabochii klass i soveremenii mir*, no. 5 (September-October 1975), pp. 21–35; and V. Zagladin, "Izmeneniya v mire i kommunisticheskoye dvizeniye," *Rabochii klass i soveremenii mir*, no. 5 (September-October 1975), pp. 3–20.

10. V. I. Lenin, *Imperialism: The Highest Stage of Capitalism* (New York: International Publishers, 1939), pp. 88–98.

11. "The Report of the CPSU Central Committee to the 26th Party Congress of the CPSU and the Party's Immediate Tasks in the Field of Foreign Policy," *Pravda*, February 24, 1981, pp. 2–9, as reprinted in *Current Digest of the Soviet Press* 33:8 (March 25, 1981), especially pp. 8–10.

12. *XX Party Congress of the Communist Party of the Soviet Union, February 14-25, Stenographic Report*, vol. 1 (Moscow, 1956), pp. 37–38, as cited in Herbert S. Dinerstein, *War and the Soviet Union* (Westport, Conn.: Greenwood Press, 1959), pp. 80–81.

13. The "five permanently operating factors" were the stability of the home front; the morale of the army; the quantity and quality of divisions; the equipment of the army; and the organizational abilities of the commanding personnel of the armed forces. See David Holloway, *The Soviet Union and the Arms Race*, 2nd ed. (New Haven: Yale University Press, 1983), p. 36; and Dinerstein, *War and the Soviet Union*, pp. 76-77.

14. See in particular David Alan Rosenberg, "The Origins of Overkill: Nuclear Weapons and American Strategy, 1945–60," *International Security* 7 (Spring

1983), pp. 3–71; and Marc Trachtenberg, "A 'Wasting Asset': American Nuclear Strategy and the Shifting Nuclear Balance, 1945–54," *International Security* 13 (Winter 1988/89), pp. 5–49.

15. Dinerstein, *War and the Soviet Union*, pp. 37–64.

16. The threat was communicated through Premier Nikolai Bulganin, who stated to British prime minister Eden that "there are countries that are so powerful that they need not attack Britain and France by naval power," but by other means, "such as rocket technique." See Chester L. Cooper, *The Lion's Last Roar: Suez, 1956* (New York: Harper and Row, 1978), p. 193.

17. V. D. Sokolovskii, *Military Strategy* (Moscow: Voenizdat, 1962).

18. See Lawrence Freedman, *U.S. Intelligence and the Soviet Strategic Threat*, 2nd ed. (Princeton: Princeton University Press, 1986), pp. 62–80; and John Prados, *The Soviet Estimate: U.S. Intelligence Analysis and Soviet Strategic Forces* (Princeton: Princeton University Press, 1986), pp. 51–110.

19. *The Military Balance: 1969–70* (London: Institute for Strategic Studies, 1969), p. 55; also see Freedman, *U.S. Intelligence*, pp. 97–117; and Prados, *The Soviet Estimate*, pp. 182–99.

20. Blacker, "Learning in the Nuclear Age," especially pp. 431–55.

21. Raymond L. Garthoff, *Deterrence and the Revolution in Soviet Military Doctrine* (Washington, D. C.: Brookings Institution, 1990), pp. 49–93.

22. Michael MccGwire, *Military Objectives in Soviet Foreign Policy* (Washington, D.C.: Brookings Institution, 1987), pp. 75–89 and 128–60; Stephen M. Meyer, "Soviet Perspectives on the Paths to Nuclear War," in Graham T. Allison, Albert Carnesale, and Joseph Nye, Jr., eds., *Hawks, Doves, and Owls: An Agenda for Avoiding Nuclear War* (New York: W. W. Norton, 1985), pp. 178–87; and David Holloway and Condoleezza Rice, "Soviet Military Doctrine and Implications for Crisis Management," in Kurt Gottfried and Bruce G. Blair, eds., *Crisis Stability and Nuclear War* (New York: Oxford University Press, 1988), p. 141.

23. See Coit D. Blacker, "The Kremlin and Détente: Soviet Conceptions, Hopes, and Expectations," in Alexander George, et al., *Managing U.S.–Soviet Rivalry: Problems of Crisis Prevention* (Boulder, Col.: Westview Press, 1983), pp. 119–37; and Blacker, "The Soviets and Arms Control: The SALT II Negotiations, November 1972–March 1976," in Michael Mandelbaum, ed., *The Other Side of the Table: The Soviet Approach to Arms Control* (New York: Council on Foreign Relations, 1990), pp. 41–87.

24. TASS-attributed report, "Leonid Brezhnev's Speech at Tula," *Foreign Broadcast Information Service* (hereafter cited as *FBIS*), Soviet Union, January 18, 1977, pp. R3-R13.

25. See "Speech by Comrade L. I. Brezhnev," *Pravda*, March 22, 1977, pp. 1-3; D. F. Ustinov, "Military Détente Is the Imperative of the Time," *Pravda*, October 25, 1977, pp. 4–5, and "Under the Banner of Great October," *Pravda*, November 6, 1981, pp. 1–3; and N. V. Ogarkov, "Standing Guard over Peaceful Labor," *Sovetskaya Rossiya*, February 22, 1981, pp. 1–2.

26. D. F. Ustinov, "To Avert the Threat of Nuclear War," *Pravda*, July 12, 1982, p. 4.

27. "L. I. Brezhnev Answers Questions from a *Pravda* Correspondent," *Pravda*, October 21, 1981, p. 1.

28. Strobe Talbott, *Endgame: The Inside Story of SALT II* (New York: Harper Colophon, 1979), pp. 57–67.

29. For useful discussions, see Abraham S. Becker, *Sitting on Bayonets: The Soviet Defense Burden and the Slowdown of Soviet Defense Spending* (Los Angeles: RAND/UCLA Center for the Study of Soviet International Behavior, December 1985), and Becker, *Ogarkov's Complaint and Gorbachev's Dilemma· The Soviet Defense Burden and Party-Military Conflict* (Santa Monica, Cal.: RAND Corporation, December 1987), pp. 1–23.

30. Herspring, *The Soviet High Command*, pp. 63–64.

31. *The Economist*, April 11–17, 1981.

32. At the time of the Cuban crisis the United States maintained approximately 1,200 strategic nuclear systems, including some 400 ICBMs, 225 SLBMs and 600 long-range bombers; by most estimates, the Soviet Union had deployed fewer than 50 ICBMs, as well as 100 SLBMs and 190 long-range bombers, for a total of between 300 and 350 systems. In all likelihood, the U.S. advantage in deliverable nuclear weapons was even greater, given the high production rates for U.S. bombs and warheads during the early 1960s. In his book *Reflections on the Cuban Missile Crisis*, Raymond Garthoff recalls one estimate (provided by a U.S. Air Force Major General) that between 90 and 100 percent of the Soviet Union's long-range nuclear arsenal could have been destroyed in October 1962 had the United States elected to strike preemptively; see Raymond L. Garthoff, *Reflections on the Cuban Missile Crisis* (Washington, D.C.: Brookings Institution, 1989), p. 160. See also Holloway, *The Soviet Union and the Arms Race*, pp. 84–86.

33. *The Military Balance: 1968–69* (London: Institute for International Studies, 1969), p. 52.

34. See figure 3-1, in MccGwire, *Military Objectives*, p. 40.

35. See, for example, Michael Sadykiewicz, *Soviet–Warsaw Pact Western Theater of Military Operations: Organizations and Missions* (Santa Monica, Cal.: RAND Corporation, August 1987); Phillip A. Petersen and John G. Hines, *Soviet Conventional Offensive in Europe* (Washington, D.C.: Defense Intelligence Agency, May 1983); and C. N. Donnelly, "The Soviet OMG: A New Challenge for NATO," *International Defense Review*, no. 9 (1982), pp. 1177–86.

36. See, for example, D. F. Ustinov, "Against the Arms Race and the Threat of War," *Pravda*, July 25, 1981, p. 4.

37. See MccGwire, *Military Objectives*, pp. 249–61; and Herspring, *The Soviet High Command*, pp. 202–11.

38. N. V. Ogarkov, *Vsegda v Gotovnosti k Zashchite Otechestva* (Moscow: Voenizdat, 1982), p. 16; and Ogarkov, "Victory and the Present Day"; see also D. F. Ustinov, "Defending Peace," *Pravda*, June 22, 1981, pp. 2-3, and "Lessons of the Great Victory," *Pravda*, May 9, 1981, p. 2.

39. Ogarkov, "Victory and the Present Day"; and N. V. Ogarkov, "Defense of Socialism: Experience of History and the Present Day," *Krasnaya zvezda*, May 9, 1984, pp. 2–3.

40. This particular quotation is from that part of Leonid Brezhnev's report to the twenty-fifth CPSU congress in February 1976 devoted to a discussion of the Soviet armed forces. See "The Report to the CPSU Central Committee and the Party's Immediate Tasks in the Fields of Domestic and Foreign Policy—Deliv-

ered by Comrade L. I. Brezhnev, General Secretary of the CPSU Central Committee," *Pravda*, February 24, 1976, pp. 2–9, as reprinted in *Current Digest of the Soviet Press* 38:8 (March 24, 1976), p. 30.

41. The list is a lengthy one. For a representative sample, see Lawrence Caldwell, *Soviet Attitudes To SALT*, Adelphi Paper no. 75 (London: Institute for Strategic Studies, 1970); Raymond L. Garthoff, "Mutual Deterrence, Parity, and Strategic Arms Limitation in Soviet Policy," in Derek Leebaert, ed., *Soviet Military Thinking* (Boston: George Allen and Unwin, 1981), pp. 92–124; *Détente and Confrontation: American-Soviet Relations from Nixon to Reagan* (Washington, D.C.: Brookings Institution, 1985); and *Deterrence and the Revolution in Soviet Military Doctrine* (Washington, D.C.: Brookings Institution, 1990). See also John Newhouse, *Cold Dawn: The Story of SALT* (New York: Holt, Rinehart and Winston, 1973); and Strobe Talbott's trilogy, *Endgame*, cited above; *Deadly Gambits: The Reagan Administration and the Stalemate in Nuclear Arms Control* (New York: Alfred A. Knopf, 1984); and *The Master of the Game: Paul Nitze and the Nuclear Peace* (New York: Alfred A. Knopf, 1988). Additional works include Thomas W. Wolfe, *The SALT Experience* (Cambridge, Mass.: Ballinger, 1979); and Harry Gelman, *The Brezhnev Politburo and the Decline of Détente* (Ithaca, N.Y.: Cornell University Press, 1986). The best of the edited texts are Alexander L. George, Alexander Dallin, and Philip Farley, eds., *U.S.–Soviet Security Cooperation: Achievements, Failures, Lessons* (New York: Oxford University Press, 1988), especially the chapters by Farley and Condoleezza Rice; and Mandelbaum, *The Other Side of the Table*.

42. Blacker, "The Soviets and Arms Control," especially pp. 56–69.

43. Blacker, "Learning in the Nuclear Age," pp. 439–45.

44. For a detailed discussion, see Coit D. Blacker, "The MBFR Experience," in George, Dallin, and Farley, eds., *U.S.–Soviet Security Cooperation*, pp. 123–43.

45. See L. I. Brezhnev, "Report to the CPSU Central Committee to the 26th Congress of the Communist Party of the Soviet Union: The Party's Tasks in the Fields of Domestic and Foreign Policy," *Pravda*, February 24, 1981, pp. 2–9, as reprinted in *Current Digest of the Soviet Press* 33:8 (March 25, 1981), pp. 12–14.

46. Roman Kolkowicz, *The Soviet Military and the Communist Party* (Princeton: Princeton University Press, 1967).

47. Timothy J. Colton, *Commissars, Commanders, and Civilian Authority: The Structure of Soviet Military Politics* (Cambridge: Harvard University Press, 1979).

48. Condoleezza Rice, "The Party, the Military, and Decision Authority," *World Politics* 40 (October 1987), pp. 55–81; Dale Herspring, *The Soviet High Command*; and Matthew Evangelista, *Innovation and the Arms Race: How the United States and the Soviet Union Develop New Military Technologies* (Ithaca, N.Y.: Cornell University Press, 1988).

49. The military learned this lesson most tragically during the infamous Stalin purge of 1937–38, when some 20 to 35 percent of the Soviet officer corps was relieved of command and imprisoned for "treason" and "crimes against the state." Many of those found guilty were later executed, including Mikhail Tukhachevsky, former chief of the General Staff and arguably the most gifted

of the Soviet Union's military commanders in the interwar period. The lesson was relearned in the early postwar era—albeit without the bloodshed—when Khrushchev, having elevated Marshal Georgi Zhukov to full membership in the party presidium (Politburo) in the summer of 1957, turned on the World War II hero several months later and fired him, allegedly for harboring ambitions to become "a new Bonaparte."

50. See, in particular, N. V. Ogarkov, "Military Leader's Creative Thought," *Pravda*, October 2, 1982, p. 3; and Ogarkov, "Defense of Socialism."
51. Ogarkov, "Victory and the Present Day" and "Defense of Socialism."
52. Ibid.
53. V. F. Tolubko, "The Ballistic Bayonets Are on Guard," *Sovetskaya Rossiya*, February 23, 1983, p. 1, and "The People's Great Exploit," *Selskaya zhizn*, May 9, 1983, pp. 1, 3.
54. Moscow Domestic Service, February 22, 1983 (*FBIS*, Soviet Union, February 22, 1983, pp. V1-V3); P. S. Kutakhov, "On Guard over Peace and Socialism," *Selskaya zhizn*, February 23, 1983, pp. 1, 3; and A. Yepishev, "Reliable Shield of Peace and Socialism," *Izvestiya*, February 23, 1983, pp. 1–2.
55. "Conference of Military Leaders in the Kremlin," *Pravda*, October 28, 1982, p. 1.
56. Herspring, *The Soviet High Command*, pp. 218–24.
57. For a focused discussion, see Brian A. Davenport, "The Ogarkov Ouster: The Development of Soviet Military Doctrine and Civil-Military Relations in the 1980s," *Journal of Strategic Studies* 14 (June 1991), pp. 129–47.

CHAPTER 2

1. TASS-attributed report, "Gorbachev Speech at Trilateral Commission Meeting," January 18, 1989 (*FBIS*, Soviet Union, January 18, 1989, pp. 8–10).
2. See, in particular, M. S. Gorbachev, "October and Restructuring: The Revolution Continues," *Pravda*, November 3, 1987, pp. 2–5; V. A. Medvedev, "The Contemporary Concept of Socialism: International Scientific Conference," *Pravda*, October 5, 1988, p. 4; and A. Bovin, "Restructuring and the Fate of Socialism," *Izvestiya*, July 11, 1987, p. 6.
3. See Bill Keller, "Gorbachev Urges Party to Pull Together," *New York Times*, July 3, 1990, p. A1.
4. Ibid.
5. This is not quite true. Stalin, when he moved against the Soviet military in 1937–38, did so by impugning the patriotism and loyalty of the officer corps. He accused senior officials of the High Command both of "wrecking" activity (economic sabotage) and outright treason (spying for Nazi Germany). The charges were absurd. See Robert Conquest, *The Great Terror: A Reassessment* (New York: Oxford University Press, 1990), pp. 182–213.
6. See, for example, E. A. Shevardnadze, "Foreign Policy and Restructuring," *Pravda*, October 24, 1989, pp. 2–4; and A. G. Arbatov, "How Much Defense Is Sufficient?" *International Affairs*, no. 4 (April 1989), pp. 31–44.
7. See "At the USSR Ministry of Foreign Affairs," *Vestnik Ministerstva Inonstrannykh Del SSSR*, no. 2 (1987), pp. 30–34; and "19th All-Union CPSU Conference: Foreign Policy and Diplomacy," *Pravda*, July 26, 1988, p. 4. See

also the speeches of Gorbachev and Shevardnadze to the twenty-eighth CPSU congress, as reported in *FBIS*, Soviet Union (Supplements), July 2 and July 3, 1990.

8. See Gorbachev, "October and Restructuring," especially section III, "Great October and the World Today."

9. The theme is apparent in virtually all major domestically delivered Gorbachev speeches, beginning in 1987, including his remarks to the January and June 1987 party plenums; his address on the seventieth anniversary of the Bolshevik Revolution in November 1987; and his speeches at the nineteenth party conference (June 1988) and the twenty-eighth CPSU congress (July 1990). It was Shevardnadze, however, speaking in June 1987, who drew the connection with perhaps the greatest force and simplicity:

> If the idea that foreign policy is an extension of domestic policy is true—and it undoubtedly is true—and if the thesis that the goal of diplomacy is to form an external environment that is favorable for internal development is correct, then we are compelled to recognize that the backwardness of our power and its steady loss of status is particularly our fault too.
>
> Beyond the borders of the Soviet Union, you and I represent a great country which in the last fifteen years has been steadily losing its position as one of the leading industrially developed countries. . . . If we are finally honest, we frequently encouraged and at times even induced enormous material investments in hopeless foreign policy projects and tacitly promoted actions which both in the direct and the indirect sense have cost the people dearly even to this day. And we coordinated foreign and scientific-technical cooperation very badly or, to put it differently, not at all. See "At the USSR Ministry of Foreign Affairs," *Vestnik Ministerstva Inonstrannykh Del SSSR (VMID SSSR)* (1987).

10. For the text of Gorbachev's speech to the Council of Europe Parliamentary Assembly on July 6, 1989, see Moscow Television Service, "Speech to the Council of Europe" (*FBIS*, Soviet Union, July 7, 1989, pp. 29–34).

11. "M. S. Gorbachev Speech at UN Organization," *Pravda*, December 8, 1988, pp. 1–2.

12. Moscow Television Service, "Gorbachev Delivers Report to the 19th CPSU All-Union Conference," June 28, 1988 (*FBIS*, Soviet Union, June 29, 1988, p. 11).

13. "19th All-Union CPSU Conference: Foreign Policy and Diplomacy."

14. See Ye. K. Ligachev, "On Restructuring of Secondary and Higher Education and the Party's Tasks in Implementing This Restructuring," *Pravda*, February 18, 1988, pp. 1–4. See also David Binder, "Soviet and Allies Shift on Doctrine, *New York Times*, May 25, 1988, p. A8; and "A Logical Step," *Argumenty i fakty*, no. 14 (October 1988), pp. 1–2.

15. See, in particular, "Speech by M. S. Gorbachev," *Pravda*, March 17, 1988, pp. 1–2; and "M. S. Gorbachev Speech at UN Organization" and "Speech to the Council of Europe."

16. See Robert Jervis, "Cooperation Under the Security Dilemma," *World Politics* 30 (June 1978), pp. 167–214, and "Security Regimes," *International Organization* 36 (Winter 1982), pp. 357–78. For a more broadly gauged discussion,

see Kenneth Oye, ed., *Cooperation Under Anarchy* (Princeton: Princeton University Press, 1986).

17. For a representative sample of the first group, see Harriet Fast Scott and William F. Scott, *Soviet Military Doctrine: Continuity, Formulation, and Dissemination* (Boulder, Col.: Westview Press, 1988), especially pp. 253–65; and William F. Scott, "Another Look at the USSR's 'Defensive Doctrine,' " *Air Force Magazine*, March 1988, pp. 48–52. For a sampling of the second group, see Harry Gelman, *The Soviet Turn Toward Conventional Force Reductions: The Internal Struggle and Variables at Play* (Santa Monica, Cal.: RAND Corporation, 1989); Edward L. Warner III, *The Defense Policy of the Soviet Union* (Santa Monica, Cal.: RAND Corporation, 1989); and Dale R. Herspring, *The Soviet High Command*. For analyses characteristic of the third group, see Michael MccGwire, *Perestroika and Soviet National Security* (Washington, D.C.: Brookings Institution, 1991); and Garthoff, *Deterrence and the Revolution in Soviet Military Doctrine*.

18. In October 1987 Soviet defense minister Yazov defined military doctrine as "a system of fundamental views on how to avert war, develop military capabilities and make a country and its armed forces ready to repel aggression. It also explains the methods of waging armed struggle in defense of socialism." See Dmitri Yazov, "Warsaw Pact Military Doctrine—For Defense of Peace and Socialism," *International Affairs* 10 (October 1987), p. 4.

19. "Communiqué of the Conference of the Warsaw Pact Political Consultative Committee," *Pravda*, June 13, 1986, pp. 1–2.

20. "On the Military Doctrine of the Warsaw Pact Member States," *Pravda*, May 31, 1987, pp. 1–2.

21. Ibid.

22. See "At the USSR Foreign Ministry Press Center," *Krasnaya zvezda*, June 24, 1987, p. 3; and "Page 13 Guest: Mikhail Moiseyev, Chief of the General Staff," *Nedelya*, no. 18 (May 1989), pp. 13–14.

23. S. F. Akhromeyev, "Watching Over Peace and Security," *Trud*, February 21, 1988, pp. 1–2.

24. "Restructuring Demands Action," *Krasnaya zvezda*, August 13, 1988, p. 2.

25. See "Marshal of the Soviet Union S. F. Akhromeyev Answers Questions from *Sovetskaya Rossiya* Readers," *Sovetskaya Rossiya*, January 14, 1989, pp. 1, 3. Akhromeyev listed the three tasks of the military-technical component of doctrine as: defining (the nature and sources of) the military threat confronting the Soviet Union and its allies; anticipating the kinds of aggression to be repelled in the event of war; and determining, in light of the above, the most appropriate composition and structure of Soviet armed forces.

26. "Yazov: 'Not Aiming at Supremacy,' " *Die Welt*, October 17, 1988, p. 1 ; and "Reliable Defense of Socialism and Peace—This Is Our Common and Responsible Task," *Narodnaya Armiya* (Sofia), October 14, 1988, pp. 1, 3.

27. D. T. Yazov, "Increasing the Returns from Military Science," *Krasnaya zvezda*, August 14, 1988, pp. 1.

28. "At the Cutting Edge of Restructuring: All-Army Conference on Military Press Organ Leaders," *Krasnaya zvezda*, March 7, 1989, p. 2.

29. *Die Welt*, "Yazov: 'Not Aiming at Supremacy.' "

30. *Krasnaya zvezda*, "Restructuring Demands Action."

31. M. S. Gorbachev, "Political Report to the CPSU Central Committee to the 27th Party Congress of the CPSU," *Pravda*, February 26, 1986, pp. 2–10, as reported in *Current Digest of the Soviet Press* 38 (March 26, 1986), p. 28.

32. Ibid.

33. "Speech by S. L. Sokolov, USSR Minister of Defense," *Pravda*, March 2, 1986, p. 6.

34. See TASS-attributed reports, "At the USSR Foreign Ministry Press Center" and "Gareyev Outlines Doctrine" (*FBIS*, Soviet Union, June 23, 1987, p. AA1); and "Of Reasonable Sufficiency, Precarious Parity, and International Security," *New Times*, July 13, 1987, pp. 18–21.

35. Use of the phrase "unacceptable damage," which the Soviets borrowed from former U.S. defense secretary Robert McNamara, was explicit and intentional. See D. T. Yazov, "The Military Doctrine of the Warsaw Pact Is the Doctrine of Peace and Socialism," *Pravda*, July 27, 1987, p. 5.

36. For the low-end estimates, see Committee of Soviet Scientists for Peace, Against Nuclear War, *Strategic Stability Under Conditions of Radical Nuclear Arms Reduction* (April 1987); the high-end estimates comported with the then current Soviet position in the START negotiations.

37. See, for example, Blacker, "Learning in the Nuclear Age," pp. 429–68; and Garthoff, *Deterrence and the Revolution*, especially pp. 49–93 and 149–85.

38. Defense of the notion of symmetry and reciprocity in the negotiated reduction of U.S. and Soviet strategic forces was fairly uniform across the military, although Marshal Akhromeyev, for one, was more attached to the latter than he was to the former. See *Sovetskaya Rossiya*, "Marshal S. F. Akhromeyev Answers Questions." The INF treaty had legitimized, in any event, the practice of asymmetrical (Soviet) reductions in the interests of achieving an equal outcome.

39. Under terms of the agreement signed by Bush and Yeltsin in June 1992, the total number of U.S. and Russian strategic nuclear warheads will decline to between 3,000 and 3,500 by the year 2003; the two sides also agreed to eliminate all MIRVed ICBMs and to limit SLBM warheads to 1,750.

40. See "Gorbachev Delivers Report to the 19th All-Union CPSU Conference," p. 11; and "The 19th All-Union CPSU Conference: Foreign Policy and Diplomacy." See also Ye. Primakov, "A New Philosophy of Foreign Policy," *Pravda*, July 10, 1987, p. 4.

41. See, for example, *New Times*, "Of Reasonable Sufficiency, Precarious Parity, and International Security"; and M. S. Gorbachev, "The Reality and Guarantees of a Secure World," *Pravda*, September 1987, pp. 1–2.

42. G. Mukhin, "From the Positions of the New Political Thinking: What Must Be Given Priority," *Krasnaya zvezda*, June 1988, p. 3.

43. One possible reason to delay, of course, was the predictable economic consequences of rapid demobilization. Discharging large numbers of officers and enlisted personnel could add to the Soviet Union's already severe economic woes by suddenly introducing into the country's labor force hundreds of thousands of people in desperate need of employment (not to mention adequate housing).

44. See, for example, A. Kokoshin and V. Larionov, "The Confrontation of Conventional Forces in the Context of Ensuring Strategic Stability," *Mirovaya*

ekonomika i mezhdynarodniye otnosheniya, no. 6 (June 1988), pp. 24–28, particularly the so-called "fourth variant."

45. Yazov, "Warsaw Treaty Military Doctrine," p. 6.

46. *FBIS*, "Gareyev Outlines Doctrine."

47. M. A. Moiseyev, "Soviet Military Doctrine: Realization of Its Defensive Thrust," *Pravda*, March 13, 1989, p. 5.

48. John G. Hines and Donald Mahoney, *Defense and Counteroffensive Under the New Soviet Military Doctrine* R-3982-USDP (Santa Monica, Cal.: RAND Corporation, 1990).

49. Ibid., especially pp. 87–100.

50. General Moiseyev raised, and responded to, these and other questions in "Soviet Military Doctrine," cited above.

51. From "The Ministry of Defense's Draft Concept of Military Reform," *New Outlook* (Winter 1990–91), especially pp. 40-42.

52. *Krasnaya zrezda*, "Page 13 Guest: Mikhail Moiseyev."

53. Ibid.

54. Ibid.

55. Of the 10,000 tanks, Gorbachev later stipulated, 5,300 would be newer, "more modern" types. The figure for combat aircraft was later increased from 800 to 830.

56. *Pravda*, "M. S. Gorbachev Speech at the UN Organization."

57. Ibid.

58. See *Military Balance 1989–90* (London: International Institute for Strategic Studies, 1989), p. 30. The figure of 4,250,000 troops is from Gorbachev's Guildhall address in London in April 1989; it did not include some 500,000 railway and construction troops, or 570,000 forces attributed to the KGB and the Interior Ministry.

59. *Arms Control Association*, "CFE Treaty Declarations," December 1990, p. 31.

60. *Sovetskaya Rossiya*, "Marshal S. F. Akhromeyev Answers Questions."

61. Moiseyev, "Soviet Military Doctrine."

62. Bill Keller, "Shevardnadze Says Moves Pave Way to 'a Safer Future' for Europe," *New York Times*, July 7, 1990, p. A1; and Craig R. Whitney, "NATO Leaders Proclaim End of Cold War," *New York Times*, July 18, 1990, p. A1.

63. Serge Schmemann, "Gorbachev Clears Way for German Unity," *New York Times*, July 17, 1990, p. A1; and Craig R. Whitney, "Kohl Outlines a Vision; A Neighborly Germany," *New York Times*, July 18, 1990, p. A4.

64. Moiseyev, "Soviet Military Doctrine."

65. See *Krasnaya zvezda*, "Page 13 Guest: Mikhail Moiseyev"; *Sovetskaya Rossiya*, "Marshal S. F. Akhromeyev Answers Questions"; and "Interview with Soviet Military Adviser Sergei Akhromeyev," *La Repubblica*, March 11, 1989, p. 11.

66. See *New Outlook*, "The Ministry of Defense's Draft Concept," pp. 38–48.

67. See especially Hines and Mahoney, *Defense and Counteroffensive*, pp. 101–10; and Edward L. Warner III, "The Evolving Soviet Military Challenge (1990)," unpublished manuscript.

68. *The Military Balance 1990–91* (London: International Institute for Strategic Studies, 1990), pp. 29–30.

69. Ibid, p. 32.

CHAPTER 3

1. The exceptions are 1980, the last full year of the Carter administration; 1981, the first year of the Reagan administration; and 1984, following Moscow's suspension of the START (and INF) talks. At some point during every other year since 1969, U.S. and Soviet negotiators were in session—even if, as in 1982 and 1983, little of real consequence transpired.

2. See, in particular, Moscow Television Service, "Gorbachev Delivers Report to 19th CPSU Conference," June 28, 1988 (*FBIS*, Soviet Union, June 29, 1988, p. 11).

3. See, in particular, Gorbachev, "The Reality and Guarantee of a Secure World"; and "October and Restructuring", and E. A. Shevardnadze, "At the USSR Ministry of Foreign Affairs," *Vestnik Ministerstva Inonstrannykh Del SSSR*, no. 2 (1987), pp. 30–34.

4. See "M. S. Gorbachev Speech at the UN Organization," *Pravda*, December 8, 1988, pp. 1–2; and Moscow Television Service, "Speech to the Council of Europe," July 6, 1988 (*FBIS*, Soviet Union, July 7, 1988, pp. 29–34).

5. At this stage, the Soviet proposal lumped American central strategic forces—ICBMs, SLBMs, and heavy bombers—together with shorter-range nuclear-capable U.S. systems, principally aircraft, deployed around the Soviet periphery; thus the formula, "capable of reaching each other's territory." It was a familiar Soviet tactic, employed throughout much of the SALT I and SALT II negotiations, although ultimately without success. The same fate was to befall Moscow's latest attempt, in the NST talks, to get a negotiating handle on these U.S. forward-based systems.

6. "Mikhail Gorbachev, General Secretary of the CPSU Central Committee, Addresses the French National Assembly and Senate," *Survival*, March/April 1986, pp. 163–64.

7. "Joint U.S.–Soviet Statement at Geneva, 21 November 1985," ibid, pp. 154–58.

8. Ibid., pp. 171–72.

9. "Transcript of Reagan's Address on Arms Reductions," *New York Times*, November 19, 1981, p. A17.

10. Between 1981 and 1983 the Kremlin formally submitted a number of proposals in INF, all of which would have resulted in the retention of at least some Soviet medium-range ballistic missile systems in both Europe and Asia, while requiring NATO to cancel its plans to deploy any and all comparable weapons.

11. In June 1982 Nitze and Kvitsinski agreed to explore with their respective governments the possibility of an INF agreement in which the United States would limit itself to 75 cruise-missile launchers in Europe (for a total of 300 systems), while the Soviet Union would consent to dismantle all medium-range ballistic missiles in the European USSR, except for 75 SS-20 missiles (deploying some 225 reentry vehicles). Moscow also would consent, under the terms of the accord, to freeze its Asian-based SS-20 force at 108 missiles. Both governments soon distanced themselves from the "Walk in the Woods" formula and the negotiations remained at an impasse. Similar initiatives, floated immediately prior to the collapse of the talks in November 1983, fared no better.

12. "Statement by M. S. Gorbachev, General Secretary of the CPSU Central Committee," *Pravda*, January 15, 1986, pp. 1–2.

13. In emboldening U.S. and Soviet negotiators to pursue an agreement that would have fundamentally restructured superpower strategic relations, the negotiating sessions at Reykjavik may be considered the precursors to the arms control discussions between Presidents Bush and Yeltsin in 1992, which resulted in an agreement in principle to reduce U.S. and Russian strategic nuclear weapons by roughly 75 percent from their peak levels in the mid-1980s. Although the Bush-Yeltsin accord may have come about in the absence of the Reykjavik experience, the negotiations in Iceland demonstrated to each side, for the first time, that spectacular progress in limiting the superpowers' nuclear capabilities was at least possible, given the requisite political will.

14. Moscow Television Service, "News Conference Addressed by CPSU General Secretary M. S. Gorbachev," October 12, 1986 (*FBIS*, Soviet Union, October 14, 1986, pp. DD26–42).

15. See "Arms Control," *Strategic Survey 1986–87* (London: International Institute for Strategic Studies, 1987), especially pp. 56–64.

16. Moscow Television Service, "Address by CPSU General Secretary M. S. Gorbachev on 'Vremya' Program," October 14, 1986 (*FBIS*, Soviet Union, October 15, 1986, pp. DD1–11).

17. Ibid. See also "In the USSR Foreign Ministry Press Center," *Pravda*, October 18, 1986, p. 5.

18. *FBIS*, "Address by CPSU General Secretary M. S. Gorbachev on 'Vremya' Program."

19. See "Excerpts from Comments by Shultz at News Conference in Reykjavik," Los Angeles *Times*, October 13, 1986, p. 4.

20. See "George Shultz Opening Remarks at Vienna Press Conference, 6 November 1986" and "Eduard Shevardnadze Statement at Vienna Press Conference, 10 November 1986," *Survival* 24 (March/April 1987), pp. 178–84.

21. See, for example, Henry A. Kissinger, "Missiles: A Zero Option Is No Choice," Los Angeles *Times*, April 5, 1987, pp. 1–2 (sec. 5); and Henry A. Kissinger and Richard M. Nixon, "To Withdraw Missiles, We Must Add Conditions," Los Angeles *Times*, April 26, 1987, pp. 1, 3 (sec. 5).

22. The INF Treaty, along with its two protocols and a summary of the "Memorandum of Understanding," is reproduced in *Arms Control Today*, January-February 1988, pp. 2–17.

23. "Summary of Data in the Memorandum of Understanding," *Strategic Survey 1987–88* (London: International Institute for Strategic Studies, 1988), p. 27.

24. Expressions of concern along these lines emerged, in fact, in the course of the Supreme Soviet's consideration of the INF Treaty during the spring of 1988. See, for example, B. Ivanov, "Discussion of the Treaty on Intermediate- and Shorter-Range Missiles Continues," *Izvestiya*, March 26, 1988, p. 5; and L. Koryavin, "Gamble on Trust," *Izvestiya*, March 26, 1988, p. 6.

25. See *Arms Control Today*, January/February 1988, especially pp. 4–16.

26. Two issues remained particularly nettlesome: the negotiation of sublimits on ICBM and SLBM warheads and the disposition of sea-launched cruise missiles (SLCMs). Regarding the former, the sides were in substantial agreement on the desirability of a limit of approximately 3,300 for ICBM warheads, but could not agree on appropriate warhead levels for SLBMs. The Soviets lobbied for a

limit of 1,800 to 2,000; the United States wanted the freedom to deploy as many as it chose (within the ceiling of 4,900). On SLCMs, the sides agreed to impose limits, but to do so outside the framework of the treaty. How to constrain these deployments, and how to monitor compliance, were, however, yet to be decided.

27. The phrase is Michael MccGwire's.
28. For the text of Gorbachev's remarks in East Berlin on April 18, 1986, see the TASS-attributed report, April 18, 1986 (*FBIS*, Soviet Union, April 19, 1986, pp. F1–9). For an analysis of the stalemate in MBFR, see Blacker, "The MBFR Experience," pp. 123–43.
29. See "Communiqué of the Conference of the Warsaw Pact Political Consultative Committee," *Pravda*, June 12, 1986, p. 1.
30. Ibid.
31. "Document of the Stockholm Conference on Confidence- and Security-Building Measures and Disarmament in Europe, 19 September, 1986 (excerpts)," *Survival* 24 (January/February 1987), pp. 79–84.
32. For a discussion of the MBFR "data-base" problem, see Blacker, "The MBFR Experience," pp. 127–32.
33. For details of the Jaruzelski speech, see Y. Grigoryev, "The 'Jaruzelski Plan,' " *Pravda*, May 11, 1987, p. 6.
34. D. T. Yazov, "On the Military Balance of Forces and Nuclear Missile Parity," *Pravda*, February 8, 1988, p. 5.
35. See, for example, Gelman, *The Soviet Turn Toward Conventional Force Reductions*, pp. 32–40.
36. *Pravda*, "M. S. Gorbachev's Speech at the UN Organization."
37. "Announcement," *Krasnaya zvezda*, December 15, 1988, p. 1.
38. "Vienna Talks Underway: Speech by E. A. Shevardnadze," *Pravda*, March 7, 1989, p. 4.
39. For the text of Secretary Howe's remarks on March 6, 1989, see *Survival* 31 (May/June 1989), pp. 275–78.
40. *Strategic Survey 1989–90*, pp. 41–42.
41. For a discussion of the "three obstacles," see Coit D. Blacker and Brian A. Davenport, *The Beijing Summit of May 1989 and the Normalization of Sino-Soviet Relations*, Pew Case Studies in Diplomatic Training (Los Angeles: Center for International Studies, University of Southern California, 1991), pp. 5–13.
42. During the final weeks of the war in the Pacific, the Soviet seized the southern-most Kurile Islands, located just to the north of the Japanese home island of Hokkaido. They did so, they argued, in keeping with agreements reached during the Yalta Conference in February 1945. Tokyo has never acknowledged the legitimacy of the territorial transfer and continues to insist that the islands of Etorofu, Kunashiri, Shikotan, and the Hamobai group belong to Japan. Prior to Gorbachev, the Soviets not only rejected the Japanese claim, but after the collapse of the negotiations on a peace treaty between Japan and the USSR in the mid-1950s, declined to admit that a territorial dispute even existed. The issue remains a very sensitive one in relations between Japan and the new Russia; when the Japanese insisted in September 1992 that the status of the so-called Northern Territories would figure prominently in upcoming discussions

between Boris Yeltsin and Japanese prime minister Kiichi Miyazawa, the Russian president abruptly canceled his trip to Tokyo.

43. "Speech by Comrade M. S. Gorbachev at the Ceremonial Meeting Devoted to the Presentation of the Order of Lenin to Vladivostok," *Pravda*, July 29, 1986, pp. 1–3.

44. Ibid.

45. Prior to the collapse of the Soviet Union, the United States had never shown much interest in negotiated limitations on naval forces and operations. With the coming to power of the Yeltsin government in the Russian Republic, however, Washington's position seemed to soften. As of this writing, discussions on naval arms control between U.S. and Russian officials remain exploratory and informal.

46. "A Time for Action, A Time for Practical Work—M. S. Gorbachev's Speech in Krasnoyarsk," *Pravda*, September 18, 1988, pp. 1–3.

47. "Press Conference in Beijing," *Pravda*, February 5, 1989, p. 4.

48. Moscow Television Service, "Speech by M. S. Gorbachev at the Great Hall of the People on May 17, 1989" (*FBIS*, Soviet Union, May 17, 1989, pp. 6–12).

49. Blacker and Davenport, *The Beijing Summit of 1989*, p. 31.

50. "USSR-Japan Foreign Ministry Talks Reported: Characterized as 'Business-like' " (*FBIS*, Soviet Union, March 22, 1989, pp. 19–20); and "Rogachev Rejects Japan's Northern Territories Claims" (*FBIS*, Soviet Union, March 29, 1989, pp. 8–9).

51. "M. S. Gorbachev Meets with S. Uno," *Pravda*, May 6, 1989, p. 1.

52. "Further on Shevardnadze-Uno Meetings in Moscow: Hint at Partial Territorial Settlement" (*FBIS*, Soviet Union, May 4, 1989, pp. 17–18).

53. See, in particular, "Yakovlev Hints New Soviet Offer on Northern Islands Issue," *The Daily Yomiuri*, November 14, 1989, p. 1; and "Yakovlev: No Miracle Solution," *The Daily Yomiuri*, November 16, 1989, p. 1.

CHAPTER 4

1. See, in particular, Colton, *Commisars, Commanders, and Civilian Authority*; and Rice, "The Party, the Military, and Decision Authority in the Soviet Union."

2. "Conference of Military Leaders in the Kremlin," *Pravda*, October 28, 1982, p. 1.

3. See, in particular, Bruce Parrott, "Political Change and Civil-Military Relations," in Timothy Colton and Thane Gustafson, eds., *Soldiers and the Soviet State* (Princeton: Princeton University Press, 1990), pp. 71–72.

4. While Chernenko seemed to place more faith than Andropov in the possible restoration of détente with the United States, denoting a somewhat "softer" foreign and defense policy line than that of his predecessor, he did not stake out a consistent position to limit or reduce military expenditures, nor did he advance any provocative ideas in the areas of doctrine or strategy to which the uniformed military might have taken exception. For a somewhat different interpretation of Chernenko's relations with the Soviet military, see Parrott, "Political Change," pp. 72–74.

5. "The Soviet People's Immortal Exploit," *Pravda*, May 9, 1985, p. 3.

6. Gorbachev, "The Political Report of the CPSU Central Committee to the 27th Congress of the Communist Party of the Soviet Union," p. 8.

7. "Speech by S. L. Sokolov, USSR Minister of Defense," *Pravda*, March 2, 1986, p. 6.

8. A. T. Altunin, "Guarding Peace and Socialism," *Ekonomicheskaya gazeta*, February 1986, p. 7.

9. *Pravda*, "Speech by S. L. Sokolov." Following several paragraphs on the "war preparations" of the United States and its European allies, Sokolov argued that "[t]he main purpose of these actions is to gain a decisive military superiority over the USSR and secure the potential to threaten to deliver a first nuclear strike. In this way the real threat of the unleashing of war against the Soviet Union and the other socialist countries is being created. We cannot ignore this fact."

10. Akhromeyev, "Watching Over Peace and Security."

11. V. F. Yermakov, "Allegiance to International Duty," *Rude Pravo*, February 21, 1986, p. 6.

12. Akhromeyev, "Watching Over Peace and Security."

13. See chapter 2.

14. "At the USSR Ministry of Foreign Affairs," *Vestnik Ministerstva Inonstrannykh Del SSSR*, no. 2 (1987), pp. 30–34.

15. "19th All-Union CPSU Conference: Foreign Policy and Diplomacy," *Pravda*, July 26, 1988, p. 4.

16. See, for example, Yazov, "Warsaw Treaty Military Doctrine," pp. 3–8; Akhromeyev, "Watching Over Peace and Security"; and D. T. Yazov, "Reliable Defense of Socialism and Peace—This Is Our Common and Responsible Task," *Narodna Armiya* (Sofia), October 14, 1988, pp. 1, 3.

17. G. A. Arbatov, "Glasnost, Talks, and Disarmament," *Pravda*, October 17, 1988, p. 6.

18. See, for example, I. Sas, "Restructuring Demands Action: Meeting of the USSR Armed Forces General Staff Party Aktiv," *Krasnaya zvezda*, August 13, 1988, p. 2; "Increasing the Return from Military Science," *Krasnaya zvezda*, August 14, 1988, pp. 1–2; "Democratization and the Armed Forces: Army General D. T. Yazov, Candidate Member of the CPSU Central Committee Politburo and USSR Defense Minister, Answers *Krasnaya zvezda* Readers' Questions," *Krasnaya zvezda*, November 18, 1988, pp. 1-2; and Sergei Akhromeyev, "Restructuring Requires Action," *Rabotnichesko delo*, December 6, 1988, pp. 1, 4.

19. Sas, "Restructuring Demands Action."

20. Ibid.

21. "Increasing the Return from Military Science."

22. Jack Mendelsohn, "Gorbachev's Preemptive Concession," *Arms Control Today* 19 (March 1989), p. 11.

23. "On the Basic Guidelines of the USSR's Domestic and Foreign Policy—Report by M. S. Gorbachev, Chairman of the USSR Supreme Soviet," *Pravda*, May 31, 1989, pp. 1–3.

24. As reported in Gelman, *The Soviet Turn Toward Conventional Force Reductions*, especially pp. 18–25.

25. See "Marshal of the Soviet Union Sergei Fedorovich Akhromeyev Answers Questions from *Sovetskaya Rossiya* Readers," *Sovetskaya Rossiya*, January

14, 1989, pp. 1, 3; Ezio Mauro, "Interview with Soviet Military Adviser Sergei Akhromeyev," *La Repubblica*, March 11, 1989, p. 11; and V. Syrokomsky, "Page 13 Guest: Mikhail Moiseyev, Chief of the General Staff," *Nedelya*, no. 18 (May 1989), pp. 13–14.

26. See, for example, S. Tokalenko, "Show Concern for Living Arrangements, Too" and P. Barabolya, "I Want To Sound A Warning," *Krasnaya zvezda*, December 15, 1988, p. 2.

27. The clearest sign of dissent was the sudden resignation of Akhromeyev, which was revealed in the Soviet press a week after Gorbachev's UN speech. Akhromeyev, who had been a forceful, if not always consistent, supporter of Gorbachev's initiatives in the military sphere, might have stepped down in protest against the reductions, believing they went too far, too fast. For additional discussion, see chapter 2.

28. On the utility of the two-year time frame, see "USSR Defense Minister Army General D. T. Yazov Answers Questions by an *Izvestiya* Correspondent: In the Interests of Universal Security and Peace," *Izvestiya*, February 28, 1989, p. 3; and M. Moiseyev, "Soviet Military Doctrine."

29. See, for example, the speech by USSR defense minister D. T. Yazov from a recorded relay of the July 3, 1989, session of the Supreme Soviet, Moscow Domestic Service (*FBIS*, Soviet Union, July 5, 1989, p. 42).

30. See "From Defensive Doctrine Positions. Colonel General M. A. Moiseyev, Candidate USSR People's Deputy, Meets Communists from the USSR Armed Forces General Staff," *Krasnaya zvezda*, February 10, 1989, pp. 1–2; Speech by D. T. Yazov (*FBIS*, Soviet Union, July 5, 1989); D. T. Yazov, "Military Reform," *Krasnaya zvezda*, June 5, 1990, pp. 1–2; and "Key Task of Military Reform: Speech by Marshal of the Soviet Union D. T. Yazov," *Krasnaya zvezda*, September 2, 1990, pp. 1–2.

31. See "Dialogue. Ask Questions!" *Komsomolskaya pravda*, February 11, 1990, p.1; N. Nikitin, "Statutory Obligation," *Krasnaya zvezda*, April 14, 1990, pp. 1, 5; S. Aleksandrov, "To Serve the People and Not Parties," *Nedelya*, no. 22 (May 1990), pp. 1, 3; "What Kind of Army Do We Need," *Krasnaya zvezda*, June 27, 1990, p. 4; "Military Reform: Generals and Radicals," *Komsomolskaya pravda*, November 13, 1990, pp. 2–3.

32. "At the Cutting Edge of Restructuring: All-Army Conference of Military Press Organ Leaders," *Krasnaya zvezda*, March 7, 1989, p. 2. The issue of costs associated with the transition to an all-volunteer force provoked continuous controversy between the military leadership and its critics. In February 1990 General Mikhail Moiseyev, Akhromeyev's replacement as chief of the General Staff, estimated the costs of an all-volunteer force at five to eight times that of the conscript system then in place. Critics of the military expressed doubts about the reliability of these estimates, noting the military's reluctance to share its methodology or to be explicit about its assumptions. See V. Litovkin, "Interview with USSR People's Deputy Army General M. Moiseyev, Chief of the General Staff of the USSR Armed Forces and USSR First Deputy Minister of Defense," *Izvestiya*, February 23, 1990, p. 3; "17 Servicemen's Draft," *Komsomolskaya pravda*, February 11, 1990, p. 1; and "Debate with Generals and Radicals," *Komsomolskaya pravda*, November 13, 1990, pp. 2–3.

33. *Krasnaya zvezda*, "At the Cutting Edge of Restructuring".

34. Speech by D. T. Yazov (*FBIS*, Soviet Union, July 5, 1989, p. 42).

35. Interview with S. F. Akhromeyev ("What Kind of Army Do We Need?"—from a special edition of "View"), Moscow Television Service, October 9, 1989 (*FBIS*, Soviet Union, October 13, 1989, p. 95).

36. Ibid. See, in particular, "Is the Army Protecting Itself" (interview with Marshal of the Soviet Union Sergei Fedorovich Akhromeyev), *Novoye vremya*, no. 15 (April 1991), pp. 12–17.

37. *Krasnaya zvezda*, "At the Cutting Edge of Restructuring."

38. Interview with army general Vitali Shabanov, Moscow Domestic Service, February 23, 1990 (*FBIS*, Soviet Union, February 26, 1989, p. 86).

39. See, for example, D. T. Yazov, "The Defense of the Fatherland Permits No Regionalism, Selfishness, or Self-Seeking," *Pravda*, November 13, 1989, p. 3; interview with USSR Defense Minister Army General D. Yazov by N. Burbyga, *Izvestiya*, March 12, 1990, p. 3; and interview with army general M. Moiseyev, chief of the Armed Forces General Staff, by N. Burbyga, *Izvestiya*, December 23, 1990, p. 5.

40. *Krasnaya zvezda*, "At the Cutting Edge of Restructuring."

41. Ibid.

42. "Constitution (Basic Law) of the Union of Soviet Socialist Republics," *Pravda*, October 8, 1977, pp. 3–6. See, in particular, chapter 5: "Defense of the Socialist Fatherland."

43. A. Uglapov and V. Romanenko, "The Army and Politics" (interview with Colonel General B. Gromov), *Argumenty i fakty*, no. 12 (March 1990), p. 34.

44. V. Kosarev, "Marshal of the Soviet Union S. F. Akhromeyev: We Must Fight for the Truth," *Krasnaya zvezda*, April 24, 1990, pp. 1–2. See also S. F. Akhromeyev, "Attacks on the USSR Armed Forces: Why," *Krasnaya zvezda*, April 8, 1990, p. 2, in which the marshal denounces the magazine *Ogonek* and its editor, V. A. Korotich, for publishing a contribution by G. A. Arbatov, titled "The Country's Army or the Army's Country?"

45. Kosarev, "Marshal of the Soviet Union S. F. Akhromeyev."

46. Aleksandrov, "To Serve the People and Not Parties," p. 1.

47. *Krasnaya zvezda*, "What Kind of Army Do We Need?"

48. Ibid.

49. See, for example, Pierre Briançon, interview with General Aleksey Lizichev, chief of the Soviet Army and Navy Main Political Directorate, *Liberation*, June 30–July 1, 1990, p. 14; "A Renewed Political Organ: What Is It to Be" (interview with Colonel General N. Moiseyev, chief of the Ground Forces Political Administration), *Krasnaya zvezda*, July 29, 1990, p. 1; and "Key Task of Military Reform: Speech by Marshal of the Soviet Union D. T. Yazov, *Krasnaya zvezda*, September 2, 1990, pp. 1–2.

50. Moscow Central Television, January 11, 1991 (*FBIS*, Soviet Union, January 14, 1991, p. 37).

51. Moscow Central Television, January 12, 1991 (*FBIS*, Soviet Union, January 14, 1991, p. 38).

52. For the text of the Defense Ministry's plan, see Dmitri Yazov, "The Ministry of Defense's Draft Concept of Military Reform," reprinted in *New Outlook*, vol. 2, no. 1 (Winter 1990–91), pp. 38–48. For the text of the principal rival plan, see Vladimir Lopatin, "Draft on Preparing and Implementing Military Reform," *New Outlook*, vol. 2, no. 1 (Winter 1990–91), pp. 51–55.

53. In July 1990 *Krasnaya zvezda* revealed that while young men in the Slavic republics, in particular, were still responding to their induction notices, their counterparts in Armenia, Georgia, and the three Baltic republics were doing their best to avoid military service altogether. In Armenia, for example, only 7 percent of those called to serve actually responded, as ordered by the army. The corresponding statistics for Georgia (27.5 percent), Estonia (40 percent), Latvia (54 percent), and Lithuania (33.6 percent) were less dramatic, but only in comparison. See N. Ter-Grigoryants, "Draft Results Not Gratifying," *Krasnaya zvezda*, July 12, 1990, p. 4.

54. Moscow Television Service, November 27, 1990 (*FBIS*, Soviet Union, November 28, 1990, p. 68).

55. Address to the nation by Vytautas Landsbergis, chairman of the Supreme Council of the Republic of Lithuania, Vilnius Domestic Service, January 9, 1991 (*FBIS*, Soviet Union, January 10, 1991, p. 54).

56. As reported on "Television News Service," Moscow Central Television, January 14, 1991 (*FBIS*, Soviet Union, January 15, 1991, p. 34).

57. Civilian members of the State Committee for the State of Emergency in the USSR included first deputy chairman of the Defense Council, Oleg Baklanov; KGB chairman Vladimir Kryuchov; Prime Minister Valentin Pavlov; Minister of Internal Affairs Boris Pugo; Vice President Gennadi Yanaev; Vasili Starodubtsev; and Aleksandr Tizyakov.

58. See Stephen Foye, "A Lesson in Ineptitude: Military-Backed Coup Crumbles," *Report on the USSR* (RFE/RL Research Institute), vol. 3 (August 1991), pp. 5–8.

59. Uglapov and Romanenko, "The Army and Politics," p. 34.

60. George Possanner, "Soviet Marshal in Vienna: Generals Back Gorbachev," *Der Standard*, May 30, 1990, p. 3.

61. Moscow Television Service, June 19, 1990 (*FBIS*, Soviet Union, June 21, 1990, p. 93).

62. Ibid.

63. V. Litovkin, "What Airborne Assault Troops Are Doing in the Capital," *Izvestiya*, September 12, 1990, p. 6; and "What People Write to Us From the Army," *Komsomolskaya pravda*, October 12, 1990, p. 1.

64. See A. Pankratov, "So Who Ordered the 'Parade'? The Special Parliamentary Commission Has Concluded Its Investigation into the Case of the Paratroopers' March on Moscow," *Komsomolskaya pravda*, November 28, 1990, p. 2.

65. See, for example, Ivan Sidelnikov, " . . . And Now They Are Intimidating Us with a Military Coup," *Krasnaya zvezda*, October 4, 1990, p. 2; Valeriy Vyzhutovich, "Political Diary: Rotting Potatoes in the Field of Abuse," *Izvestiya*, September 30, 1990, p. 1; and N. Belan, "If Only to Make a Bit of a Fuss: From a Competent Source about the 'Military Coup,' " *Sovetskaya Rossiya*, September 29, 1990, p. 1.

66. The available evidence suggests that the conspirators acted sooner than they intended because of the planned signing of the new union treaty, negotiated over the preceding several months by Gorbachev and the leaders of ten of the Soviet Union's fifteen constituent republics. When the signing ceremony was moved up several days, to August 20, Yanaev and his confederates appear to

have accelerated their plans, leaving important details unattended. The result, while perhaps not inevitable, was predictable.

67. "Tanks from Elite Division Back Yeltsin" and "General Kobets Defects?" *RFE/RL Daily Report* (Radio Free Europe/Radio Liberty Research Institute), no. 157, August 20, 1991, p. 1.

68. Foye, "A Lesson in Ineptitude," p. 7.

69. Ibid.

70. "Yevgeniy Shaposhnikov: 'I Sensed Something Was Wrong, But I Had No One to Share This Feeling with on the Morning of August 19," *Komsomolskaya pravda*, August 27, 1991, p. 3.

71. The Soviet press alleged after the coup that Moiseyev had countersigned the enabling orders issued by Yazov, thus implicating him directly in the conspiracy to overthrow Gorbachev. As of this writing, Moiseyev's exact role during the aborted coup remains something of a mystery. His removal as chief of the General Staff within several days of Gorbachev's return to Moscow would seem to suggest, however, that senior political figures—especially Yeltsin—did not believe his protestations of innocence.

72. Boris Pugo, minister of the interior, committed suicide on August 22.

73. Among the more tragic outcomes of the failed coup was the suicide of Marshal Sergei Akhromeyev on August 24. In the note that Akhromeyev left behind he apparently complained that "everything" to which he had devoted his life was in the process of being destroyed. Akhromeyev, Gorbachev's military adviser and former chief of the General Staff, was not directly implicated in the attempt to oust Gorbachev, although his stance toward the actions of the Emergency Committee was, at best, ambiguous.

CHAPTER 5

1. An apparent reference to the song, "I Did It My Way," first made popular in the 1960s by the American artist Frank Sinatra.

2. The description of the negotiations that resulted in Germany's unification in October 1990 as the "2 Plus 4" talks refers to the active participation in that process of the two German states (the Federal Republic of Germany and the German Democratic Republic) and the four victorious powers of World War II (the United States, the Soviet Union, the United Kingdom, and France), which, under the terms of the Yalta and Potsdam agreements (1945), enjoyed particular rights and responsibilities regarding Germany throughout the postwar era.

3. Condoleezza Rice, using the "2 Plus 4" negotiations on German unification as a case study, examines the effect on Soviet decision-makers of what she terms the shift in the "supergame" of world politics, following the fall of the Berlin Wall in November 1989 and collapse of Soviet-supported regimes in Eastern Europe in the months thereafter. See Condoleezza Rice, "Soviet Policy toward German Unification: Implications for Theories of International Negotiation," forthcoming.

4. Also important to Gorbachev was bringing to an end the profound rift between Moscow and Beijing—a conflict that had seriously handicapped Soviet diplomacy and complicated the country's military planning for more than thirty years. Gorbachev pressed aggressively for the normalization of Sino-Soviet

relations almost from the outset of his leadership, calling in 1986 and again in 1987 for settlement of the differences dividing the two countries on the basis of reciprocity and mutual respect. In 1989, at a summit meeting with Chinese leaders in Beijing, he achieved his goal, although at a price—the withdrawal from Afghanistan and the virtual abandonment of the Soviet's Vietnamese allies—that previous Soviet leaders had refused to pay.

5. Take, for example, the argument that the American military challenge during the 1980s essentially drove Gorbachev to embrace radical reform. The U.S. military buildup was indeed important in shaping Soviet policies, but it was the looming economic crisis in the Soviet Union that made it so. To be convincing, such an argument would have to demonstrate that when faced with comparable challenges in the past, Soviet leaders responded in a similar fashion. The historical recorded suggests otherwise.

During the late 1940s, when confronted with the U.S. nuclear monopoly, the Soviet government under Stalin ordered a crash program to develop atomic weapons of its own. In 1949 Moscow detonated its first atomic device; in 1955 it successfully tested a two-stage thermonuclear weapon. More telling, perhaps, was the Soviet response to the Kennedy-McNamara military buildup during the first half of the 1960s; far from seeking to de-escalate the superpower military competition then developing, the Brezhnev-Kosygin regime authorized a major increase in defense expenditures and over the course of the succeeding decade and a half deployed nuclear and conventional forces on a massive scale, outbuilding and outdeploying the United States in virtually all categories of weaponry.

Twenty years later, Gorbachev opted for a fundamentally different strategy—that of convincing the United States to abandon its own buildup in exchange for far-reaching Soviet concessions. While he may have been tempted to pursue the same hard-line strategy, at least initially, the manifest weakness of the Soviet economy deprived him of that option; by the second half of the 1980s the Soviet Union could not cope with the military and technological challenge then being mounted by the United States.

6. Robert Gilpin, *War and Change in World Politics* (Cambridge: Cambridge University Press, 1981).

7. The proposition is a contentious one. See, for example, the exchange between John Mueller ("The Essential Irrelevance of Nuclear Weapons") and Robert Jervis ("The Political Effects of Nuclear Weapons) in *International Security* 13 (Fall 1988), pp. 55–90. See also John Mueller, *Retreat from Doomsday: The Obsolescence of Major War* (New York: Basic Books, 1989).

8. C. John Ikenberry and Charles A. Kupchan, "Socialization and Hegemonic Power," *International Organization* 44 (Summer 1990), pp. 283-315. I am grateful to Gregory Mitrovich, a Ph.D. candidate at the School of International Relations of the University of Southern California, for first suggesting to me the possible relevance of the Ikenberry-Kupchan framework to my work on the Soviet Union (as well as to his own research on the origins of U.S. containment strategy).

9. Ibid., p. 285.

10. Ibid., p. 284.

11. See, for example, Breslauer and Tetlock, eds., *Learning in U.S. and Soviet Foreign Policy*.

Suggested Readings

Bialer, Seweryn, ed. *Inside Gorbachev's Russia: Politics, Society, and Nationality*. Boulder, Co.: Westview Press, 1989.

Colton, Timothy J. and Thane Gustafson, eds. *Soldiers and the Soviet State: Civil-Military Relations from Brezhnev to Gorbachev*. Princeton: Princeton University Press, 1990.

Dallin, Alexander and Condoleezza Rice, eds. *The Gorbachev Era*. Stanford, Cal: The Stanford Alumni Association, 1986.

Dallin, Alexander and Gail Lapidus, eds. *The Soviet System in Crisis: A Reader of Western and Soviet Views*. Boulder, Co.: Westview Press, 1991.

Hewett, Ed A. and Clifford G. Gaddy. *Open for Business: Russia's Return to the Global Economy*. Washington, D.C.: The Brookings Institution, 1992.

Garthoff, Raymond L. *Deterrence and the Revolution in Soviet Military Doctrine*. Washington, D.C.: The Brookings Institution, 1990.

Hanson, Philip. *From Stagnation to Catastroika: Commentaries on the Soviet Economy, 1983–1991.* New York: Praeger, 1992.

Herspring, Dale R. *The Soviet High Command, 1967–1989: Personalities and Politics.* Princeton: Princeton University Press, 1990.

Mandelbaum, Michael, ed. *The Rise of Nations in the Soviet Union: American Foreign Policy and the Disintegration of the USSR.* New York: Council on Foreign Relations Press, 1991.

MccGwire, Michael, *Perestroika and Soviet National Security.* Washington, D.C.: The Brookings Institution, 1991.

Index

ABM Treaty (1972), 24–26, 41, 103,
185; and the Basic Principles of
Relations Agreement, 40; and deterrence, doctrine of, 25–26; and
qualitative improvements in air
defenses, 32–33; and the Reykjavik
Summit, 104, 105, 106, 107, 108;
and SDI, 98, 100
"Absolute" weapons, concept of, 23
Academy of Sciences, 17, 155
Afghanistan, 169; invasion of, 43,
44, 59, 64, 193; withdrawal from,
132, 134, 135, 139
Africa, 15, 52
Agriculture, 58, 148
Akhromeyev, Sergei, 49, 70–72, 77,
82, 84, 154, 225n73; and attempts
to depoliticize the armed forces,
169; and the conscript system,
165, 223n32; and civil-military
relations, 150; and ethnically-based
conflict, 173; proactive stance of,
with regard to the debate over doctrine, 156, 157, 160; resignation
of, 124–25
Albania, 186

Allied military intervention of
1918–1919, 17
Altunin, A. T., 153
Andropov, Yuri, 10, 94, 191, 221n4;
and Ogarkov, 49; and the Rey-
kjavik Summit, 112; and civil-
military relations, 148–49; reform
program of, elements embraced by
Gorbachev, 152–53; and SDI, 100,
101
Arbatov, Georgi, 157
Argumenty i fakty, 169, 177
Armenia, 82, 172, 173, 184
ASEAN (Association of Southeast
Asian Nations), 134, 138
Asia, 6, 81, 130–39; and the
Brezhnev era, 15, 52; and INF,
110, 135, 218n10, 218n11; and
the international system, notion of,
15; and the Reykjavik summit,
110. *See also* specific countries
Azerbaijan, 82, 172, 173, 184

Baker, James, 127
Baku, 172
Baltic states, 168, 173–74, 179

Basic Principles of Relations
Agreement, 40
Belarus, 82, 143, 182, 184, 185
Beijing Summit, 137
Berlin, 20
Berlin Wall, 129, 194, 196, 202,
226n2
Black Berets, 173
Black Sea, 179–80
Bolsheviks, 16–17, 18, 178, 213n9.
See also October Revolution
Bombers, 28, 37, 42; Blackjack, 32,
85; and the Reykjavik summit, 106
Brezhnev, Leonid, 39, 73, 185–86;
address in Tula (1977), 27; address
at the twenty-sixth CPSU congress,
27; acquisition of an assured retaliatory capability under, 24; and
arms control in Asia, 132–33; and
the Basic Principles Agreement, 40;
civil-military relations under,
45–51; Constitution (1977),
168–70; corruption under, 152;
and the danger of nuclear war,
94–95; death of, 10, 44, 49,
147–48; doctrine, 64; and détente,
44; and deterrence, 23, 20–26, 36,
48, 49, 53, 91–92; dogged pursuit
of "absolute security" under, 93;
era, 10–54, 90, 92–93, 149–50,
152, 155, 164; Economist on, 29;
failure of, to exercise oversight of
the military establishment, 67; and
the international system, 14–17;
and INF, 101; and keeping the nuclear threshold in Europe as high
as possible, 35; and the perceived
weakness of Soviet military posture, 30; refusal of, to sanction
military cuts and make bilateral reductions, 30; and SALT II, 31, 99;
and theater military forces, 37
Britain, 126
Budapest Appeal, 117
Bulgaria, 19, 115, 128, 129
Bundeswehr, 83
Bush, George, 89, 128, 142, 196–97;
and the creation of CIS, 189; and

the Malta Summit (1989), 188–89;
and Yeltsin, 75, 143, 218n13
Byelorussia, 189

Cambodia, 134, 135
Capitalism, 18, 195; and Gorbachev's
vision of a "common European
house," 115–16; and the impor-
tance of economic power and
technological clout, 60; and the in-
ternational system, 15, 16, 60; and
socialism, irreconcilability of the
interests of, 15, 16–17; and the
Soviet economy, state of, 30
Carter, Jimmy, 27, 28, 31, 99, 153
Castro, Fidel, 189
Caucasus, 167
CDE (Conference on Disarmament in
Europe), 118, 119
Ceauşescu, Nicolae, 64, 116, 186
Censorship, 183–84, 206
Central Group of Soviet Forces, 154
CFE Treaty (Treaty on Conventional
Armed Forces in Europe), 3,
91–92, 119, 135, 185, 194, 196;
and arms control in Asia, 131,
135; and the collapse of Soviet
power in Europe, 121–29; scope
of, description of, 141–42; sum-
mary of, 184. See also
Conventional forces Chernenko,
Konstantin, 10, 89, 94, 96, 221n4;
appointment of Sokolov, 150;
death of, 10, 20; and Ogarkov, 49;
and civil-military relations, 148;
and SDI, 100
China, 38, 81, 130–39, 226n3
Choice, freedom of, 64–65, 66
CIS (Commonwealth of Independent
States), 82, 182, 189, 201
Civil-military relations, 6, 67, 87,
147–52; and the Brezhnev era,
45–51, 147–48, 168–70; Chernenko and, 148–49; and the
December 1988 initiative, 160; and
the disintegration of the Union
(1989–1991), 161–75; "loosely
coupled," 145; and the politics of

military reform (1985–1989), 152–61

Civil war (1917–1920), 18

Class: conflict, as inevitable, 16; and Gorbachev's reforms, 63–64, 66; and the international system, 14–17, 38, 44, 63–84, 195–96, 205

CoCom (Coordinating Committee for Multilateral Export Controls), 203

Cold war, 83, 92, 111, 114–29, 163, 184–85, 188; and the conclusion of the START Treaty, 142; the constraining effects of nuclear weapons, 202; and the economic impact of the arms race, 94; post–, era, 184, 203; winding down of, and the need for a conscript army, 164

Colton, Timothy, 4, 46

Command-and-control arrangements, 22, 24

Committee for the State of Emergency, 144, 175–76, 180–81; civilian members of, list of, 224n57

Confidence and security-building measures, 116, 117, 118, 123; and arms control in Asia, 133–34

Congress (United States), 185

Congress of People's Deputies, 158, 162–63, 168–69, 194

Conscription, 161, 163–71, 172, 174, 223n32

Conventional forces, 39, 52, 159, 96; and arms control in Asia, 134; bilateral reductions in, 30; and the Budapest Appeal, 117; and deterrence and "conventional options," 25; and extraterritoriality, 166–67; and Gorbachev's December initiative, 80, 64, 81, 84–85, 124–25, 135–36, 159–62, 197, 222n27; and the independent ground–force command, 29; and INF, 110, 112; and NATO and the Warsaw Pact, 34–37; and the restructuring of the armed forces, 78–79, 80–85; and the shift in emphasis from offensive to counteroffensive

postures, 78–79, 85; and the Stockholm Accord, 118, 119; and sufficiency, concept of, 73, 76, 156. See also CFE Treaty (Treaty on Conventional Armed Forces in Europe)

Conventional Stability Talks (Mandate Talks), 120, 121, 122, 135

Corruption, 152, 190

Communist Party of the Soviet Union (CPSU), 10, 62, 89, 200, 205–6; and attempts to depoliticize the armed forces, 168–69; and the Brezhnev Constitution, 168–70; Central Committee of, 168–69, 170, 177–78; corruption in, revelations of; election of Gorbachev as general secretary to (1985), 1, 6, 10, 89, 96, 114, 140, 146, 152, 188, 191; nineteenth conference of (1988), 5, 63–64, 213n9; prestige of, and decline of, 140; twentieth congress of (1956), 17; twenty-sixth congress of (1981), 27; twenty-seventh congress of (1986), 62–63, 65, 73, 117, 133, 149, 153; twenty-eighth congress of (1990), 58, 62, 213n9

Council of Europe, 63

Council of Ministers, 158

Coup d'état(s), 50; against Ceauşescu, 64, 116, 186; against Gorbachev, 144–46, 150, 151, 175–82, 200; against Khrushchev, 10, 11, 30, 90, 147, 150, 151

CSMBs (confidence-and-security-building measures), 118

Cuba, 20, 30, 189

Cuban missile crisis (1962), 20, 30, 210n32

Czechoslovakia, 64, 79, 80–81, 115, 122, 128, 129, 154, 186; forces stationed in, 141; and INF, 184

"Data–base" problem, 121

Defense Department (United States), 33

Democratization, 62, 86, 178; in Eastern Europe, 79, 116, 187; and the disintegration of the Union, 161; and the international system, 205

Deng Xiaoping, 136

Depoliticization, 163–71

Détente, 38, 89, 137, 153–54, 221n4; and the CFE Talks, 128; and Eastern Europe, 128, 188–89; and Gorbachev's vision of a "common European house," 115–16; Reagan and, 44; and SALT, 41

Deterrence, 36, 94; "assured destruction" model of, 97–98; and Brezhnev era, 23, 20–26, 36, 48, 49, 53, 91–92; and civil-military relations, 48, 49; "minimum," 74; and the concept of sufficiency, 73–74, 75

Distribution systems, 58

Double Zero, 110

Draft. See Conscription

Early-warning systems, 22, 32–33

Eastern Europe: and democratization, 79, 116, 187; and Gorbachev's restructuring of the armed forces, 80–81, 83–84; and Gorbachev's vision of a "common European house," 115–16; and MBFR, 120, 121; liberation of, Gorbachev's posture towards, 64–65, 185–87; and the revolutions of 1989–1990, 79, 87, 116, 128–29, 130, 141–42, 161, 185–89, 196, 202, 205; and the Sinatra Doctrine, 187; and the 2 Plus 4 negotiations, 188. See also CFE Treaty (Treaty on Conventional Armed Forces in Europe); specific countries; Warsaw Pact (Warsaw Treaty Organization)

East Germany (German Democratic Republic (GDR)), 79–81, 83, 115, 117, 122, 128–29, 186; and CFE, 141; collapse of, 188; and INF, 184

Economy, 55–66, 86, 190–98; and the American economy, as a model, 12, 54; and the Andropov reform program, 152; and the Brezhnev era, 12, 30, 51–54, 58, 59, 61, 86, 147–48; and Eastern Europe, 116, 120; and economic inequality between developed and developing countries, 95; and economic reform as a catalyst for revolution, 191–98; and economic "shock therapy," 192; and the economic toll taken by military spending, 2–3, 94, 95, 120, 197; and the failure of Gorbachev's reforms, 198–201; and the international system, 60, 203–4; and limits on Gorbachev's capacity to maneuver internationally, 140; and market economies, 57, 62, 192; and the politics of military reform (1985–1989), 152–61; and popular support for the Soviet system, erosion of, 152. See Perestroika

Economist, 29

Elections, 162, 206

El Salvador, 189

Emergency Committee, 144, 175–76, 180–81; civilian members of, list of, 224n57

Engels, Friedrich, 13

Environment, 95

Estonia, 168, 172, 174

Ethnic relations, 6, 86, 140, 172–73, 190

Etorofu island, 138

Evangelista, Matthew, 46

Extraterritoriality, 163–71; definition of, 165–66

"Fallacy, of the last move," 53

500-Day Plan, 194

Forces, "correlation of," concept of, 16, 52

Ford, Gerald R., 26, 41

"Fourth-generation systems," 42

France, 98, 102

Frunze Military Academy, 181

Galosh system, 32

Gareyev, Makhmut, 69–70, 77

Garthoff, Raymond, 3, 25, 210n32

GATT (General Agreement on Tariffs and Trade), 203

General Staff, 162–63, 171, 176, 182, 198–99

Geneva summit, 98, 99–103, 104, 119, 135

Georgia, Republic of, 82, 167–68, 172, 174, 184

Gerasimov, Gennadi, 187

Germany (Federal Republic of Germany), 20, 34, 150, 184, 191; and German unification, 64–65, 83, 187–88, 196; fall of the Berlin Wall in, 129, 194, 196, 202, 226n2; and World War II, 19, 149

Gilpin, Robert, 201

Globalism, 11, 14

GNP (gross national product), 158

Gorbachev, Mikhail: address to the Council of Europe (1989), 63; address to East Germany's Communist Party (1986), 117; address to the French National Assembly, 98; address to the twenty-seventh CPSU congress (1986), 62–63, 65, 73, 117, 133, 149; address to the twenty-eighth CPSU congress (1990), 58, 62, 213n9; address to the United Nations (December 1988 initiative), 80, 64, 81, 84–85, 124–25, 135–36, 159–62, 197, 222n27; announcement of cutbacks in military spending (1989), 57; announcement of moratoriums on deployments (1985), 97; announcement of the withdrawal from Afghanistan, 134; coup attempt against, 144–46, 150, 151, 175–82, 200; election of, as general secretary (1985), 1, 6, 10, 89, 96, 114, 140, 146, 152, 188, 191; Krasnoyarsk speech, 134–35; remarks to the nineteenth CPSU conference, 5, 63–64, 213n9; report to the Council of Europe (1989), 63; suspension of nuclear tests, 97, 102; vision of a "common European house," 115; Vladivostok speech, 133–34, 135

Gosplan (State Planning Commission), 57

Grachev, Pavel, 181

Gromov, Boris, 169, 177

Gromyko, Andrei, 1, 28, 89; and civil-military relations, 149; and the Shultz-Gromyko Statement (1985), 100, 101

Group of Seven, 5

Growth rates, 58

Hazing, 164

Helicopters, 127, 128

Helsinki process, 134–35

Herspring, Dale, 46, 50

Hines, John G., 77–78

Hiroshima, 18, 97

Historical determinism, 13

Hokkaido island, 137

Honecker, Erich, 188

Howe, Geoffrey, 126

Human rights, 105

Human idea, common, concept of, 63

Hungary, 79–81, 115, 128, 129, 141, 186

ICBMs (intercontinental–range ballistic missiles), 12–13, 59, 85, 98; and the Cuban Missile Crisis, 210n32; and deterrence, concept of, 21–22; and the Kremlin's posture in Europe, 35–36; as "survivable" nuclear forces, 21–22; and the Reykjavik Summit, 106–7; and SALT, 22, 31–32. See also START (Strategic Arms Reduction Treaty)

Iceland, 105, 107. See also Reykjavik Summit (1987)

Ikenberry, C. John, 204–5, 206

IMF (International Monetary Fund), 203

Imperialism, 12, 38, 60, 63, 195; and accommodating the nuclear revolution, 26; and civil-military relations, 46; and deterrence, 20, 21; Gorbachev's denunciation of, at a May 1985 Kremlin meeting, 148; and the international system, 16, 17; as a "threat to socialism," and military analyses, 153–54

India, 131

Indochina, 134

Industrial infrastructure, 2, 57, 58, 61

INF Treaty, 3, 39, 42, 79, 87, 89–91, 99–114, 194, 196; and arms control in Asia, 135, 218n10; and the Double Zero, 110; "end-game" in, 108–14; and the Geneva summit, 100–103; and Gorbachev's announcement of moratoriums on deployments, 97; and the "Gorbachev legacy," 185; inspection procedures, 112; and the NST, 97, 99; and the Rey-kjavik Summit, 104, 105, 106, 107, 108–10; Soviet walkout from, 89, 96; and START, separation of, 109; summary of, 184; Zero Option, 93, 102–3

Infant mortality rates, 51

Inspection procedures, 112, 118, 127

Institute for USA and Canada Studies, 155, 157

Institute of World Economics and International Relations, 155

Interim Agreement on Offensive Weapons (1977), 40

International system, 14–19, 44, 67, 93, 195–96; and the Basic Principles Agreement, 40; created after World War II, 65; and economic power, 60, 103–4; new conception of, and Gorbachev, 61, 62; and the socialization process, 204–5, 206

Izvestiya, 179

Jackson, Andrew, 14

Japan, 130, 132–35, 137–39, 155, 191; and the Beijing Summit, 137; and the Northern Territories issue, 132, 134,137–38, 220n42

Jaruzelski, Wojciech, 122, 128

Jefferson, Thomas, 14

Kantemirov Tank Division, 180

Kazakhstan, 143, 185

KGB (Committee for State Security), 170, 180

Khrushchev, Nikita, 150, 160, 163, 186, 206; address to the twentieth CPSU congress (1956), 17; and the Brezhnev era, 10, 14–15, 17, 20, 29, 30, 34, 45–46; and the Cuban missile crisis, 20, 30; formula of, for war with the West (one-variant strategy), 34; and the independent ground–force command, 29; and the international system, notion of, 14–15; and Marxism-Leninism, 14; ouster of, 10, 11, 30, 90, 147, 150, 151; and Zhukov, 212n49

Kiev, 169, 177

Kobets, Konstantin, 180

Kohl, Helmut, 83, 141

Koldunov, Aleksandr, 150

Kolkowicz, Roman, 45

Kommunist, 7

Kommunist vooruzhennikh sil, 7

Korea, 89, 130, 133, 202. See also North Korea; South Korean Airlines Flight 007, 89, 130

Kosygin, Alexsei, 10, 14, 191

Krasnaya zvezda, 7, 46, 124, 170, 179, 224n53

Krasnoyarsk, 32–33, 131–35

Kravchuk, Leonid, 182, 189

Kulikov, Viktor, 177

Kunashiri island, 138

Kupchan, Charles A., 204–5, 206

Kurile Islands, 137, 220n42

Kuriyama, Kakakazu, 137

Kvitsinsky, Yuli, 102, 218n11

Landsbergis, Vytautas, 174

Latvia, 168, 172, 173, 174

Lenin, V. I., 7, 16–17, 62, 165. See also Leninism

Leningrad, 180–81, 182

Leninism, 13, 14–15, 61, 63 Life expectancy rates, 51

Ligachev, Yegor, 64
"Limited war," concept of, 21
Literaturnaya gazeta, 194
Lithuania, 168, 172–75
Lobov, V. N., 181
Lopatin, Vladimir, 169–70

Mahoney, Donald, 77–78
Main Inspectorate, 50
Main Political Administration, 170
Makashov, A. M., 177, 178
Malta Summit (1989), 188–89
Manchuria, 132, 136
Mandate Talks, 120, 121, 122, 135
Mao Zedong, 132, 133
Market economies, 57, 62, 192
Marx, Karl, 13, 62. *See also*
  Marxism
Marxism, 13, 14–15, 61, 63, 115
Mazowiecki, Tadeusz, 116, 128
MBFR (Mutual and Balanced Force
  Reduction negotiations), 42, 117,
  120, 121, 124, 127
MccGwire, Michael, 33
Medvedev, Vadim, 62
MiG-27J Flogger aircraft, 37
Ministry of Defense, 46, 124,
  150–51, 155–56, 163, 197; ap-
  pointment of Shaposhnikov as
  head of, 181–82; and attempts to
  depoliticize the armed forces, 170,
  171; and the conscript system,
  164–65; and the coup d'état
  against Gorbachev, 175–76, 178,
  179, 180; draft program of military reform, 171–72; and
  ethnically-based conflict, 173; and
  Lithuania, 173–74; and the ouster
  of Yazov, 181; and theater military forces, 34–35
Ministry of the Interior, 172, 173–74
Minuteman missiles, 31
MIRVs (multiple independently targetable reentry vehicles), 12, 31, 32
Moiseyev, Mikhail A., 77, 78,
  79–80, 82–84, 170; appointment
  of, as Akhromeyev's successor,
  124; and the coup d'état against
  Gorbachev, 181, 225n71

Moldova, 82, 174, 184
Mongolia, 81, 136
Moratoriums, 97
Moscow News, 194
Moscow Writers' Union, 52
MX missile, 42

Nagasaki, 18
Nagorno-Karabakh, 172–73
National Guard, 166
Nationalism, 163, 190, 202
Nationalities question, 51
NATO (North Atlantic Treaty
  Organization), 34–37, 88, 96, 149;
  and arms control in Asia, 130; attempts to sow dissension between
  the U.S. and, by the Andropov
  leadership, 89; and the Budapest
  Appeal, 117–18; and the collapse
  of the Warsaw Pact, 85; and the
  December Initiative, 197; and the
  "de-nuclearization" of Europe,
  110; Dual Track decision, 35–36,
  44, 102; and first use of nuclear
  weapons, 25; and the Geneva summit, 102; and German unification,
  83, 187–88; and Gorbachev's recasting of Warsaw Pact military
  doctrine, 68–69, 75; and Gorbachev's restructuring of the armed
  forces, 82–83, 85; and Gorbachev's vision of a "common
  European house," 115–16; hard
  line toward, and international support for domestic reform,
  incompatibility of, 92; and INF,
  184–85, 218n10; and MBFR, 42,
  117, 120, 121; negotiations on
  conventional forces, *see* CFE Treaty
  (Treaty on Conventional Armed
  Forces in Europe); 1990 London
  Summit session, 83; possible war involving, and civil-
  military relations, 46, 47; and
  the politics of military reform
  (1985–1989), 155, 160; and the
  Reykjavik summit, 109; Soviet
  "imitation" of, Shevardnadze on,
  155; and START, 184–85; and the

Stockholm Agreement, 119; and the Warsaw Pact's PCC, 68–69; Warsaw Pact threat to, magnitude of, at the start of the 1980s, 52
Nazism, 149
Nedelya, 79, *170*
Nicaragua, 189
Nitze, Paul, 102, 218n11
Nixon, Richard M., 26, 40, 41
Nomenklatura, 145
Northern Territories issue, 132, 134,137–38, 220n42
North Korea, 131, 135, 138
NST (Nuclear and Space Talks), 96–114
Nuclear-free zones, 133–34
Nuclear Nonproliferation Treaty (1968), 143

October Revolution, 6, 16–17, 18, 55, 70, 206
OECD (Organization for Economic Cooperation and Development), 203
Ogarkov, Nikolai, 27, 37, 47–51, 57–58, 147–48, 150
106th Airborne Division, 180
Ownership, public vs. private, 16

Parameters, "need-driven" and "threat-driven," 197–98
Peasantry, 16
Perestroika, 4–5, 62, 72, 146, 180; failure of, 193, 200
Pershing missiles, 36, 89, 102, 111
Philippines, 133
Phnom Penh, 135
Podgorny, Nikolai, 10, 14
Poland, 79, 116, 122, 129, 130, 185–86; and economic "shock therapy," 192; and INF, 184; and the Polish Roundtable, 64, 128; Solidarity in, 43, 128
Politburo, 6, 64, 154, 178, 192, 194
Pravda, 7, 27, 46, 157, 193–94
Presidium on the Supreme Soviet, 10
Pricing system, 192
Proletariat, 16, 17, 63

Propaganda, 15, 97
Pyongyang (North Korea), 131, 138

Qichen, Qian, 136

Radar systems, 32–33
RAND Corporation, 77–78
Reagan, Ronald, 89, 90, 135, 153, 190, 196; and civil-military relations, 49; December 1987 Washington meeting with Gorbachev, 113; defense buildup under, 3, 153, 59, 190, 226n4; election of, 27, 44; and the "endgame" in INF, 109, 111; and the Geneva Summit (1985), 99–104; May 1988 visit to Moscow, 124; and the NST, 97; and the Reykjavik Summit, 104–8; and SALT, 27; and SDI (Strategic Defense Initiative), 97, 98, 99, 100, 104, 106, 107, 108; skepticism of, toward Gorbachev, 149–50; and START, 113; and Tolubko's support for the Strategic Rocket Forces, 49
Realpolitik, 13
Red Square, 150, 178
Regional conflicts, 95, 105, 166–71, 172–75
Religion, 6, 173, 190
Reykjavik Summit (1987), 103–8, 109, 112, 218n13
Revolutions of 1989–1990, 79, 87, 116, 128–30, 141–42, 161, 185–89, 196, 202, 205
Rice, Condoleezza, 46, 226n2
Rogachev, Igor, 137
Romania, 64, 115, 116, 128, 186
Roosevelt, Franklin, 14
Rude Pravo, 154
Russia, 82, 143, 185. *See also* Russian Federation
Russian Federation, 1, 144, 176, 177, 180, 182, 184; and economic "shock therapy," 192
Russian republics, 199, 224n53; bid for political independence, 172–75, 179, 182; and extraterritoriality, 166–71; former, and the CFE

Treaty, 184; former, and START, 185; and Gorbachev's proposed union treaty, 225n66. *See also* specific republics
Ryazan, 178
Ryzkhov, Nikolai, 158

SALT (strategic arms limitation agreements), 11, 22, 25, 88; and the Brezhnev era, 11, 27, 28; and deterrence, doctrine of, 25; explanation of, to the Soviet public, 40; and fourth-generation systems, 42; and the INF Zero Option, 102; and the Interim Agreement, 40–41; Reagan as a critic of, 27; SALT I, 39–45, 96, 218n5; SALT II, 28, 31–32, 39–45, 96, 99, 102, 218n5
Samsonov, Viktor, 180, 181, 182
SDI (Strategic Defense Initiative), 98, 99, 103–8, 198; and the Geneva Summit, 100, 101; and the Reykjavik Summit, 105, 106, 107, 108
"Security dilemma," 65, 66
Sejm, 128
Senate (United States), 185
Shabanov, Vitali, 167
Shaposhnikov, Yevgeni, 181–82
Shevardnadze, Eduard, 62–64, 72–73, 94, 188; and arms control in Asia, 136, 137; and CFE, 124, 125–26; and civil-military relations, 154–55; on foreign policy as an extension of domestic policy, 213n9; and INF, 109, 110–11; and the liberation of Eastern Europe, 186–87; and Reagan, 98; remarks delivered to a Foreign Ministry–sponsored conference (1987), 155, 157; and Yazov, 124
Shultz, George, 89, 109, 110–11
Shultz-Gromyko Statement (1985), 100, 101
Shushkevich, Stanislau, 182, 189
Sinatra Doctrine, 187
SLBMs (submarine launched ballistic missiles), 32, 32–33, 106
Sobchak, Anatoli, 181

Socialism, 23, 25; and the Brezhnev era, 11, 12–13; and capitalism, irreconcilability of the interests of, 15, 16–17; and Gorbachev's vision of a "common European house," 115–16; and the revolutions of 1989–1990, 116; and the task of "socialist construction," 11
Socialization process, 204–5, 206
Sokolov, Sergei, 73, 150, 153–54, 155, 221n9
Sokolovskii, V. D., 20–21
Solidarity, 43, 128
South Korea, 133, 135, 138, 139
Sovetskaya Rossiya, 179
Soviet navy, 12, 37–38, 52, 85, 167, 169. *See also* Submarines
Space-based weapons, 74, 98–101, 103–8, 198
SSBN (ballistic missile submarine program), 32
Stalin, Josef, 12, 13; and nuclear weapons, 18–19, 226n4; purge under (1937–1938), 212n49, 213n5
START (Strategic Arms Reduction Treaty), 3, 39, 42, 75, 88–89, 90–91, 97, 194, 196; and CFE, 142–43; and the collapse of the Soviet Union (1991), 143, 185; conclusion of (July 1991), 142–43; and the Gorbachev legacy, 189; and INF, 109, 113; and NST, 96, 109; summary of, 184–85; and the Reykjavik Summit, 109; Soviet walkout from (1983), 96
Stavropol meetings, 83
Steel production, 57
Stellar-navigation systems, 12
Stockholm Accord, 118–19, 123, 135
Stoph, Willi, 188
Strategic Rocket Forces, 47, 49, 147
Submarines, 13, 24, 28, 32–33, 42, 85, 106. *See also* Soviet navy
Sufficiency, concept of, 4, 73–76, 84, 86, 122, 197–98; and the CFE Talks, 125, 126, 128; and Gorbachev's December initiative, 125,

126; and the politics of military reform (1985–1989), 153, 156, 160
Supreme Soviet, 162, 165, 171
"Survivable nuclear forces," 21–22
Suslov, Mikhail, 10, 59

Tadjikistan, 173
Taman Motorized Rifle Division, 180
Tbilisi, 167, 172
Tbilisi-class aircraft carriers, 85
Terrorism, 202
Third World, 131
Titan missiles, 31
Tolubko, Vladimir, 49
Trade, 105, 136, 138, 203
Transportation systems, 58
Trud, 154
Truman Doctrine, 202
Tula line, 27–28
2 Plus 4 negotiations, 188, 226n2

U.S. News and World Report, 159
Ukraine, 82, 143, 174, 182, 189; and the CFE Treaty, 184; and START, 185
Ulan Bator (Mongolia), 136
United Kingdom, 102
United Nations, Gorbachev's address to (December 1988 initiative), 80, 64, 81, 84–85, 124–25, 135–36, 159–62, 197, 222n27
Uno, Sosuke, 137
Ural Mountains, 68, 102, 117, 126, 136, 177
Ustinov, Dmitri, 27, 50, 59, 150
Uzbekistan, 173

Verification, 128. See also Inspection procedures
Vietnam, 131, 132, 134, 135, 138, 202
Vladivostok, 41, 131–35
Voennaya mysl'(journal), 19
Volga-Ural military district, 177

"Walk in the Woods" proposal, 102, 218n11
Warsaw Pact (Warsaw Treaty Organization), 25, 34–37, 67, 88, 96,

149; adoption of military doctrine (May, 1987), 77; and arms control in Asia, 130; and the Brezhnev doctrine, 64, and the Budapest Appeal, 117–18; collapse of, 85; and Gorbachev's restructuring of the armed forces, 83, 85; and Gorbachev's vision of a "common European house," 115–16; and INF, 110; invasion of Czechoslovakia, 64; June 1986 statement, 153–54; June 1987 statement, 68, 69–70; and MBFR, 42, 117, 120, 122, 127; military doctrine, Gorbachev's recasting of, 67, 68–70, 75, 77; Political Consultative Committee (PCC), 68–69, 73; possible war involving, and civil-military relations, 46, 47; and the revolutions of 1989–1990, 116; and the Stockholm Agreement, 119; threat to NATO, magnitude of, at the start of the 1980s, 52. See also CFE Treaty (Treaty on Conventional Armed Forces in Europe)
Western Theater of Military Operations, 49
Working class, 15, 16–17, 195, 200
World Bank, 203
World War I, 18, 86
World War II, 37, 60, 65, 86, 90; and appearance of nuclear weapons, impact of, 18–19; and Germany, 19, 149; first noncommunist ministry in Poland since, 128; international system created after, 65

Yakovlev, Aleksandr, 62, 137–38, 154–55, 186–87
Yalta Conference, 220n42
Yanaev, Gennadi, 177, 179–80
Yazov, Dmitri, 70, 71–72, 77, 84, 155–59; and attempts to depoliticize the armed forces, 170; and CFE, 123–24; and the conscript system, 164–65; and the coup

d'état against Gorbachev, 175–76, 179–80, 181, 182; definition of military doctrine, 214n18; and ethnically-based conflict, 173; and extraterritoriality, 167

Yeltsin, Boris, 1, 189; Bush and, 75, 143, 218n13; and the coup d'état against Gorbachev, 144–45, 176, 180, 181; and economic "shock therapy," 192

Yermakov, V. F., 154

Young Communist League, 52